underground film

parker tyler

underground film *a critical history*

grove press, inc., new york

Designed by Damienne Grant

Grateful acknowledgment is made to the following for the use of stills reproduced in this book: Brandon Films Inc., Cinema 16 / Grove Press, Inc., Contemporary Films / McGraw-Hill, Inc., *Film Culture*, Film-Makers' Distribution Center, Film-Makers' Cooperative, the Museum of Modern Art, and Andy Warhol Films, Inc.; also: Robert Beavers, Stan Brakhage, Mary Ellen Bute, Shirley Clarke, Charles Henri Ford, Storm De Hirsch, Gerard Malanga, Paul Sharits, and Jack Smith.

contents

The Underground versus the Taboo on Reality / 1

The Exploding Peephole of the Underground / 9

Toward Exhibition and Exhibitionism / 17

Popularizing Peepshows: the Infantile Gimmick / 24

No Establishment at all? / 32

Underground Climb: from Exhibitionism to Art / 35

Underground Infantilism: Surfacing Superstars / 45

Superstar Space: the Playroom / 51

Can the Technician Escape the Pad? / 60

The Pad Can Be Commercialized / 64

Performing Children, Performing Madmen / 72

The Paranoiac–Critical Kick / 83

The Pad's Predecessor: an Archetype / 91

Underground Film Is Primitive Film / 102

Where the Rub Is / 106

The Abstractness of Avant-Gardes / 111

The Avant-Garde Laboratory / 116

Dotting the Eyes of Distortion / 122

Psychedelic Anamorphosis and Its Lesson / 129

Dotting the Eye of History / 132

Film Aesthetics: Rampant and Purist / 141

The Plot Thickens—but Seriously / 143

The Plastic Pulse Ticks On / 151

In the Pad: Plastique versus Surplot / 157

Hard-core History / 164

The Ethics of Film History / 177

The Population Explosion and the Remedy / 185

Basic Film Forms / 191

History and Manifesto / 197

The Shape of Things to Come? / 221

Coda / 236

Filmography / 241

Photographs following page / 122

the underground versus the taboo on reality

To taboo reality—modern civilization has long considered that a crime against mankind, against human society. Science and the newspapers alike are dedicated to outlawing such a taboo. It may seem odd, then, that a book dealing with the history of the Underground Film should begin by suggesting that the film camera has for one of its most neglected functions that of invading and recording realms which have to some degree remained taboo—too private, too shocking, too immoral for photographic reproduction. Why hang up Underground Film, which has entered (after about a dozen years of conscious striving) an era of shining publicity, with something that has the reputation of being a sneak function? A voyeur camera! Don't Underground filmmakers believe the subject matter of their cameras is worth the light of projection any time, anywhere, with as large an audience as possible? No peepshows . . . nothing the police have any good reason to forbid . . . and if what is shown is rare, tempting, unusual, thrilling, it is only.

1

because big commercial film has so long neglected its natural opportunities.

One could say that the ever growing organism of Underground Film, in order to surface in more and more places, must convert the "squares" of the world, must initiate those who hold back through timidity on one hand and loyalty to the old-fashioned stereotypes on the other. Maybe a little history will help illuminate the point. Once there was no Underground, nominally speaking, there was only an "avant-garde," an "experimental film," a "poetic film." Today in the United States there have been widely publicized transformations that have called up new labels (usually bestowed by exponents of the movement) such as the Independent Film and the New American Cinema. But it is significant that the term most generally accepted, Underground, actually comes from the domain of political and military activity. From all this, it might be assumed that the avant-garde has indeed taken on fresh energies. What is indisputable is that it has earned, in its present forms, an unprecedented public acknowledgment and a certain popular acceptance.

Necessarily these facts give rise to the question of the nature of the thing thus newly acknowledged. For instance: Is the avant-garde, as a concept, the permanent renewal of creative activity in a given art medium, and does this radical renewal represent, as some have argued, a principle of "permanent revolution" in the arts? The answer to this query must be reserved till various issues regarding Underground Film have been settled. One all-important issue is complex: that of content in relation to form, actual result in relation to conscious aim. Still another is the relation of today's Underground film forces to the traditional concept of art itself, a concept much damaged in this century. Moreover, the science of ethnology distinguishes culture from art. Can anti-art, as a new "revolution," actually be (as certain early-century movements such as Dadaism might imply) a new form of culture itself? Instantaneous answers to these questions must be postponed for the sake of arguments yet to be offered here.

One empiric fact is that, so far as public exhibition goes, two things have helped achieve the successful change from the old avant-garde film labels to the new ones: organized publicity and the organized effort to obtain subsidy from private individuals as well as from the big foundations. Thus modern economic pressures, as well as a new political awareness and instrumentation in the domain of culture, have changed the moral temper of the old avant-garde, which tended to be deliberately elite and exclusivist. Assiduous promotion of the new avant-garde elements has been conducted like parallel efforts to obtain charitable support for all varieties of the causes known as worthy.

In the arts this is not a new phenomenon in itself but one of the well-grounded features of modern capitalist society. "Little magazines" and "little theaters" have always been run partly or wholly on private subsidy by editors or owners as well as by campaigns to obtain support from those who have money to spare and are willing to part with it so that the arts may prosper. The non-profit-making organization, for several decades, has drawn help from sources which welcome the chance to reduce their taxes by making tax-deductible gifts.

If I emphasize the economic status of Underground Film (though it is still the Cinderella among the aidable arts) it is to point to one channel which largely accounts for its belonging to those art "establishments" which exist on subsidy rather than on commercial profits. The American Film Institute has been in existence since 1967, and since 1968 has been awarding grants to individual filmmakers as well as students of the film. Before that independent filmmakers were the most neglected group seriously engaged in exploiting a given medium; above all, the artistic aims of independent filmmaking remained in the shade because those of documentary filmmakers had won preference over them in the eyes of big foundations awarding grants for filmmaking.

Undoubtedly this relative neglect was due to the famous taint of commercialism that perennially clings to the "art" of filmmaking. As a popular art (now rivaled by television, which so freely borrows from it), the film has lain under suspicion through the decades as an "entertainment" rather than an "art" form. Moreover, as large as the group of film experimentalists may appear, the general public has tended to believe that, in contrast with commercial film, its products are "amateurish"— and amateurish exactly because members of this group cannot afford the means to make technically efficient films even if they know how. The truth is that, as little aid as the American film experimentalists received in the thirties and forties, the best of them disproved that lack of means was an insuperable handicap to efficient technique. Indeed, one of the chief factors to recognize in the current ascendancy of Underground Film is that artistic ingenuity is not to be equated with the material means of filmmaking; on the contrary, a great pride of the true avant-garde filmmaker is that he can produce extraordinary effects through manipulations that in themselves are not costly. This is apart, of course, from how serious or how significant his basic artistic aims may be.

The Underground filmmaker, despite all the hullabaloo about his products during the past few years, is still radically underprivileged so far as the wherewithal to make feature-length films is concerned. Laboratory costs are higher than ever and the increasing use of large casts makes the payment of actors a problem. Furthermore, the very fact of the rise of prestige provided for the avant-garde by the surfacing Underground encourages more people to make films, and practicing filmmakers to invent more and more elaborate projects. Many individuals whose names are already prominent in the Underground movement, therefore, are poorer than ever in proportion as their opportunities logically have increased with their prestige. All the same, one must admit that if paltry profits have been made, in the commercial sense, much more money has lately been spent on independent filmmaking of the more radical order—aside from the increasing number of large independent film projects whose backers expect financial profit.

By now it must be clear that the "taboo on reality" which I began by invoking has a good deal to do with the sheer physical possibility that theoretically lies open to the avant-garde—now turned into the supersurfacing Underground—and also with the size and quality of audiences able to appreciate what Underground films have to offer. One of the bad habits of modern society is to place too much emphasis on technical accomplishment (this will be a leading theme in the following pages), and of course big commercial film has nurtured this bad habit in film audiences. Technical flash and professional splash have been exactly what "entertainment film" has substituted for serious themes and truly artistic treatment. Respect for those qualities remains a vice even among the film buffs who recognize the "art of the film" and pretend, as well, to measure the extent to which the avant-garde, in its Underground upsurge, has "come up" to this art.

An example is the recent dialogue with Alfred Hitchcock reported by François Truffaut in his book, *Hitchcock*. A bigtime director of film kitsch, Hitchcock is very clever ("classically" clever), but a maker of entertainment films that should not be mistaken for serious art (or, for that matter, for serious anti-art). So Truffaut's book, whatever technical or psychological interest it may have, is pure blague in its assumption that Hitchcock is a serious film artist.

My aim in this book is not to write a history in the ordinary sense of supplying an encyclopedia of information. I want to show, rather, what the exact personality of the Underground

5

Film is, and how its traits, getting so much attention these days, exist in a historical perspective by which they must be evaluated. The in-groupers, the film buffs, the super-hipsters who form the Underground Film's cheering sections are sometimes just as far from understanding the realities of the current avant-garde as those who think that Underground films are the pretentious products of very wild, nasty-minded amateurs. In this situation the "camera" of criticism must itself compete in voyeurism, for no truth worth the name can be achieved without criticism of both sides of an argument. To exalt the Underground as the faultless and incomparable gift of the 1960's to the film art would be as simple-minded as the resolution of an advertising agency to use all its best talents to exploit the product of the newest account.

Suppose we devote a little space to considering just what true "reality" might be in regard to *film as such*; for example, in the pivotal distinction between fact and fiction. Philosophers and aesthetic theorists have long held that a fiction (e.g., something made up rather than evidently factual) is designed to tell the truth in a more or less symbolic, always appropriate, and usually condensed form; in other words, "truth" is not simply a literal or verifiable matter, it also exists in the domain of pure fiction. Serious thinkers have often phrased the issue (especially in contemporary times) as that of a basic dichotomy between science and art: literal truth is reserved to the category of science, formal or symbolic truth to the category of art. The point that deeply concerns anyone who is concerned about film nowadays is that this division into categories of truth as the specific properties of different modes of thought (essentially different attitudes toward life) harnesses all possible phenomena into the terms of one quality of a medium or another. For example, the "scientific" medium is rational, mathematical, constantly subject to test and verification; it is very concrete, but only as words and numbers and algebraic formulas are concrete. One might say of scientific media that they are either abstract in form and concrete in substance, or concrete in form and abstract in substance, according to whether the medium exists only in the mind or on paper, or is being demonstrated in the physical world. On the other side, artistic media are more or less irrational, tend to obey a logic of the senses and emotions rather than the mind, and are "abstract" insofar as a work of art is not to be tested for authenticity by any strict reference to the physical world—to "life as it is," to statistical facts. A fiction, in brief, must be taken for granted as true without verification. This does not mean that meanwhile the critical intelligence is inactive; constant automatic reference compares one work of art to others and to the sum of experience which life has afforded a given commentator.

Obviously the perpetual inquiry of philosophers tends to modify, perhaps contradict, such neat symmetrical conclusions —and precisely on the basis of human experience on all its levels. One modern school, existentialism, would place us where "reality" is beyond media as media may be divided into scientific and artistic types of truth. Existentialism implies a great homogenizing of the life experience into a theoretically monolithic current, where all the forms are basically soluble, merging into each other without set frontiers. If it were not for the very specific and concrete problems of modern socialist states, one could say that existentialism is the official socialist philosophy, making all classes, kinds, nations, colors, and so on into one human entity. Unities in philosophy—except where purely transcendental ideas obtain—mean the concentration of vast areas of reality into a certain great form. Religion, with its nuclear idea of a god or gods from whom the world emanated, is one such form. Science itself is a form that regards all matter, its behavior and interrelations, as subject to systematic scrutiny and corresponding codification into various sorts of patterns: physiological, biological, astronomical, etc. Art would be a

7

form in which any coherent body of symbols makes a legitimate medium provided the symbols represent the fictions of the imagination. In other words, art is the universal, or great, form using the imagination as an infinitely plastic medium.

At first glance this aspect of our discussion may seem a far cry from the role of the camera as voyeur, the image with which I started and which seems to me so important a factor in the evolution of the film medium. Motion pictures brought to the still photograph the only element, the reproduction of motion, that was lacking to simulate life itself. No matter how complicated an art (indeed, a fine art) the film may become, this elementary charm of witnessing life as it happened or may still be happening outstrips in closeness to reality, to life "as it is," any other medium containing representations of the natural world. The visual image is more immediate in communicative terms than the word, either printed or spoken—and anyway, for some time now the film has also possessed the spoken word, absorbed it. As for the visual imagery of the stage, it exists within a literally confined space of which the spectator is always tacitly aware, no matter how many mobility devices are used to create a sense of spatial expansion. The stage cannot hope to achieve what the film achieves without effort: the illusion of being a window opened on the world itself. And not only does the world move; the window also moves *in* the world.

the exploding peephole
of the underground

Now all this, which seems basic in describing the spell of the film medium, may seem banal in reference to a very recent phenomenon like the Underground Film. Surely all such considerations can safely be taken for granted? Yet just here lies a challenging paradox. It is not even that many avant-garde films are still silent, or very sparing of dialogue or commentary, or have a simple musical accompaniment; the issue does not depend on technical variations that specialize or limit the medium. If, then, actual reality, the whole objective life of the world, is what interests us here, and if the film is the perfect medium to reveal it (that is, to incarnate it for the purpose of contemplative enjoyment as distinguished from direct participation), why should the camera ever be welcomed by an audience, or exploited by a filmmaker, *as a voyeur*?

The answer is that the whole concept of voyeurism implies that reality contains certain taboo spheres—and especially where the naked eye is concerned; where *seeing* is the same as

9

believing. There is a multitude of conventions of good taste (still, strangely enough, observed) which prevent our speaking of or displaying certain things. To the imagination and the reason, supposedly, all is "visible," at least if we obey the simple rule of modern candor about all aspects of life. At the same time there is a point at which, aesthetically no less than documentarily, there is nothing like the naked eye for satisfying both curiosity about facts and the sense of pleasure. Hence the frontier separating what is easily or normally seen and what it is desirable to see is flexible for a virtually infinite number of reasons. And this situation always appears absurdly ironic whenever the subject of the voyeur, which implies the sight of "forbidden things," is evoked. Absurdly ironic? Yes, because the existence of the camera eye implies *an optical omniscience from which nothing can be concealed,* since it is able to reproduce both microscopic and telescopic effects, with the result that all barriers between spectator and spectacle necessarily seem arbitrary and artificial—a mere matter of "stage illusion."

Naturally, then, a classic function of all independent films, avant-garde and otherwise, has been to provide "peephole excitement." But of course such films have not been the only agents of such revelation. In my book *The Hollywood Hallucination* I pictured Hollywood as a sort of mundane Olympia, where men and women led the "ideal" lives of gods and goddesses, so that the trivial (or at least trivialized) film stories about them amounted to voyeuristic viewings of their private lives parading in the symbolic form of fiction. Here was a case —that of the commercial fiction film—where reality was a myth hiding snugly inside more or less cheap and obvious imaginative formulas. On the other hand, I contended, movie-going in this respect was a sort of fun-game (to me it was an absorbing Surrealist pastime), and insofar as a film work could be explained by this pattern it could still be called a charade.

One of the most positive things achieved by Underground

the exploding peephole of the underground

Film in what was roughly the first decade of its recognized existence, 1957-67, was recognition of the value of the film work as a charade, in relation to two developments rising independently in the plastic arts: Happenings and Pop Art. The Happening was—and continues to be in expanded forms—a theatricalization of the painted picture, first by making painting an environment or surrounding décor, and second by introducing human action into this environment—spectator action, I mean, which can even move, like the film camera itself, from point to point. The irrational, fragmentary, usually enigmatic, and generally mocking nature of this action * is a simple reassertion of anterior twentieth-century developments in painting and object making: Dadaism and Surrealism. The classic Cubists themselves (Braque, Picasso, Juan Gris) started using newsprint, string, and "things" other than just paint on their canvases. Under the influence of Surrealism the plastic surface became more and more high-relief until Happenings released it into three actual dimensions. It is only apt that in recent years painters' studios have become the slummy scenes or environments of planned Happenings.

Theatrically the Happening corresponds to the improvisation of actors who make up their own plays rather than follow a given script. They may be given a rough idea of a theme but from then on they are on their own. This may not always be literally so in Happenings, though such is the mystifying content and unco-ordinated style of many Happenings that it seems so. It is all part of the experimentalism of the twentieth-century theater, which eventually became related to the psychodrama, in which psychiatric patients are urged to reconstruct their private dilemmas in dramatic form, to set forth their inner stories; in other words, the psychiatric patient has risen from his supine position on the clinical couch and

* As in the film of Claes Oldenburg's Happening, *Fotodeath*, and Raymond Saroff's *Happenings I* and *II*.

11

started to recall dreams and half-remembered, half-understood experiences in terms of pantomime and even words.*

At the same time something about Dada and Surrealism resists the effort to interpret an artist's works as dreams are interpreted. The main shift via Happenings has been to separate the dark "Surrealist act" from passion, from the idea of necessity, since those elements would imply gratification, motivation, coherent impulse. I think the Happening has been intellectually inspired by a strange entente between Dada-Surrealism and abstractionism. The abstract movement to some extent resents the intrusion of Expressionism (that is, passion and content supplied by motive) as too much an indirect moral affirmation of life through aesthetic strategy. Therefore the Happening developed as a pseudo-scientific verification of the *absence of content in life*; it grew specifically from the aggressive desire of instinctive abstractionists to be delivered from life performance by emptying physical behavior of all coherent motive while retaining natural shape (the forms of relations between and among people and things), only to distort that shape by irrationally breaking up the normal contents of physical action.

A Happening resembles life in the way that a dream resembles it: the elements are all literally recognizable. The difference is that (a) the elements as psychological manipulations don't operate in a normal rational context, and (b) they are self-sufficient ends in themselves, and (unlike dreams) not material for symbolic interpretation. Re-entry to the world of actual human motivation is barred to them; inevitably, then, they become gratuitous moral excrescences, solemn put-ons. This is clear from the tendency of Happenings to frame themselves in the actual world, to appear in public places as "demonstrations." It is a sort of adult make-believe, releasing people from real life the way the fictions of the playroom release children from

* See my article, "An American Theatre Motif: the Psychodrama," in the *American Quarterly*, Summer 1963.

real life. The mistake children make (so the Happening-abstractionists reason) is to make playacting resemble life too closely and logically. If art cannot be purified of content and become an alternate reality—this experiment seems to have been made by the aesthetic movement, and failed, at the end of the nineteenth century—why not purify life itself, treat it in plastic terms as if it were substantially a nonhuman abstraction whose resemblance to ordinary human occupations is accidental, a sort of illusion or delusion?

But the hardest thing for a very radical idea to do is to stay very radical. The dialectic movement of history in process tends toward numerous compromises, if only because of the latent inner human contradiction which seems to abide in the most ambitious, world-defying philosophies. Pop Art, with its reliance on photographic processes for its plastic effects, has been very close in spirit to the popular fiction film according to that film type's own ambiguous yet deep affinity with the comic strip. This kinship, in the shape of the rough, robust satire which is more and more prevalent, has come to the fore during the same decade—the sixties—that the avant-garde film has acquired its Underground personality. One factor to be noted is the way in which connoisseur taste has been altered (and perhaps degraded) by the upsurging success of Pop Art, which came on the scene almost in step with the reawakening of the avant-garde film in the late fifties. Just as the Surrealist game of movie-going, which became a cult, meant a certain conscious condescension toward the vulgar as a source of value, so neo-Dada and Pop Art revived the caricature of the common, the making of a potential fine art into the campy sort of sport initiated by the Dadaists in the early twenties.

The direct influence of the movies on the Parisian aesthetes for whom Dada was an intellectual toy became apparent in one of the earliest avant-garde films, René Clair's *Entr'acte* (1924), in which the filmmaker was associated with the Dada painter,

Francis Picabia. This film had the tone of Dada camp and the basic form of the primitive film archetype, the chase, in which everybody joins. That the rollicky action is mainly concerned with farcing a funeral expresses the adult impulse to revive the irreverent licence of children toward "serious" things such as death. Dadaism in word and picture was an art of more or less serious joking, a profound inversion of the elite attitude that enjoyed the privilege of all elites: making fun of the best as well as the worst, even exploiting the worst at the expense of the best. Such revolutionary movements always occur in the arts when the inner content of a style exhausts its credit in its own eyes and seeks vital replenishment in culturally contrary sources.

Dadaism and Surrealism, the latter more positive and a dialectic version of the former, exploited the "bankruptcy" of the fine arts by seeking a refinement of the unrefined. They saw how silly were the very early "art films," which simply employed famous French stage stars to gyrate in front of static cameras. These revolutionary art movements seized on neglected writers such as the Marquis de Sade, who had been considered only a very distinguished sex maniac, as well as on pop subjects such as the Keystone Kop comedies of American films and (even as Pop Art today) on advertising art itself; the latter was touched up as a plastic conceit which the Dadaists dubbed ready-mades: Marcel Duchamp's mustachio'd *Mona Lisa* (a small reproduction of the original) remains the most memorable ready-made.

But the epitome of the Dada-Surrealist spirit, circa 1924, was realized in Clair's *Entr'acte*, conceived to occupy the intermission between acts of a Swedish ballet presented in Paris, *Relâche* (No Performance Today). The very title of the ballet typified the spirit of waste and sabotage that was part of the destructive wit of Dada-Surrealist works and that was revived in the collage and assemblage art of later decades, which used cheap commercial objects and junkyard supplies as its main ingredients. The theatrical purpose behind such things as *Entr'acte* (whose chase is after a runaway hearse) and Jarry's play *Ubu Roi* (whose hero is a brutal clown) was to create scandals by committing outrages against both artistic form and moral conventions. This spirit was faithfully carried forward in the famous avant-garde films *Un Chien Andalou* (1929), *L'Age d'Or* (1930), and *Le Sang d'un Poète* (1930). Dali remarked of *Un Chien Andalou*, on which he collaborated with Buñuel, that they "would plunge [it] right into the heart of witty, elegant and intellectualized Paris with all the weight of an Iberian dagger."

Of course there is a signal difference between the recognized Underground film works of the sixties and the sum of avant-garde films up to 1930, and the difference lies largely in the attitude toward craftsmanship. Even today neo-Dada collage and assemblage, whatever their importance, are carefully composed objects showing plastic harmony and pattern—built, as it were, to last. Many contemporary Underground films, on the other hand, seem flung together and justify their nickname of "fetish footage," a term echoing the raw footage of film known as the rushes; that is, all the exposed reel from which the final film is supposedly edited. Fetish footage may even be regarded as a sort of pun: the kind of erotic fetishism which, like that for the human feet, abandons totalities and more usual areas for details, and dwells on them compulsively, whimsically, endlessly. Fetish footage, as something presented to audiences as a film, is basically the literal exposure of a private hang-up, whatever the hang-up may be. Instead of being carefully edited, with economy of plastic form in mind, these Underground films are shown entire, thus seeming inflated episodes, at best, and leading to the unarticulated "solid time" of Andy Warhol's fixed-viewpoint camera that developed in 1963. Many such films sound the improvisatory note I spoke of in regard to Happenings and psychodramas.

15

underground film

In Warhol's early films the situation is given à la tableau vivant, and whatever happens (or doesn't happen) thereafter is mostly up to the entranced actors, who never—intentionally, anyway—move beyond range of the fixed-forever camera. To the spectator it is somewhat like a comprehensive view through a large keyhole: eavesdropping on eventlessness. "What's happening" may well mean something seemingly minimal from the purely visual standpoint. This is why Warhol, despite the temptation to "package" his work for commercial exhibition, intentionally steers away from "editing," from all devices that would make the material look shapely or dependent on "technique." Such attentiveness to form itself would shift emphasis from the feeling that a film camera, basically and finally, intervenes in the flow of ordinary life and shows us an ordinary piece of it. The more extraordinary the "stolen" piece of it, the more exciting the stolen glimpse. Supposedly! The question must remain as to how close to both inner and outer reality the visible action manages to be.

toward exhibition and exhibitionism

All these shifts in the evolution of the avant-garde film will be
taken up more extensively in later pages. Our emphasis now is
on the film camera as the vehicle of forbidden subject matter—
subject matter which, in the avant-garde view, is forbidden to
high artistic and social levels as well as to mere decency (or
supposed decency) and good taste. The Paris avant-garde that
promoted the showing of *Entr'acte* wished to create a scandal
by disrupting the values of good taste in every segment of the
theater-going public. The very fact that a *movie* was being used
to embellish a theatrical performance was then a calculated im-
pertinence. The means of *Entr'acte* in several instances were
pointed enough. One was a ballerina, a reference to the ballet
being performed, photographed from directly underneath: evidently she danced on a floor of glass under which the camera
was directly stationed, so that one had a glimpse of her rather
inelegant panties. Naturally, frequenters of the ballet know
that in the lifts the most intimate parts of a ballerina's body,

17

while closely sheathed, become visible. However, the film camera often means concentration on detail and selected angle, so that here, in *Entr'acte*, was a parody of the childish impropriety of eavesdropping or taking a forbidden peek. Nowadays this parody seems outmoded and naive because of the more and more deliberate, straightforward licence that is steadily dissolving the visual taboo which has prevailed historically in public spectacles.

The gap between Dada *impudence* and Underground *glare* is measured accurately by the recent work of Carl Linder, an independent filmmaker regarded as a member of the Underground. Heavily preoccupied with eroticism, Linder has composed long passages of nothing but visual intimacy with sheathed female crotches; the very fact that they are sheathed makes the camera's prolonged preoccupation voyeuristic. The general aim of the historic *Entr'acte* was not anatomic revelation, veiled or naked; rather, it concerned the camera's brazen positioning, which was ostentatiously voyeuristic. Historically the camera as a breaker of visual taboo is distinct from the camera as a new source of visual information. The ballerina in *Entr'acte* is then shown wearing a beard. (There are two stories about "her" identity; one is that she was impersonated by Jean Borlin, leading dancer and choreographer of *Relâche;* the other, that the painter Picabia impersonated her.) Not only is her dignity being attacked but also her sexual integrity. This was part of the game, the conceit, of a revelation of taste that was specifically an inversion of good taste.

There are positive distinctions to be made between filmic Dada, circa 1924, filmic Surrealism, 1929-30, and Underground avant-garde films (mostly American), 1957-69. Yet plainly René Clair's bearded ballerina was in some ways a precursor of the transvestite heroines of films in the Underground sixties. Actually the Surrealists, headed by André Breton, bothered to "come out against" homosexuality, but this did

toward exhibition and exhibitionism

not prevent the poet Paul Eluard from getting into comic drag, with negligee and blond wig, in a Dada skit called *Vous M'Oublierez* (1920), in which Breton also performed. In *Flaming Creatures* (1962), Jack Smith's banned film, a grotesque cunnilingual rape is committed on a lone undefended woman by a man (not in feminine costume), aided and abetted by a bevy of transvestite males who, disheveled and naked, handle each other's limp genitals. The theme of violent outrage in the avant-garde tradition was here set forth as sadistic sex in which, oddly, frustration supplied a good deal of the flame's heat.

One is reminded of the famous shot near the opening of *Un Chien Andalou*, the film made by Luis Buñuel in collaboration with Salvador Dali, in which the theme of optical assault is savagely stated by drawing a razor blade (in a close-up) through a naked eye. A man wields the razor and the victim is a woman. (The reader may be relieved to know that the actual eye used, when the slicing was photographed, belonged to a dead donkey.) The ambiguous compliment paid the female sex was typically Sadian in spirit. In Buñuel's next film, *L'Age d'Or*, from which Dali retired at an early point, aggressive infantile sex is much more specifically exploited as part of adult precoital play. The film's high moment, however, is a Sadian assault on religion, for Buñuel makes Jesus Christ preside over Sade's *120 Days of Sodom*; the orgies themselves are skipped for a view of Jesus, the master debauchee, leaving the Château with his fellow sadists when the session is over.

What marked the early avant-garde spirit in Europe, before it spread to the United States, was a consciously immoral savagery, partly sadistic, partly intellectual satire: a grinning, elite sort of grimness. Religion and love were the two main objects of the mock-epicurean attack. In *L'Age d'Or* a couple give way to their mutual erotic impulse while part of a religious pilgrimage and start doing it on open ground, then and there. When the police, backed by the clergy, interfere, the male is

19

collared but escapes official detention and visits his mistress' home, where a formal party is going on. Soon he scandalizes everyone by assaulting (not sexually but like a furious child) the hostess and others and going utterly berserk.* The general effect is that of some prodigious and most unlikely farce—one not played for laughs. The camera is a voyeur in being uniquely privileged to witness one of those weird moments when social decorum is trampled underfoot by an adult yielding to infantile impulses out of sexual frustration. This situation, no matter how grotesque and funny, has an essential seriousness that gives *L'Age d'Or* a lasting Underground dignity.

For decorum's sake, up to now, people in most social strata still politely suppress violent or merely positive impulses that would make them ridiculous or compromise them morally. One of the strongest motifs in Underground films is the drive toward sloughing off civilized dignity and indulging amoral naked impulses in the sight of all; performers spontaneously do things which form a spectacle for others in the film as well as for the hypothetical audience. Since such action so often lacks a significant context (looks "gratuitous") and is not part of a plot, the performers tend to have the spontaneity of life rather than the "acted spontaneity" of a theatrical performance. This kind of performing is weakest in effect when the style is inept and frivolous and the actors, in consequence, seem exhibitionistic. Even when inspired with a covert wit, the more implausible a speech, gesture, or act, the more conspicuous and aggressive its look.†

* *Wild in the Streets*, a commercial film inspired by the youth revolt of today, has its teenage hero going berserk in his family home (the folks are away) and then by a series of fabulous events becoming President of the United States. In a still newer commercial film, *If* . . . , what was once avant-garde fantasy, the schoolboy daydreaming of Jean Vigo's *Zéro de Conduite*, assumes the significance of an existential myth: a program of action that is political, violent, and murderous in the comic-strip manner.

† The Living Theatre has made this deliberately inept style of performance an issue of the new stage art, but its stronghold remains the Underground Film.

toward exhibition and exhibitionism

It is true that many Underground films dispense with a craftsmanlike attitude and indulge in fetish footage which looks like so many golden moments of self-exhibition. The film itself may lack positive qualities to the extent of reducing it to the filmmaker's personal "ad." The more amateurish and inexpressive the actors, the less raison d'être an implicit situation seems to have. The most spineless of such films can pretend to be spoofs, but here again is an aspect in which the film camera's subject matter invites the exact coefficient of the voyeur-spectator. Not merely the audience is seeking peephole sensations, so are the actors and filmmakers who provide numerous films that correspond to sex shows and are aesthetically too little above the commercial nudie films shown on Forty-second Street in New York.

A vivid case in point is an Underground film called *I, a Man*, in emulation of the Swedish commercial film *I, a Woman* (which is better, incidentally, than a mere nudie film). When I attended a private screening of *I, a Man* the information was that it was a Warhol production, although the genesis of the idea and the apparently improvised dialogue is said to emanate from Tom Baker, a young man impersonating his own hero. In any case, unlike the sex film whose title it imitates, the Underground film has no plot whatever, being simply a sequence of seduction scenes unified only by the fact that the male is always the same one. There is much casual nudity in both sexes, a good deal of lovemaking (however much faked), and some ostensible frustration. To say the total effect is lifelike would be to assert that life is mostly dull with some interesting moments. *I, a Man*, having the authentic air of cinéma vérité, can surely be said, considering its subject matter, to fit the voyeuristic category.

In 1968 Warhol's chief assistant, Paul Morrissey, a filmmaker in his own right, directed a film called *Flesh*. Although it is like Warhol's work in many ways, it still manages to impart

21

the outline of a story to its portrayal of a young hustler's life. It stumbles a bit, but because it is coherent in a fairly conventional way, *Flesh* enjoyed what is perhaps the longest off-Broadway run of an Underground film. Its success is due partly, of course, to the personality of the hustler as played by Joe Dallesandro, a youngster with a photogenic face and curiously natural poise to his whole physique (which is small but neat and shapely). He too is shown in the nude, taking athletic poses for an artist, and also in bed with several nude or seminude women. He hustles males but is married to a girl and is not above letting a female whore go down on him (an action we witness from directly behind him as he stands in his underwear, and which is pretty convincing). Actually, the only parody here is provided by the incidental presence of a pair of female impersonators who, seated to one side, coolly chat through the fellatio scene. Otherwise there is a truly confiding air of vérité about it all, down to the last bit of action when the hustler, in bed with his wife and her pregnant girl friend, casts a very sleepy eye at lesbian demonstrations between the two females. Many technical things in Morrissey's film are sloppy, including a generally atrocious sound track. Yet one may pick out felicitous things, too. *Flesh* thus shows forth as a modulation of fetish footage toward attempts at formal coherence and filmic significance. Warhol disapproved of the film's formal editing, its story shaping. Morrissey (while his mentor and chief was hospitalized recovering from his gunshot wound) had been guilty of a kind of lèse-majesté.

One may as well prophetically conjure, right now, with the threat to Warholism and fetish footage that is already showing up in Underground film cameras. Somehow spectators can't get over being acclimated to "stories," so that all the vérité atmosphere that can be crammed into cameras is not proof against a series of related events which approximate what is known, historically, as "experience." At this stage of the avant-garde evolution various revolutions of taste tend to scant the story for the illustrated slogan and simple pictorial propaganda. Yet I don't mean that politics per se always dictates the propagandistic subject matter. Perennially active, the propaganda tends to be that of absolute freedom in love and the given privilege of all varieties of offbeat sex. Filmic evidence of the latter type is being shown all over New York these days as a "life style," as if what millions of people over the globe have been doing in bed for uncountable centuries had at last earned a place in the moral vocabulary. Thus the statistical prominence of the fetish-footage sort of film also carries with it a charge of phenomenal *moral* importance. Its strictly filmic (or what we may call its artistic) significance is altogether a different matter.

popularizing peepshows: the infantile gimmick

Of course the fetish-footage works are among the worst, not the best, of any given year's Underground crop. But the ratio of badly made, uninspired Underground films increases, alas, with every year. I do not mean that all of them fail to be transiently entertaining—far from it—yet they are very uneven in quality and lack importance *as films*. The reason must be found for so precipitate a degenerate growth of the Underground, and this reason, not far to seek, is integral with the Underground breakthrough of recent years. In fact, it is uncritical permissiveness—and this is precisely the moral stance of the child who stages absolute rebellion against his parents and all adults. He asserts the right of doing as he pleases, regardless. It is impossible to ignore this insistent phase of Underground psychology: it is childish self-indulgence.

To understand Underground Film, we must realize that it is an expression which, after 1960, gained much impetus as a group idea. It was part of the universal youth movement, and like a progressive school for modern children it felt (and feels) that nothing among outgoing emotions should be suppressed. It is the democratic ideal of free expression slanted specifically toward the indeterminately young and thus toward the relatively inexperienced and unproven. In the Film-Makers' Co-operative, the distributing system conceived by Jonas Mekas,* every young filmmaker gets *unlimited credit* for good intentions, so that regardless of his ability to realize his ideas, regardless of the ideas themselves, the fact that he wants to use film as a medium of self-expression is, in advance, the chief virtue of whatever he may produce. The current avant-garde has a vice: wish-fulfilment psychology masquerading as a system of aesthetic values.

A momentarily embarrassing irony cropped up in Underground history when Stan Brakhage, one of the film movement's superstars, inaugurated a one-man revolt. Out of the blue, a letter from this filmmaker arrived for Jonas Mekas, withdrawing all collaboration from the Film-Makers' Cooperative and its Film-Makers' Cinémathèque. "I cannot, in good conscience," Brakhage wrote—as quoted in a mimeographed report circulated by the Coop—"continue to accept the help of institutions (for that is what they have become) which, thru the imbalances of the works of unaesthetic and thoughtless self(ish) expression they do mostly distribute and show-forth, have come to propagate advertisements for forces which I recognize as among the most destructive in the world today: 'dope,' self-centered Love, unqualified Hatred, Nihilism, violence to self AND society. . . ."

Rather dazed and a little angry, but still "tolerant," Mekas

* Cinema 16, the film society which became the nation's first large distributing organization concerned chiefly with avant-garde films, was temporarily eclipsed in the 1960's only because of the Coop's comprehensively uncritical policy. These two remain the movement's chief distributing organizations. Next in importance are Canyon Cinema Cooperative, on the West Coast, and Audio Film Center, which also distributes classic commercial films. See note pages 248-249.

25

and his governing board could do nothing but assent (with a formal expostulation) to Brakhage's withdrawal. It was not many months before the old group spirit prevailed in the rebel's bosom. After all, he had reason to be grateful because, ever since the sixties began, Mekas' magazine, *Film Culture*, had been the chief publicity medium for Brakhage and other Underground filmmakers. In 1962 Brakhage had received the magazine's annual Independent Film Award and the organization had issued a large monograph devoted to his writing and his films. Finding himself without an immediate showcase for his work, and living isolated with his wife and children near Boulder, Colorado, he had a change of heart and rejoined the ranks suddenly and quietly, with no questions asked by either side.

The temper tantrums of children arise and pass off in much the same way. Moreover, I imagine that Brakhage had found especially rankling the unexpected and instant success of Andy Warhol's films, which in a couple of years gained more publicity than Brakhage's had in ten years. Warhol too had been taken to the heart of *Film Culture* and the Cinémathèque and had duly received the magazine's annual award. Both adult and infantile jealousy can be, at times, extraordinarily childish. The phenomenon of Warhol was probably especially stinging to Brakhage, who had emerged from the old avant-garde tradition of technically acute and resourceful film-making. Warhol had, among other things, rolled back the history of the film to certain artless, primitive beginnings (paradoxically artificial in effect) that would be obnoxious to anyone bred on the ingenuities of the historic avant-garde.

Brakhage's *Desistfilm* (premièred at Cinema 16 in 1955) was the first important beatnik film with the air of a spontaneous Happening. Disarmingly candid in depicting youth in the simple occupation of getting high, being tricksy, and then running harmlessly wild, it was influential and prophetic—and, happily, quite brief. In his earlier period, besides earning a living by working on science-research films, Brakhage also did a lot of wandering. Yet he never ceased making his films and trying to decide about love and marriage. Like Maya Deren, he was wise enough to undertake spates of barnstorming with his films at colleges and film societies all over the country. But when he at last found an ideal mate, he married her, and when there were children it seemed expedient for him to settle down rather than go on with his wandering. A large foundation grant helped him decide to remain on the land in Colorado; after that came the explosive withdrawal from the Cinémathèque.

For his part, Warhol provided in every way a contrast to his rival: bachelorhood, an unintellectual temperament, verbal inarticulacy, secretiveness, much dependence on collaborators, an abiding air of goggle-eyed voyeurism in his films. It is illuminating to compare these two conspicuous Undergrounders, one (Warhol) so calculatedly naive and untheoretical, the other (Brakhage) so calculatedly sophisticated and theoretical; both already long past chronological adolescence. Taking a retrospective view, suppose we try to assess their work as objectively as possible. Whereas Warhol's films tended to move at major physical retardation, Brakhage's tended to move at major physical acceleration. In this contrast their styles are equally distinctive and can be equally irritating. If Warhol seems to have solved the problems of his radically restrained movement better than Brakhage has solved those of his radically propelled movement, it is because the former is simply do-nothing while the latter seems to do too much, too fleetly, and without enough rhythmic control or variety. During Warhol's first three years of filmmaking, from 1936 to 1966, an inner slow motion, like an implosive weight, surrounded and framed off the slightest willed motion of his performers. On the other hand, nearly all the activity of Brakhage's perpetual-motion style is in his camera, which dives, swoops, caracols, stops transiently in its tracks, and—when situated in a moving automobile, as in *Anticipation of the Night*—provides an extra, monotonously jiggling counterpoint.

Generally speaking, the human action in Brakhage's work, through rapid cutting, close-up frames, and under- or over-exposed film, is fragmented and abstracted into light and color patterns even when the action is identifiable and fairly coherent. In contrast, until very lately Warhol's films have been content (the camera being at a technically antiquated standstill) with the minutest moves of beings who may be so inanimate, for minutes, that they actually seem drugged. Warhol's rejection of the mature vocabulary of filmic effects, including varied editing rhythms, may remind one of a young child's trancelike, arbitrary fixation on certain objects. The very different streamy-dreamy rhythm of Brakhage's work is surely provocative and serves up unexpected—all too momentary—beauties. To me this style seems to come from the filmmaker's subservience to an only partly controlled, will-o'-the-wisp nervousness of pulse beat; but a psychological, not a physical, pulse beat.

To hear Brakhage's claim that *Anticipation of the Night*, the film out of which his present style grew, is governed by the musical design of Beethoven's Seventh Symphony is simply to be impressed once again with how mortally crippling a hold the cult of abstraction can get on modern artists in all media. Even if this completely silent film has been edited according to that great symphony's rhythms, it does not necessarily mean that the total sum of movements within the film frames has a proper correspondence to Beethoven's music. Moreover, after repeated viewings of the film, I cannot detect in it a consistent rhythmic organization of its own. Only crude infantile compulsion, seemingly, can account for the filmmaker's marked obsession with racing rhythms. It seems no accident, then, that the overall pattern of *Anticipation of the Night* concerns an

popularizing peepshows: the infantile gimmick

adult male's hallucinations of young children, either sleeping babies (who seem to dream of animals) or tiny tots absorbed in endlessly spinning on amusement-park whirligigs. As for plot, like the great majority of Underground films, this film is content with incident and episode to shape its message.

Warhol's anti-film has meant a significant anticlimax for the avant-garde movement because it represents a primitivism lodged in the limitations of film's strict technical beginnings. Why, in fact, did the very earliest films in history (fond of showing chases) portray slapstick and lively, at times speeded-up, action? Why did they exhibit, like stage magic, the same magic transformations (trick editing) that eventually led to the surreal effects of the first avant-garde films of Europe? Partly because, surely, they were trying to overcome the handicap of a technical instrument (the film camera) which, then just born, could not perambulate, move perceptibly into close-ups, isolate detail clearly or easily, or continuously follow the pattern of an action through space—all things which in the technical adulthood of the movies have long been mastered. Aside from all magical effects (animation of inanimate matter and trick editing to produce supernatural behavior), filmic movement once existed entirely in *what* the camera photographed, not *how*, and thus not in the camera itself; nor, till the first decade of filmmaking had passed, did film achieve itself in the laboratory, where it is now edited to give it narrative shape and final plastic interest. At first only the studio set-ups changed from action to action (or, as on the stage, from scene to scene); gradually several viewpoints within one set established an elementary interest and variety in the given action. Today in the avant-garde (one thinks of Markopoulos' intensive use) many technical effects, such as multiple exposure, are achieved in the film camera during the shooting.

When film history is assessed in relation to the avant-garde as climaxed and anticlimaxed by the Underground, it is surprising how much the strength and distinction of current developments depend on a *rejection* of sophisticated technical means and of sophisticated aims in general. At first glance this may seem to have a purely economic basis—and naturally, it does most assuredly have an economic cause. But the major reason is a "cause" in the moral sense and in the sense associated with revolution. In many, many ways Underground Film represents the cause of the underdog as not merely underprivileged in economic means but underprivileged also (despite subjective delusions) in talent and general culture. Is this the old "making a virtue out of necessity"?

However kindly or unkindly viewed, it is a great big toddler, the Underground Film. Something of a small titan, it is noticeably underprivileged. The last, of course, is my own word; in the eyes of Underground ideologists this attribute is construed as the expression of a natural privilege such as "poetic" talent. Strength in numbers is merely ancillary to such large benign theories. Shining epithets are integral with the ideological blarney of the movement, the Underground's unabashed lyricism of self-praise. In Mekas' prose it is like a fond papa's lullaby. (An interesting point is that while Mekas himself, by the clock, gets older and older, his ideas get younger and younger.)

A number of independent filmmakers of the sixties, coming straight out of beatnik and hipster environments, take pride in assuming that primitive camera work, deteriorated film, indifferent lighting, nonacting, and other purely atechnical things are not imposed by lack of means to buy equipment, hire actors and so on, or by inexperience, but are chosen as expressions of cultural, even quasi-aesthetic prejudice. The photographically and emotionally shaggy films of Ron Rice and of Jack Smith are outstanding examples of this pseudo-economic (or pseudo-aesthetic) viewpoint. Up to this very moment Mekas (who, incidentally, is called the "guru of Underground Film") denies

popularizing peepshows: the infantile gimmick

that economically his organizations are a "success," although
by now a small part of the movie-going public has the impression—true or false—that they are. There is a tendency inside
the movement to underplay any actual commercial breakthrough, such as Warhol's with *The Chelsea Girls* (1967).
Nevertheless, there has been a significant expansion of the
Underground among the art theaters.

Influential weeklies such as *Time, Newsweek,* and the *Village
Voice* have given Underground Film a great deal of space in
the past three or four years, and have more than once saluted
it for "surfacing." Even the *New York Times* has repeatedly
written up Underground Film developments and considers
Mekas a public figure worth being interviewed. Such things
(whatever their importance) could not have been anticipated
before the sixties. Previously the openings of even the most
ambitious avant-garde films were very seldom reviewed. Today,
at least a second-string reviewer is delegated to cover most
feature-length items and occasionally even mixed programs
of short works. Sometimes this happens because the big films
have begun to open in art theaters around New York, but it is
not always for that reason. People tend to respect even cradles
when their occupants have the muscles of Gargantua.

no establishment at all?

The Underground Film is not predominantly or necessarily the expression of a beatnik cult. The point is that it *encourages* beatnik expressions through its practical rule of universal tolerance. The moral note struck has a good deal to do with the revolt against the Establishment that predated the rise of the Underground Film and centered during the fifties in the plays and novels of England's Angry Young Men. It also received a strong current of influence (as the 1958 Underground film *Pull My Daisy* proves) from the prose and poetry of the Beat Generation that appeared in the late fifties and that celebrated, to borrow Jack Kerouac's own formula, the milieu of the dharma bums.

The avant-garde film, for that matter, has always opposed itself to professional slickness and popular film formulas and always disdained the "costly look" as such. This has been its ineradicable aim as representing the standards of a *pure* art. Yet, as we see when inspecting the unique cultural revolt

32

no establishment at all?

of the Dadaists and the Surrealists, this century has brought
into question exactly the purity of art and has made material
poverty irrelevant to spiritual poverty. The anomaly peeps
out when we read in a recently published survey of American
Underground films a whole chapter devoted to "The Underground Establishment." Does this term signify that an *art*
Establishment is meant? Aesthetics, however, is not a province
of the naïve author of the book, which amounts simply to a
miniature encyclopedia of the avant-garde film.* In all seriousness one might ask: Was the drastic revision of culture inaugurated by Dada-Surrealism after all only a palace revolution—that is, an "academy revolution"? Also, are those same
historic movements (which of course encompass the film) just
another case of contesting the seats of the mighty? The election
of Jean Cocteau to the Académie Française might well give us
pause over this question.

If one ethical trait is characteristic of the twentieth century,
it is that social theory—rooted in political revolutions from
that of France to that of Russia—has tended to prohibit the
very psychology of Establishments. Many objective ironies are
meshed with this supposed prohibition, not the least being
the existence of Establishment forms,—political bureaucracies
—in socialist as well as fascist states. Nevertheless, a dominant
tendency of popular thinking in our time is anti-Establishment,
not merely in opposing existent Establishment orders, but by
negating the very concept of Establishment. The forces in
avant-garde films which have been named Underground conspicuously if tacitly support a code that would outlaw Establishments—that is, destroy forever the political validity of the
Establishment idea.

Curiously enough, the Underground film movement, regarded in this light, can be identified as having traits of both

* *An Introduction to the American Underground Film*, by Sheldon Renan. E. P.
Dutton and Co., New York, 1967.

Anarchist and Communist philosophy. The catch is that, considering its best predecessors in American avant-garde film, the movement has taken specifically *formal virtues* as the object of destruction, and has done so not autocratically, by rigidly excluding those virtues, but by using its universal-tolerance code. Valid formal virtues therefore manifest themselves in the movement as a minority, not a majority. In the mouth of an authoritative Underground spokesman, "A film is a film is a film" means that anything amateurishly (i.e., lovingly) recorded on film is a legitimate object for public exposure. Hence ultrapermissiveness achieves an ironic triumph by also welcoming the work of nominally Underground filmmakers who take great technical pride in their products and aim at creating films that, whatever their true virtues or defects, have both filmic craft and a poetic style. Among such filmmakers are Stan Brakhage, Gregory Markopoulos, Ed Emshwiller, Kenneth Anger, Charles Boultenhouse, and (until recently) Willard Maas. By association the non-technical ones profit from this chameleon atmosphere and the technical ones suffer.

For example, the Underground critical Establishment is slower to accord filmmakers of the craft group an official honor such as the yearly *Film Culture* award. Markopoulos, though he had been working before the advent of men like Warhol and Ron Rice, had to wait until seven other filmmakers had been honored before receiving that award in 1967. Analyzing to what degree the achievements of the Underground Film are artistic and to what degree otherwise is an unavoidably complex subject, if only because *art as such has nothing to do with the reigning Establishment procedures.*

underground climb: from exhibitionism to art

The main strength of the Underground Film per se (not simply as a variety of avant-garde film) is currently to use the camera as the self-sufficient reporter of vital activity. It is as if to say: The technique and the form do not matter, only the message matters. And yet here the message is what makes the medium look messy—*that* is the ultimate message! The Underground has enshrined the camera as a wild, willful, inquisitive eye, disposed to give graphic publicity to everything that has remained taboo in the realm of popular commercial films, even the most serious and artistic among them. If it were not clear that such men as Fellini, Antonioni, Godard, and Truffaut must be rejected by the Underground canon, then the American Underground would hardly be what it is—what it pretends to be and sometimes, significantly, can be.

I shall now risk a general formula for the key term of voyeur which I have proposed as one of the main drives of the Underground camera. Perhaps the voyeur camera can be equated with the avant-garde without damaging the integrity of the really valuable—that is, artistically vital—elements of the avant-garde and its tradition. Remember that art itself is *expensive*. It is expensive since it must draw heavily and primarily on the capital of individual genius. The organized American Underground Film is anticapitalistic in this sense. It is no accident that Andy Warhol's films, during his first three years of making them, were mainly group endeavors and that throughout those years he functioned with very little directorial power, leaving script and the coaching of actors largely to others, while using the paltriest methods of editing. He is a filmic *auteur* by default. In fact, a Warhol pride and distinction has been the projection of solid time on the screen, where not only is clock time uninterrupted in form, but the takes themselves are (so far as possible) made without interruption. Owing to amateurish contingencies, of course, sometimes Warhol had to cheat—and this meant more than just stopping while the camera was being reloaded. I have heard the boast, from a close associate of Warhol's, that at one period a "film" was shot at the Factory (Warhol's loft studio) "every day."

Ours is the sneaking time of the voyeur and also the voyeur's tragic "poverty": the peephole is his makeshift but necessary field of "stolen" vision and an absolute limit to this field. This may seem, at first sight, a rather biased view that does injustice to well-intentioned candor in Underground films. I hasten to cite Stan Brakhage's series of sex and birth films as illustrations of something unquestionably bona-fide and entirely without suspicion of lubricity. As for their "exhibitionism," let that be the final issue. From the psychological angle these brief films (two of which confront the act of giving birth in full light and full color) may be thought of as scientifically valuable: a bold use of the documentary film. Yet they have a personal touch; in fact they look like sophisticated home movies on the happily hip side.

underground climb: from exhibitionism to art

"Why did Brakhage make them?" is a legitimate first question. The first, *Window Water Baby Moving*, is extremely candid and straightforward. We see the mother, Jane Brakhage, in late pregnancy and then in childbed; we see the attending doctor, the opening vulva, the birth itself in most details, and then (the camera being, one was told, in the hands of the mother) the father, Brakhage himself, in a fleeting state of jubilant delirium. In its way, a cozy little film. Is it not like an automatic diary, a record of his couvade by Brakhage the filmmaker? The hand-held camera, one feels, does not have much grace, and moreover does not pretend to have any; here is a small lyric of privacy whose originality is in the public visibility of the subject rather than any subtlety of handling it. Surely it is not without meaning that at the Living Theatre in New York, when a program of films by the Gryphon group (to which Brakhage then belonged) was given at the end of the fifties, the late Maya Deren emerged from seeing *Window Water Baby Moving* with a vociferous protest.

It was a little astounding to hear a senior member of the avant-garde ranks so "anti" about a modest film done in perfect good faith,* but Miss Deren was objecting that woman's privacy had been deliberately, tactlessly invaded. Human birth, she declared, is a mystery and especially a feminine mystery. Though herself a scholar of primitive ritual, she did not sympathize at all, here, with the male couvade that Brakhage was celebrating.

Without regard either to aesthetics or to the possible sacredness of certain physical mysteries, it could be argued in Brakhage's behalf that he was, at worst, exercising the father's privilege of being at the bedside when his wife was

---

* Deren and Brakhage had been uniquely "pure" among prominent avant-gardistes in never having used sound accompaniment of any kind for their films; Miss Deren's last film, *The Very Eye of Night* (1959), however, had a music score by Teiji Ito.

bearing him a child. The point I am bringing out, however, is the voyeuristic agency of the camera in these birth films. The same point applies to a conjugal film by Brakhage, which, however, is (tactfully?) underlighted or underexposed, giving a shadowy and confused effect. The filmmaker's manner of shooting is usually, as here, overcasual and rather "hasty" in look, so that no special quality of mystery renders the vagueness as poetic. Thus the emergent message of such films is their novelty in terms of according public exhibition to what has been considered strictly domestic and private. Recently, in *Love Making I to IV*, Brakhage has gone much further in voyeuristic candor.

I think it notable that several years earlier, when Brakhage turned his voyeur camera on himself to film a masturbation fantasy, *Flesh of Morning*, he produced a much more craftsmanlike and genuinely poetic film; this one has some moments of doubtful taste but on the whole it is a precision-tooled product among the small number of really memorable films created by the Underground. The whole content of masturbation, with its anticlimax of futility and infertility, becomes present. The last sequence of shots is the protagonist's sight of small children playing in the suburban street below his balcony; inevitably they symbolize possible souls whose life his ritual habit makes impossible. Throughout *Flesh of Morning* occur those moments of pure magic for which the genius of the film has become famous. Yet Brakhage was highly impulsive then; he soon extradited the compulsive rhythm of thrust and recoil to the free rhythms of a restless camera eye.

The relevance of these works to cinéma vérité as a school of film should not be overlooked. Cinéma vérité (when genuine rather than faked or mimicked) may be an openly announced, often publicly practiced form of eavesdropping, like asking someone, entirely without notice, to sit, walk, and/or talk for his portrait. A hidden camera may also be used, and this would seem the only guarantee of genuine cinéma vérité. Yet such a guarantee is in order only if one assumes that individuals being photographed without their knowledge necessarily behave otherwise than if they were aware of it. On the other hand, if individuals are eager to be photographed (and/or interviewed), one can only assume that they wish to publicize what they do naturally, willingly, and ordinarily. Otherwise they would enact put-ons and cinéma vérité would be fraudulent.

A striking case of Underground-publicized privacy arrived at the Fifth New York Film Festival (1967) in the shape of an ambitious film by Shirley Clarke. According to her statements at the press conference in Philharmonic Hall after the screening, everything about the film, titled *Portrait of Jason*, is bona fide. The subject's identity is very real and he pretends to be no one, on and off the film, except himself, even though "Jason Holliday," as he explains, is a fictitious name by which he has lived for many years. When asked by a member of the press whether Mr. Holliday might be liable to prosecution "for things he said he did" in the film, the director replied, "I don't think so . . . besides, he could be lying." The fact remains that by every visible and audible token Jason Holliday is not lying, although perhaps (it may occur to the spectator-auditor) he may be "exaggerating."

Art too is said, if sometimes inaccurately, to exaggerate. The fact remains that the true cachet of *Portrait of Jason* is that it portrays a real-life individual who is willing to admit publicly everything which (especially in the case of a homosexual) it has been considered socially desirable to keep secret or a fact known only to one's close circle of friends. There can be no question of the subject's absolute complacence, even his joy, in having his film portrait done. Once he suddenly avows what a "lovely thing" is happening to him (he makes remarks throughout to the director and a male friend beyond camera range) and virtually swoons away with the ecstasy of it. Well

39

may he prize the opportunity to surface from his underground existence: nothing but his face and figure are seen during the film's 105 minutes and there are, I admit, few moments of boredom.

An "open interview," *Portrait of Jason* provides a climax for the Underground film camera as a morally sanctioned, altogether self-righteous voyeur whose findings are meant for public consumption. Indeed, it seems that a new social game (not unlike certain parlor predecessors) must be called Public Confessions and that universal applause is its natural reward. The European Underground sensibility satirized vérité interviewing in *Sweet and Sour* (1963),* directed by Jacques Baratier, who uses a hoked-up documentary style to lampoon such things as walkie-talkies and the obsession of ordinary people with hearing themselves on tape and seeing themselves on film. In *Sweet and Sour* there is a club of cinéastes devoted precisely to recording their own psychodramas. Being European, Baratier is more intellectually sophisticated than the American Underground about the moral machinery of this type of "filmic passion." He shows that the voyeur camera as a symbol of the Underground (in all its senses including the id and the libido) could not have become the force it is today without corresponding exhibitionism in the persons and actions shown. As a collective movement, then, Underground Film is simply a new, radically inspired revision of the home movie. Significantly, the subject of *Portrait of Jason* had had a solo nightclub act which he invariably failed to put across. All such frustrations are now magically wafted away by the mechanics of the Underground.

Warhol knew what he was doing when he chose the episode of fellatio as a subject for a thirty-minute silent film. It too has the honorary solid time, although it shows more than one detail. For much the greater part of the film, however, the

* Seen at the First New York Film Festival.

camera allows us (as if it were a handicapped peephole) to see only the head of the passive partner in this sexual act, the blond, leather-jacketed youth being blown. The suspension of animacy that provides a tension of boredom in many Warhol films is here modified by the built-in suspense of the prelude to orgasm. Any "aesthetic" quality of *Blow Job* (1964) must be carefully picked up from second to second by those connoisseurs devoted to watching the faces of their lovers. There is a psychological expansion, therefore, to the voyeur camera's peephole as distinct from an actual expansion.

Here, for example, the active sexual partner, prohibited from optically enjoying the register of sensation on the youth's face owing to the physical arrangement of this particular act, had the opportunity, once the film was printed, to follow without interruption the sensations his work had produced insofar as the subject's face had reflected the excitation of his penis. I doubt very much if Underground Film would be nearly what it is today without its defiance of legal taboos regarding exhibition of the sexual act—not to mention the defiance of optional moral taboos and taboos of good taste. Such taboos have been notably relaxed, during the sixties, not only because of Underground pressure but also because of pressure above ground. Sophisticated filmmaking—especially in France, Sweden, and Denmark—has been steadily preparing what is normally classed as sexual privacy for a champagne launching on the open sea of the film screen.

At the moment this preparation applies to homosexuality as well as heterosexuality and involves not merely the tolerance of official motion picture codes but of the law courts themselves. The only three exceptions to legal permissiveness toward the Underground, to my knowledge, have been those occasioned by Jack Smith's *Flaming Creatures*, whose undisguised (though futile) manipulation of male genitalia was the technical cause for the Police Department's banning of this film's public showing in New York; Jean Genet's *Un Chant d'Amour,* prohibited by verdict of the state of California and the U.S. Supreme Court; and Warhol's new *Blue Movie (Fuck).* Smith's latest film, *No President,* an even more daring exploitation of the themes in *Flaming Creatures* (minus cunnilingual rape and plus political burlesque), had a one-performance première in New York which quite escaped the notice of the police. Though *Un Chant d'Amour* is much more sophisticated than *Flaming Creatures,* its homosexuality is both pointed and blunt, and being set in a prison, it makes much of "peephole" sensations.

The up- (and in-) surge of Underground Films has revised, to some extent, the role of the motion-picture exhibitor, who may be called the middleman in a daisy chain of which the two end men are apt to be exhibitionists: the filmmaker and the film made. In case someone unfamiliar with Underground films doubts the naïveté of the fiilmmakers' personal exhibitionism, an unvarnished example ought to be cited. We are well acquainted with the new candor of commercial films (illustrated as long ago as 1949 by an incident in the neorealist *Bicycle Thief*) that permits glimpses of little boys obviously taking a pee in the street. We have also witnessed the majestic extension of visual free speech that stages scenes in which urinals are visible and men stand at them conducting a conversation. So far as I know, however, no adult male was presented to the public in profile with urine stream visible until one of the Kuchar brothers, in one of their playful Underground films, left his car on the road and relieved himself in the open. I hardly need add that the incident was pedantically uninvolved with the plot action. It remains one of those sublime Underground gratuities for which the audiences at the New York Film-Makers' Cinémathèque so patiently stay in their seats.

I was about to continue, "All camping to one side," and so on. But I reflect that camping is here to stay for some years in the domain of entertainment undergrounds, where surfacing is always expected instanter. In any case, serious criticism and art must do the best they can for themselves, as they have always had to do. There are valid precedents for the voyeur camera within the history proper of the avant-garde film; a few historic instances have already been mentioned. But Cocteau's *Le Sang d'un Poète*, first shown in Paris at the same time as *L'Age d'Or*, canonized the concept of the voyeur *as avant-garde*. This was accomplished by the ritual journey of its suicidal and self-abusive hero-poet, who enters the Hôtel des Folies as if in a dream and proceeds to view certain mysteries through the keyholes of doors along one of its corridors, mysteries involving love, death, and art. His ultimate suicide is symbolic, not real, a point deplorably misunderstood by the rich elite whose money sponsored Cocteau's film. When it was learned that a group of society people, to be included in the film as occupying a theater box, were in effect applauding a poet's suicide as if it were a theatrical spectacle, the film's sponsor, the Vicomte de Noailles, forbade Cocteau to incorporate the applauding incident in the film: he himself and his wife had amiably consented to be among those in the theater box. Cocteau used his ironic wit for revenge. The scene was reshot with, this time, a female impersonator as the leading society lady.

It is a pungent fact that a society girl of the present, Edie Sedgwick, one of Warhol's superstars, has none of the squeamishness of Cocteau's friends. In the film *Vinyl* Miss Sedgwick, seen sitting languidly at one side, is an obviously if quietly interested audience of the film's action. The "action" (miniaction would be a good general term for it) is a miniature sadomasochistic melodrama conceived by Warhol's principal script writer, Ronald Tavel (author of the play *Gorilla Queen*). It shows two male superstars, Gerard Malanga and Tosh Carrillo, indulging half playfully, half in earnest, in a naughty fiction about Leather Boy exhibitionism. Latent homosexuality is the gimmick and, as filmed, it is largely a sagging, sillified charade. While Malanga as the central character has some good moments of miming and does a superb rock-'n'-roll dance solo, the whole action is such a transparent parody that it might have been filmed in a large closet with people snatched from the street to fill out the cast. Part of the transparency is that all the speaking actors are looking at so-called idiot cards, printed speeches held up beyond camera range. The lines had not been memorized, or at least when the film was shot the actors were not in a condition to recall them.

Once we see Miss Sedgwick, who during the film takes a couple of turns rock-'n'-rolling with Malanga, abruptly rise from her seat and disappear, to return after a few minutes to her former place and attitude. Actually, as I learned much later from Malanga, she had simply left to go to the bathroom. But by accident, as we observe when she vanishes, she had been shielding Carrillo (then in the background), who was engaged in applying a candle flame to various spots on the naked flesh of a tied-up adolescent male, who in turn looked vaguely agonized. In Warhol's factory of film fantasy peepholism is a contingent and casual occupation as well as an obsession, and it must take its chance with competing drives, including any artistic impulses that may be loitering on the premises.

Miss Sedgwick was also given roles that demanded more acting ability, but (judging by the way she did them) very little more. That's part of Underground chic: *Underact!* It's another slap at professionalism, which opens the way to overacting.

underground infantilism:
surfacing superstars

Being a Warhol superstar who apparently still had not quarreled with him over acting fees or proper credits, Edie Sedgwick occupied, with a growing number of others (Mary Might—now Woronow—International Velvet, Bridget Polk, Ondine, Ultra Violet, and Viva), a peculiar category. A superstar may merely play himself or herself, perhaps ad-libbing for the purpose; he may also recite lines from a script, or occasionally read them from the idiot cards; or, with coaching from the director, he may improvise according to agreed-upon themes. The line between life and theater, reality and fiction, is not so much blurred as deliberately, cursorily informalized. The step from one to the other is taken with a casual flair or nonflair for mimicking the feelings of vague, somewhat surreal situations whose lurking absurdity or camp "poetry" is supposedly available to the spectator.

45

This is a definition of one variety of camp: satire which is funny because it makes no effort to imitate anything well; rather it is a calculated semislander by a parodist with his own sub rosa personality to exploit. If he should sound, and look, desultory, it's because he's being "natural," he's avoiding the look of put-on. The parodist's own personality does not have to be exploitable in the theatrical sense; his performance is more apt to be an "interesting failure," like those of children or very young people with the delusion that their antics are genuinely gifted and superior to the stuff of the performers they take occasion to imitate. In *Portrait of Jason,* for example, the subject (who seems thirtyish, perhaps fortyish, rather than twentyish) explains to us about the nightclub act he could never put across and proceeds to give us imitations of Mae West, Scarlett O'Hara (Vivien Leigh), and others.

The imitations, in a way, are *too* honest, *too* accurate—and why not, then, really talented? Because they lack that worldly essential which the French express in the word *chic.* The chic of parody (in contrast to that of underacting) is to have a certain detachment from what is parodied; to exaggerate just enough to make the target amusingly ridiculous. Mr. Holliday is too much Mae West inside himself; he wants too much to *be* Mae West, too little just to *imitate* her; the same applies to his Scarlett O'Hara. His is the child's delusion of grandeur when it desires to take over adult functions, to eavesdrop on them and then simulate them; this is a magic that will make the child into a man or woman. A similar case is that of another superstar, Mario Montez, whose female-impersonator act (seen several times in Warhol's films) is theoretically inspired by Maria Montez, a second-rate divinity of a previous Hollywood era. Straight-camp cult articles on this deceased actress have appeared in *Film Culture.* Jack Smith is one of her cult admirers.

Yet Montez himself, though interesting as a female impersonator, has even less resemblance to Maria Montez than to Jean

Harlow, whom he actually impersonates in the Warhol films
Screen Test I and *Harlot*—the latter title an obvious play on
the star's name. If one remarks to an Underground buff that
usually Montez' drag act (rated by drag-act standards) is pretty
bad, he will reply that that is the point, it is part of the beauty
of the parody that the parodist be inept. Mario Montez does not
impersonate Maria Montez; he "is" (that is, wishes to *be*)
Maria Montez. It is camp existentialism.

Warhol's scripts, near-scripts and nonscripts (the last based
on ideas of his own) are assuredly not unique among Underground films, in which "actors" often seem to be going through
their own daily routines, whether campy or not. This is true of
much of *The Chelsea Girls*, despite the fact that it had a script
by Tavel. In this film the male actor, Ondine, has a lengthy
monologue that is more manic than, but seemingly just as autobiographical as, that of Jason in Shirley Clarke's film. The
shaggier sort of Underground invention just naturally takes the
shape of a Happening rather extensively planned—partly improvised by the performers (these sequences have a psychedelic
tinge), partly inspired by a spirit of parody and self-parody.
The secret significance of many Underground films lies in *what*
is parodied; most often this is found to be some character or
plot situation, some style or familiar gimmick, from popular
films of other decades—films seen in the filmmaker's childhood.

Adolfas Mekas' *Hallelujah the Hills*, one of the first Underground films to make a show of surfacing commercially, was a
romping travesty, sometimes nostalgic in tone, of ancient Hollywood formulas and was put together less like a plot than an
anthology. In the thirties and forties there was a cult of admiration for Grade B Hollywood exotica (the films about the Cat
People, for instance). They were usually supernaturalist thril-
lers made by professionals but influenced by a Poësque sort of
Gothicism that easily lent itself to weird surreal effects with
an avant-garde air. A talented avant-garde filmmaker, Curtis

47

Harrington, came to grief when he tried to revitalize this same Hollywood brand of exotica with a film called *Night Tide*, its title echoing a line of Poe's.

In another Underground area, the dharma-bum films of Ron Rice, one can perceive the survival of the routines of Hollywood tramp comedians (outstandingly in Taylor Mead's role in *The Flower Thief*). In certain Underground gimmickry a parody of patriotic melodrama bears resemblance to the lunatic romps of the Marx Brothers, only now the actors are not in comic uniforms, as if the parody were part of real life, not a movie fiction. There is an Underground gem in Rice's *The Flower Thief* in which a group of the dharma bums (Rice calls them apostles of dazendada: dadaists of Zen) are found suddenly, as if spontaneously, parodying the famous film shot of the raising of the American flag on Iwo Jima in World War II. Such things are decidedly hip and still get a rise, however cool, from the audience that attends Underground films most faithfully.

There is a more vulgar sort of Underground film which becomes a vehicle of a kind of opportunism, something less genuine than a personal exhibitionistic drive or the desire to articulate some frenzied, ingrown fantasy (like Jack Smith's). This less important trend is well exemplified with two films: Mike Kuchar's *Sins of the Fleshapoids* and Ron Rice's *The Queen of Sheba Meets the Atom Man*. It is painfully plain that such films are idiot-grin camp versions of commercial pop films—part science fiction, part Poe thriller, and in sum devastatingly hip. The very statements supplied by the filmmakers to publicize them are parodies of the most blatant advertising copy known to Hollywood commercialdom. They may literally say "dig." It is to be hoped that one does dig, for that's the camp of it. The aim of these films is, by being mildly obscene, to expose the stealthy eroticism and sadism of commercial science fiction. Now such an aim is strange, if only because all hip moviegoers have grasped as much for decades. What have the howls and whistles of teenagers at the screen performances of Dracula and the Wolf Man meant through the years if not aroused sexuality ready for a rampage?

Hence the efflorescence of Underground exploitation of this same arousable sexuality by people in their twenties (by, that is, technical adults) surely deserves attention and analysis. To put the point directly, a sort of parody of Underground hipsterism —Robert Downey's *Chafed Elbows*—enjoyed a marathon run at a small East Village theater and drew the praise of some of the New York professional Establishment critics. Since it is handled by the Film Distribution Center as well as by the Film-Makers' Cooperative, *Chafed Elbows* can be regarded as part of the acknowledged canon. Mr. Downey is quoted in the Cooperative's catalogue as follows (apparently from a letter of camp advice to his distributors): "As for *Chafed Elbows* . . . if I were you, I wouldn't let anybody over 40 years old in the theatre unless they're accompanied by a teenager."

Why forty and not thirty? Teenage hippies and near-hippies claim not to trust anyone over thirty. *Chafed Elbows* is the off-beat of the offbeat, being a scrupulously coarse and inept, wildly far-out lampoon on honest Underground coarseness, boldness, and ineptitude. Where Ron Rice is relatively naïve, Robert Downey is relatively sophisticated, but with the supposed dividends of value reversed. *Chafed Elbows* is—though the expression is almost tautological—an Underground burlesque. I should say it is quite impossible that an Underground film which Bosley Crowther, Judith Crist, Archer Winsten, and *Cue* all saw fit to praise could rightly belong to the bona fide Underground. The film's effort at style is significant: it tries to out-kindergarten the kindergarten's view of the adult world.

And yet the whole point of Underground parody (perhaps take-off is a better word) is that known, stable definitions and classifications don't hold in the fluid, perpetual-motion, endless accretion-excretion atmosphere followed by the Underground ideologists who follow Mekas—and nearly all of them, consciously or unconsciously, follow Mekas. By their ideology any juvenile sort of buffoonery (sacred to show-off youth) equals "poetry," and there are no shades or grades of buffoonery, aesthetic or otherwise; there are only fond epithets uttered in a vacuum, fond superlatives, fond fondling. Here is the crucial weakness of all that passes for Underground film criticism as generally practiced. I have already noted that technical polish, in the filmic sense, is virtually an affront to hippie and beat morality. A film easily gets called a masterpiece whether or not it follows any rules of filmic (that is, artistic) form. And when it does happen to approximate such rules (but in vain), it may still get called a masterpiece.

superstar space: the playroom

Surely an enlightened critic of things in general is the Italian novelist and essayist Alberto Moravia. In *L'Espresso* (Rome), Moravia has come quite near the essence of the Underground's superstarred aim by calling the substance of *The Queen of Sheba Meets the Atom Man* "a way of life." (Nowadays it is called life style, altogether a flattering expression.) He writes: "The beat hero is a nihilist, let us say of Anglo-Saxon species, clowning, ironic, full of humor (a little bit Keaton, a little bit Chaplin, a little bit Tati)—but the Negress, in contrast, is all affirmation of life, from her head to her feet. Completely naked, she moves about the apartment on elephantine hips; she uses the electric razor, makes a phone call, plays with a cat, ends by improvising a clownlike, affectionate fight with the beat, and then, after a grotesque ball, both of them, in an embrace, collapse amid the mishmash of the pad. The film describes, poetically, a way of living. The film is a protest which is violent, childish and sincere—a protest against an industrial world based on the cycle of production and consumption."

underground film

These words, I grant, are unusually lucid to be said in honor of an Underground film. Yet despite Moravia's intellectuality his account is a little too "square." One can imagine "protests" against the industrial world much more to the point and a description more to the true point of this whimsical protest. Why the special shape and quality of it—certainly "childish and sincere" but with a definite character bias? It is a passive fantasy in which the pad is the child-adult's playroom.* Moreover the beat hero is transparently homosexual, the woman at least conspicuously offbeat, undoubtedly the pair are wild travesties of old Hollywood stereotypes—not only of personality comedy like Chaplin's but also of the space-adventure serials and the films of such queens of campy sex as Maria Montez. This film is indeed a way of life: a way of living over again, with preposterous let's-pretend, the fixating hallucinations of popular movies when one was a teenager or still licking lollipops.

Why, too, is the action of such films so much like the Happening, with instant props, instant parody, instant fun? Because the whole home-movie ambience of Underground films depends on lack of professional means as well as lack of professional aims. The economics of the matter are primitive in more than one sense. One needs only a "fix" (not a drug necessarily but at least a dose of self-administered euphoria), a camera, some lights, and a few rolls of film. The Underground platform is that this very primitive solution of equally primitive needs is per se a monument of virtue. Poverty of means is a poetic gaud, like an Indian-bead necklace on a hippie's chest. If not a "work of art," it is just as good as one—and why not even better? Many films are conscious parodies of unconscious parodies; commercial films show increasing inclination in the past two decades to parody themselves—as for example *Sunset*

---

* Films by Red Grooms were among the first to deliberately parody the archaically broad and artificial attempts of the earliest screen comedies: the result is a kindergarten vaudeville invented as a camp by adults.

Boulevard, Beat the Devil, the camp Westerns, and the recent
burlesques of the James Bond movies. To top them all came
Barbarella, queen of those commercial films which have
dropped all pretense of satire to assume that comic books can
provide a life style for in-group sophisticates.

The very conception of space—the space in which extraordinary and marvelous things happen—is significant in the self-
parody sort of avant-garde film. Provided a filmmaker is ingenious and creative enough, the marvelous can take place in
an ordinary-sized room or a small studio set of obvious dimensions. Cocteau could do it, so could Buñuel and Dali, and an
American avant-garde filmmaker such as Maya Deren. But such
film stylists had *poetic ideas*; that is, ideas poetic not only in
terms of metaphors (literature) but in terms of theater, and
specifically film. There are multiple filmic ways of magically
expanding space. The most elementary is the editing leap from
one scene to another, but this itself may be accomplished in a
great variety of ways depending on the exact aim and context.
Often the space in which the parody-marvelous takes place (the
"fleshapoid" and "atom man" sort of film) has little change of
scene and lacks both the illusion of far physical space (an easy
trick of film) and the imitation of mental space, which is
absolute. There are various ways of inventing cosmic space, for
instance, besides showing views of the starry heavens and seeming to penetrate immense distances. Filmmakers as diverse as
Stan Brakhage, Bruce Conner, and Ed Emshwiller have done it
by recognizing that mental space (created by montage and
accumulated by rapid editing) can signify the cosmic quality;
that is, be a passage through seemingly boundless space. Conner has a very ingenious way of doing this, in *Cosmic Ray*, by
making the speeded-up movement of his images look vertically.
extended, as if flashing amidst space like a launched rocket.
This is all the more phenomenal because most of his subject
matter is strip-tease female nudes. With *Relativity*, Emshwiller

53

(also preoccupied with erotics) creates a sort of *Finnegans Wake* cosmos purely with a montage of visual metaphors. Just as there are no walls or closed doors to the active mind, the cosmos has none. Film's perfect fluency of movement can easily emulate "doorlessness."

What Moravia calls the mishmash of the pad ("where things happen" in Underground films: someone's bedroom or studio) can magically convert its literal boundaries into unlimited space simply by not betraying the shallowness of the spatial unit in which the camera is situated. This was done in a brilliant way in two films by Charles Boultenhouse, *Dionysius* and *Handwritten*, by suppressing all sense of background and letting the performers work against dark shadows which silhouette their lighted figures. The fact that the themes are mythological, the action in *Dionysius* mimed and danced discontinuously, naturally expands the impression of both temporal and physical space. Boultenhouse dramatized this by giving us ambiguous shots of the studio lights which pun for the moon and visions of working cameramen who serve as a chorus. In *Handwritten*, starry space is beautifully suggested by combining camera action with words and symbolic props; the main concept of the film derives from Mallarmé's *A Throw of the Dice*. Some Underground filmmakers, such as the science-fiction parodists I have mentioned, wish, on the contrary, to exploit the camp of it by illuminating the smallness of the closed space which subjectively (to the actors) is delusion-of-grandeur space. And what, exactly, is delusion-of-grandeur space? Various drugs, of course, have a faculty of making any given space look more expansive and attractively navigable than it is. But drugs can supply only one of the more favorable conditions for the sort of space I mean. This space is that of the child violently, grimly, and with "comic relief" playing the game of being grown-up. Equally it is the space of the adult playing in the same way the game of being a child.

superstar space: the playroom

The real-life Hell's Angels are still playing Cowboys-and-Indians on motorcycles. True, many of them are quite old enough to know better, but so are most of the criminally insane, committed to institutions, old enough to know better. At times what Moravia calls the violent, childish and sincere does not seek expression in mere play or harmless exhibitionism, as in films, but through destructive acts in life, only a small ratio of these being on the political-idealistic level. Kenneth Anger's emblematic film called *Scorpio Rising* (of course a phallic metaphor) shows the intimate connection among Hell's-Angelism, idolatrous sex, childish violence, and fascism. While some of the realistic space of *Scorpio Rising* is the open road and we do indeed see militaristic Leather Boys speeding along, the symbolic space is a Leather Boy's bedroom den where he "moons" amid the fetishes adorning his walls and reads comic books. The step from there to the open road is also symbolic in that, according to Anger, it involves a death wish—final release into infinite space. When, toward the end of *Scorpio Rising*, we see a group leader haranguing on a rostrum, we have an image of Hitlerian hysteria, urging youth on to sacrifice itself in death. Sexuality per se has been concretely transmuted and superseded. Death, not Sex, rides the motorcycle.

An adult-infantile complex governs many actors as it governs many actions in recent Underground films; literally, the actors are past adolescence but cultivate the style and emotive reflexes of determined teenagers, sophisticated by the awareness of representing a cult. The cult has exactly the same adjectives as the films: "new, American, underground, independent, loving, poetic"—and "poetic" should be read "hippie-psychedelic." Warhol's actors, for example, all relatively young (thirtyish at most), do not have the tribal quality of hippies but belong to the superstar set with theatrical ambitions. It would be indelicate to try to ascertain Taylor Mead's age, not to mention Mario Montez'; for all I know, the latter may be astonishingly young. But the former is as obviously a child-man as Harry Langdon or the early Chaplin. What signifies is their Young Attitude. Consider that mini- and microskirts are parodies of the classic skirt length of little misses from four to eight. Miniskirts used to be seen on grown-ups only at kiddie parties, at one time a favored Hollywood social festivity.

This dwelling on infantile traits may offend some serious-minded Underground filmmakers, and quite rightly. Yet an infantilism veering between paranoid compulsion and unfettered euphoria cannot be ignored as a decisive Underground trait. What is in question is its basic structure and its importance.

This phase of Underground inspiration has yielded a number of strange and interesting documents but very little memorable art. As a "sensibility" it has poetic resonances that are genuine enough, and it is psychologically and socially important as the chief link between the elder avant-garde and the avant-garde of the present, the Underground. We can only view the pathological behavior of the hero of *L'Age d'Or* as symbolic invention, and sophisticatedly ambiguous; this hero (he could be forty) is a product of puritanical frustrations, his libido ostensibly maimed, his id cheated, by the great bourgeois-capitalist conspiracy, against which, like a petulant child, he stages his personal "revolution." Is this to take Surrealism at more than its face value? I think that is the best way to take Surrealism. In type, this man's erotic realism, so laughably grotesque, is not at all far from Chaplin's compulsive responses to attractive women or Harpo Marx's (presumably harmless) sexual idiocy; both were childish sex reacting directly to objects of desire. Buñuel's hero, on the other hand, has all the *outward* marks of an ordinary adult and takes the physical stance of a virile, vindictive, and amoral male.

The oral sexuality attributed to infancy is heavily displayed in Warhol's *Harlot*, where the "endlessly" repeated eating of a banana—at a pace of excruciating leisure and gourmet voluptuousness—is an overt stand-in for the subject of *Blow Job* given a campy dose of symbolism. Provided you can get to its center and stay there, *Harlot* proves a perfect camp. As to filmic and psychological structure, neither can be properly separated from the objects which preoccupy behavior in Underground films. *Harlot* is a tableau vivant of two men and two women (one of the latter Mario Montez in drag) draped obstinately on a couch, lasting an incredible, mildly amusing, mildly exacerbating seventy minutes of fiendishly sparse animacy; its "events" are like milestones on the highway and chiefly (as accompanied by an ad-libbed, pure camp dialogue between invisible men) the eating of bananas extracted tantalizingly from various caches by Montez.

The search-for-love is a prominent, remarkably sustained theme in the history of the avant-garde film; this means, among other things, exploration of the actual space in which love is to be found: Antonioni, in commercial film, has memorably done such explorations. A slow pace is common to the very diverse films of Warhol and Gregory Markopoulos, both of whom treat love in some of its far-out, far-in humors. The principal difference between them is that Warhol's action tends to stay put, self-entranced, with minimal gesture, while Markopoulos' action moves through continuous, literally geographic space at a semi-tranced rhythm, hieratically, as if all life were some veiled sort of love ritual. Markopoulos' later films have a new rhythmic technique of single-frame changes, which build a lightning-like swiftness into ordinary movements so that human movement acquires an internal "relativity" dimension: a treadmill dynamics (back and forth) inserted into ordinary straightforward movement. With Warhol, trance action looks intoxicated, drugged; with Markopoulos as with Maya Deren before him, trance action looks somnambulistic, hypnotized. As late as 1967 Markopoulos' use of single-frame action was overschematic and his general plots not various enough to properly sustain interest. But this technique has great filmic quality and can create thrilling moments that are like dance. Referring to the past and anticipating the future, it causes time to vibrate, to assume a complex rhythm.

For someone accustomed to the infantile-adult complex of Underground Film, it is always a relief to encounter something outside the patterns of systematic infantile regression. At the same time Underground infantilism has a dark power, a kind of terror, a mysteriously indefinable space: the strength of youth not *re*gressing but *pro*gressing, however blindly. It is just that the film camera becomes too incidental an instrument for this force that is (again to quote Moravia on Ron Rice's film) "a protest . . . violent, childish and sincere." Underground Film is part of the arsenal of the curiously self-reliant, curiously triumphant, rebellious youth of our times. This filmic youth is as blind as the classical Cupid and gropes inside its environments, which are taken for granted without measurement or understanding; the only attempt is to passively transform them through fantasy.

Time is such a crucial factor in Underground Film exactly because of the great tension between wishing to grow up and wishing to stay put, a tension developed by youth at various stages of its growth. Youth, that is, desires from its future the added power and independence of the adult, but also, from its past, the special privileges and nonresponsibility recalled as true of childhood. This subjective state bestows on youth a peculiar and ambiguous objective orientation in space. One of the founders of Dada, Tristan Tzara, who made poems of mere sounds and incomprehensible "words," wrote in 1916, the year of Dada's inception, "Art was a game, children assembled words that ended with the sound of a bell, then they shouted and wept their verses and put doll's shoes on them." Tzara was referring to the mature art traditions as an abandoned child's game, something in the rapidly perishing past then being replaced by the iconoclastic Dadaists. But at least it was a game with an objective medium ("verses") and thus had rules and conventions (the theater). Now, after Dada, the "game" in the Underground is improvisation, and, not being the improvisation of professionals, it can be suspected of being no game except the game of life. One gets as much out of life as possible—and to hell with art as a formal problem!

The Dadaists' sort of aggression was youth's characteristic denial of its immediate parentage. In imaginatively attacking and overthrowing the adult, the child *becomes* the adult. The Old Testament myth of David and Goliath is a poetic paradigm of this eternal combat and ideal rebirth: youth forever victorious. Since so typical a myth as that had political connotations, so had the Dadaist revolt and so do Underground films today. Yet we must make sure of certain important distinctions.

First of all, there is no true and stable orientation of such a doctrine in life or in art. An Underground film such as Jonas Mekas' *Guns of the Trees* is unquestionably a work of political and social protest. But it is badly wanting in formal structure, personal touch, and ideas (filmic or otherwise), and quite lacks the emotional directness and intellectual astringency of the old Dada spirit. Where Dada was fierce and flighty but concise, Mekas is prosaic, loose, sentimental, and vaguely hysterical. No longer does true quality matter (since the game of wit, rules, and winning is *really* gone); only naked, literal-minded statistics matter. Whatever human sweetness and pathos manage to come through in Mekas' long film all disappear into the mishmash of the mental pad. We are back in the psychic playroom, where art is a camp charade, an artless masquerade, or a negative spasm of despair.

can the technician escape the pad?

It would be valuable to do more than try to explain the infantile psychology that motivates and dominates so much Underground filmmaking. Can the Underground "aesthetic," for example, be isolated as a pure psychic mechanism? Is it just unmoored, ill-contrived, film-factoried psychedelics? Something may be gained, I think, if we turn to an Underground style which tends to be pure and to lack any overt content of an infantile character, like the pad or playroom.

Take the short films of Peter Kubelka, a forty-five-year-old Viennese who was founder and curator of the Oesterreichisches Museum in his native city. Kubelka did a one-minute and a one-and-a-half-minute film, each printed five times for exhibition on one reel; that is, we get the same film, precisely gauged to a modern-music sound track, continuously repeated four times. The titles are *Adebar* (1956-57) and *Schwechater* (1957-58). *Schwechater* uses the simplest basic material—people drinking beer—while Adebar is composed of people dancing around in a discothèque. Various treatments of the photographic image give its simple repeated movements, with a sharp contrast of light and shadow, an abstract look. Kubelka worked patiently and long on the most minute adjustments of visual rhythms to a metronome-like sound. We find Brakhage saying that, compared with Kubelka's, the work of others often looks like "some *football* tactic or other," and further, "His films exist *outside* the art-as-a-game scramble."

Lacking musical variety, Kubelka's type of rhythmic visual repetition is bound to seem compulsive and tempts us to evoke in comparison the naked rhythms of sex, which, experienced objectively, may well seem monotonous. The more isolated a rhythm from any particular context of importance, the more compulsive it must seem, whether or not associated with sexual sensation. The "musical" interest of Kubelka's films is modern in the sense that it suggests variations of mere metronomic, rather than musical, time. I think we must account for the fascination of watcher-listeners with Kubelka's work as we must account for the comparable attention given Warhol's marathons of miniaction. Kubelka's field of vision is much tighter chronologically, being literally a very small slice of movement that shifts and continues indefinitely—like, indeed, ballroom dancing itself.

In the context of modern life, especially that around the arts as practiced in various playgrounds of bohemia, this fluid time naturally brings to mind the new phenomenon of psychedelic time: the automatic expansion of consciousness by drugs which makes something normally trivial, small, passing, and nonrhythmic look large, important, enduring, and rhythmic. This is the chemical aesthetics that I have already implied is typical of Underground film works. Again, I do not mean that Kubelka or his watcher-listeners are in the habit of taking drugs to get themselves in the right chemical state for the reception of his films. On the contrary, I insist that there is a Drug Attitude along with a Youth Attitude, and that both are encouraged and crystallized by what psychology has long known as auto-suggestion, here practiced by members of a sensibility cult.

All one needs to do to achieve this dilation of sense-re-ception is to exclude certain experiential factors of the emotions —indeed, to scant a wide field of them—and concentrate on the purely formal rhythms of sight and sound organized into a unit by Kubelka's camera and sound track. The general effect, when it takes place, is rightly to be called hypnotic. It is quite logical to argue for an aesthetics of such hypnosis, as Brakhage and Mekas in their respective ways argue for it—but it is not in-evitable to do so. When Kubelka's films are criticized from a noncult, nonhypnosis viewpoint they become very narrow ex-ercises in a sort of ciné-dance of repetitions. Just as under cer-tain drugs or perhaps actual hypnosis (we think of a snake fascinating a small animal) a human subject may find the greatest "aesthetic" reward in the simplest repetitive movement of some object or objects, provided the movement is rhythmic, so, exactly, may a viewer of Kubelka's films decide, if suffi-ciently indoctrinated with the Brakhage-Mekas creed, that "Kubelka is the world's greatest film maker" (Brakhage) and that his "cinema is like a piece of crystal, or some other object of nature: it doesn't look like it was produced by man" (Mekas). The latter means that by photographic processing and editing, moving human figures can become like concrete natural "abstractions" such as crystals.

There is no need to remark further on Brakhage's verdict, but about Mekas' figure of speech one may add that the elements of a Kubelka film (human dancers) are identifiable, and so long as this is so, one may recall that while man formu-lated dance rhythms, he did not make his own limbs or create the quality of chiaroscuro. He merely invents with these things, manipulates them. A crystal, on the other hand, is either self-formulated (nature) or God-formulated, but its visual consti-

62

tuents in either case are identical; they are *only* themselves. So long as the spectator may either deliberately or automatically isolate human function from Kubelka's dance figures, they may look crystalline and crystalline only, but as soon as one imputes to this filmmaker's rhythmic organization of dance figures the meaning of human functions, one sees what a shallow trick is involved. The great thing in film, like the great thing in a novel or a painting, is to make a complicated human action, a complicated human individual, "look like a crystal." If it *were* a crystal, it would be purely ornamental. Kubelka's aesthetic is crystallization by direct reduction and abstraction: a drastic deprivation and fragmentation of human content.

For some years now machines of colored light have been projecting (whether or not recorded on film) this sort of effect. Marcel Duchamp did it several decades ago by filming revolving discs which he had designed, the film being called *Anemic Cinema*; the word "anemic," of course, is an anagram of cinema and here a wittily pointed one. Sometimes the overlapping colored circles suggest an image-motif, a wine glass. When the discs are in movement there is an illusion of a third dimension that brings out the presence of the wine glass and seems to give volume to each spiral movement.* Dada was not known for its modest charm, but with this pseudo-cinematic gimmick Duchamp accorded it just that. As for the abstract style, Dada writers did it with gibberish, Gertrude Stein with near-gibberish; they made poems of sound, poems of word sounds in which very elementary visual figures appeared. In film, Kubelka proves that such spatial reaches can look very small—as small as a pad.

---

* The discs were placed on a turntable and, when in action, filmed in black and white; thus the "anemic" role of cinema in this case.

the pad can be commercialized

A recent film, *The Trip* (1967), is a popularized, literally Hollywoodized version of an Underground film, in that its whole action concerns the ritual of hallucinogenic pleasure and pain, with the hallucinations copiously visible. Yet an important factor makes this film ineligible as Underground—or, for that matter, as avant-garde. Like the documentaries which have shown us lunatics and all the sordidness of their sequestration, *The Trip* makes fantasy not a creative product of the mind, but a chemical product of the body acting on the mind. In also showing us the surrounding "normal" reality, it compromises the "surreality" of the young hero's mental visions which occupy most of the film. True, a great deal of real filmic ingenuity is required to "reconstruct" the typical fantasies which obsess the subject here, supposedly under the influence of a drug (presumably LSD or mescaline), which we see him take in liquid form.

An impressive thing about these same fantasies is the way they are inflected toward the supernatural horror films of Hollywood. Item by item, one identifies the hero's acute sensations (both wonderful and frightening) with traditional Hollywood stereotypes taken from the Poësque and Dracula/Frankenstein sort of thriller-diller. No matter what the medium or local field of the enterprising imagination, the danger always to be avoided is stereotyped fantasy, the sort the mass public often favors. My critical writings have frequently been concerned with the theme of movie-going as a ritual of hallucination with a special hypnosis: the freedom to dream and unconsciously interpret figures and events on the screen in purely subjective terms. Through the years the peculiar spell of movie-going has cut across all cultural and intellectual strata, with the result that a special nostalgia about things filmic has left a residue of respect, even admiration, among the truly cultivated.

We have already seen, in these pages, how much the revival of avant-garde energy has derived from a more or less nostalgic, more or less satiric reference to prized memories of old movie-house experiences. In filmic practice this has led to the blurring of filmic as well as avant-garde values, a blurring the more confused by the self-parody style. Where does the cycle of either real or surreal values end—and begin? *The Trip* gives this confused impression, the reasonable inference being that drug taking is exactly what sanctions the blur as well as its bizarre ingredients. In our psychedelic era it has been learned that the mind itself, interpreting the transmuted organism in which it is lodged, *is a film*, and so is the pad, which can be turned into concrete psychedelic environments by actions and a little anti-interior decorating (Happenings and so on). The old magic-carpet function of the film is now a mental function which the film is used to report in documentary manner.

No less, and unfortunately no more, has been the aim and achievement of a moneyed young man named Conrad Rooks, who, finding himself going to pieces under the influence of drugs and alcohol, took a "sleep cure" and made a film about it, *Chappaqua*. The film is in an Underground mold on a luxury scale: its maker could afford all the expensive laboratory effects by which poor Underground filmmakers are tempted (the same ones passed up by Andy Warhol) but which can't be indulged except through dingy and makeshift splendors. Although *Chappaqua* has for actors William Burroughs and Allen Ginsberg, arrayed in official psychedelism, and even Jean-Louis Barrault, it lacks true ideas and a true filmic imagination. Most Underground films lack the same things while their poverty of means helps to conceal the uncomfortable truth.

Kenneth Anger is one of the more talented Undergrounders, but about two years ago, after having all the footage of a new film, *Lucifer Rising*, stolen at a benefit showing, he reacted—so the whole story goes—with calamitous shock, and as a sort of Surrealist joke he placed a full-page announcement in the *Village Voice* (New York) as follows:

IN MEMORIAM

KENNETH ANGER

Film Maker 1947–67

Meanwhile he had had telegrams sent to friends announcing his death. Privately he told acquaintance that the stunt was meant to symbolize his protest against the existing systems of patronage available to filmmakers; there is never enough, he feels, to make a decent film on. There is much to be said for Anger's reasoning, but it must be admitted that in 1964 he received a ten-thousand-dollar grant from the Ford Foundation to make a film which eventually he had to discard. Still, he was undefeated. Resourceful as another magician, Dr. Caligari, he devised a swift, ingratiatingly manic eleven-minute film of magic-ritual sight and sound from reserve footage of his stolen film, calling it *Invocation of My Demon Brother*, in which in fact he plays the magician.

It must not be supposed that delusions of grandeur are confined to the technically psychopathic or to the frustrated egos of the untalented. These very pages attest to quite the opposite. Yet what both *Chappaqua* and *The Trip* reveal is that drugs do induce people of modest talents to acquire an exaggerated sense of self-assurance, which may endure beyond the range of a single "trip" and assume the general lineaments and scale of—it's easy to to guess—a feature film. What happens to the chemicalized imagination of *The Trip's* hero has the roughest sort of order, which actually is controlled from the outside by the script writer and director, who might here be termed "dream makers." The film's authors have been true to psychedelic form by using an unplotlike progression: telescoping, errant, fragmentary, without any special rhythm. The hero, a recent divorcee trying to adjust to new love opportunities, is periodically pursued in his fantasies by two black-swathed phantoms on horseback who bear an embarrassing resemblance to Ku-Klux Klanners; at the end, however, as in the climax of a dream in which mysterious identities are at last revealed, the phantoms, on unmasking, are found to be only "the two women in his life." The discovery is remarkably unexciting from the dramatic viewpoint, if only because it has no visible consequences. The "trip" is over; it's just the end of the line. Of course, anticlimaxes of this sort are to be expected from drug taking.

Judging by *The Trip*, Hollywood's self-parody impulses are so compulsive as to become paranoid, and naturally much of the terror experienced by the psychedelic subject here is of the paranoid sort typically provoked by drugs. But we don't have to judge by *The Trip* alone. In general, and without the help of intoxicants, the Surrealists cultivated paranoia as an aesthetic sensation; their paranoia relates, in fact, to a special theory of Dali's which will be discussed a few pages farther on. More pertinently here, the situation in *The Trip* happens to repeat that of a female divorcee in a low-budget independent film, *The Savage Eye*, made in 1959 by Hollywood professionals evidently bored with their standard routines. The real difference between the approaches of the two films (duly affecting their respective techniques) is that the female divorcee's "hallucinations" result from her desperate efforts to find distraction—perhaps a "solution"—in such garden-variety emotional and mental bouts as those offered by a yoga studio, a faith temple, a gambling casino, a strip-tease burlesque, and (like a nightmare) a drag ball. The divorcee of *The Trip* experiences a pure horror dream with intermittent out-of-this-world ecstasies. The emotional tones are different, but the moral status of the confused, wandering, frightened, thrilled individual psyche is the same in each film. The unpsychedelized subject of *The Savage Eye* notably fails to get any *lovely* thrills: all turns out to be pain and disappointment. There you are! *Drugs* have made pure fantasy into a Hollywood commodity at last.

The producer of *The Trip*, Roger Corman, had already been responsible for translating some Poe stories into the fantasy-expertise of big filmmaking, though these would not have been undertaken without the rape-murder-and-madness standby of such extravaganzas. Unfortunately the attention to the techniques of hallucination does not rescue these films from their natural vulgarity; no more, we must add, do the statistical conventions of acid-head fantasy rescue *The Trip* from just as old and reliable patterns of vulgarity.

The question logically comes up of what, conceivably, is the distinction between *The Trip* and an Underground film, aside from Corman's professional budget. It's not just that *The Trip* is luxuriously slick in montage effects (so is *Chappaqua*) and not just that generally it's commercially lavish. As for the former, certain Underground filmmakers (Emshwiller among them) can get effects just as elaborate, and less expensively, because they don't have to have highly paid specialists do them: they know how to do them themselves. The essential difference is, rather, that the Hollywood film asserts the reality of an extra dimension while Underground films are sound, and superior, in assuming that the imaginative dimension should cover and subsume all dimensions. The fictive hypothesis in art is—that is, should be—absolute. True, certain modern artists (Pirandello comes to mind) have assumed in the imaginative dimension itself a struggle between concepts of reality—that is, an existential struggle—but this meant, and means, only one thing and it seems necessary to repeat it: The artist's imagination in this era has reached a crucial point of self-doubt.

Thus what I propose for the relation between Underground films and a film such as *The Trip*, which recognizes the borderline between illusion and reality while exploiting the former, is that Underground Film regards the reality/illusion dimension seriously enough to pretend—even as lunatic or drug addict—that what really matters is not the peripheral reality but the central illusion. A struggle, let us say, is always present (just as the struggle between desire and its fulfillment seems to be a permanent state), but programmatically the Undergrounders take the side of illusion and attempt to breed and interweave and transplant this illusion so that, like drug addiction, it may become, or seem to become, the daily round of life. *Illusion is what really happens.* This is why all varieties of Underground Film are curiously "documentary" instead of "artistic." If they fail of major illusion, they at least document the traditional social activity of making life itself into a work of art, with the result (doctrinally considered) that art as such becomes a superfluous occupation. Morally, one might be supposed to continue a well-known search: that for the Earthly Paradise.

But there is another angle, and I daresay it is closer to all the facts of life. So long as the ultimate issue remains suspended, so long as film is simply a formal medium (as it is if it remains film and is shown in theaters and in the home), so long will Underground film remain frustrated art *and* frustrated life. Perhaps no Underground work illustrates this more convincingly, in its plodding, literal-minded way, than a film that earned sympathetic attention as a Special Event at the Fourth New York Film Festival, Peter Emanuel Goldman's *Echoes of Silence*. This film is unpretentious, remains sober in viewpoint, and concerns itself with a young male protagonist and a few equally young females who are poor and seem to be drifters, with no particular occupation but hunting love and occasionally smoking pot. They are all, even when engaged in bed, notably frustrated and spend most of their film time looking dispirited. None, apparently, can find—or at least keep—the right person, so that an atmosphere of sheer sex hunger dominates almost the whole of the work's seventy-minute running time. Technically, *Echoes of Silence* is another (here modestly) shaggy film, but it is not a hopeless bore because it has unusually sensitive camera work, though no special effects, while the humble people it shows have a convincing authenticity. Nobody here has superstar ambitions and nobody suggests a put-on, either savage or mild. The best and most revealing scene takes place in one of the galleries of the Metropolitan Museum of Art. The sex-hungry young hero is really cruising, not really looking at the pictures, while several young women in whom he shows interest are at least pretending to be looking at the pictures. If there is one truly delicate factor in the film's atmosphere, it is that everyone seems steadfastly if rather passively to be "holding out" for just the right person. The streets are full of candidates but somehow these don't count. The point about the scene in the museum is that the highest art becomes meshed with the fatal alienation of the modern environment.

So long as Underground Film assumes that it can replace art with a sort of frustrated art or frustrated life (whichever one wants to call it), just so long will Underground filmmakers remain in the unique "aesthetic" position of drug addicts and lunatics—those who, recognizing all too well the dichotomy between reality and illusion, deliberately embrace illusion-as-reality, no matter how many practical embarrassments or formal contradictions this view may objectively entail. This is why the true history of the Underground Film as well as the avant-garde film begins with *The Cabinet of Dr. Caligari* (1919) and a few other predecessors.

performing children, performing madmen

That the reader may not get me wrong, I had better furnish some detailed demonstration. The child and the lunatic, to be sure, are sources of much interest and charm, being (at the very least) highly instructive as subjects of study. I have no wish at all to demean Underground films by isolating their infantile and lunatic traits. On the other hand, how striking is the elementary plight of the quietly desperate young people in *Echoes of Silence!* They seem infantilely incapable of breaking out of the daily treadmill of sex hunger; at times they look as apathetic as potential withdrawal-types. They are neither, these young people, admirable nor extraordinary; nor, just as plainly, are they "mad." Admiration is sometimes the least tribute that may be paid to those who technically may be called mad, and yet it happens that without a consideration of technical lunacy, the history of Underground film would lack one of its vital orientations. Lunatics, admittedly, are not all of a piece as interestingly instructive subjects. Magicians have falsely been considered lunatics and so have others who projected dreams which came scientifically true, the result being that "madmen" overnight became rational men to be loaded with honors. In brief, many radical innovators may first come to notice as mere lunatics.

A perennial, rock-bottom problem of the race, nevertheless, is the criminally insane: those who contribute nothing to life but horrible and destructive, sometimes mortal acts and are then, nowadays, usually incarcerated for life. A modern custom is to applaud such acts as the moral retribution deserved by the race's own history of official crimes, such as genocide and the large-scale massacres of wartime. Documentary film—like Underground Film, which it touches at certain points—is becoming more and more candid, along with the growing realism of modern society and its persistent moral conscience. As nudity is more and more printable on commercial as well as Underground film, so is the figurative "naked truth" in the columns of magazines and newspapers. Currently, even very extreme limits are being stretched (for example, "frontal nudity," however subliminal) as to what can be viewed in movie theaters. At the Fifth New York Film Festival, in 1967, the board of judges governing the main program debated whether a film called *Titicut Follies* should be shown in the big hall because of objections brought up by individual members: one was the feeling that this outspoken documentary was short on artistic presentation, another the fact that, since its subject was revelations about a hospital for the criminally insane, it might prove shocking to a minority of any large audience.

Since the state of Massachusetts thought itself compromised by the filmmakers' candid camera, it sought to block this film's public release by court order; however, in the very nick of time for showing in the smaller auditorium at the Festival (that of the Library of Performing Arts, at Lincoln Center), the judicial decision went against the state. The whole assault

of *Titicut Follies* on the moral and visceral sensibilities of
spectators had been withheld from the problematical mercies
of the audience in the big hall. Without preamble, *Titicut Follies* opens with a sort of vaudeville turn performed by three
men who, one guesses, are inmates of the hospital; eventually
an M.C. who also occupies the stage appears to be on the hospital staff, where seemingly he is in charge of recreation activities. The three performing men, whether amateurs or former
professionals, are obviously childishly pleased to be exhibiting
themselves. Later in the film the recreation leader joins a colored man at the microphone in a gay song number. This theatrical entertainment, the "Follies," threads the action as a grimly
gay leitmotif.

For an individual to gain comparable access to the inside
of this hospital would take much wire pulling and a good deal
of management while on the premises. Now the general public
is automatically privileged to occupy a voyeur's comfortably
safe and detached seat. No serious researcher wishing to study
conditions at the Bridgewater, Massachusetts, hospital would
be satisfied with this seat, naturally, but it is quite adequate as
a voyeur's vantage point: one of its chief advantages is that one
can leave it on impulse without fuss.

There is a sense, then, in which *Titicut Follies* rates as an
Underground film: one might call it a psycho-nudie peepshow.
Like many cameras that pretend impartiality, that of *Titicut
Follies* leaves open the question of the spectator's reaction. One
can as easily get morally dismayed as viscerally repelled by the
sights of Titicut—the very name (actually that of the locality)
has sinister possibilities of symbolism. Is not this hospital veritably an "underground" of modern society? It is exactly the
sort of thing which persons of dainty sensibility (and perhaps
some moral cowardice) wish to avoid knowledge of, just as
numerous citizens think it useless as well as disagreeable to

become personally acquainted with life as lived in the ghettos of the world.

An indispensable theme of my argument in this book is the value of denudation in the integument of Underground Film. Underground films tend to attract audiences held captive by their loyalty to the Underground idea, who sadomasochistically remain in their seats (some as fascinated voyeurs) to view supposedly pleasant or supposedly unpleasant truths whose main and indisputable virtue is their status as candidly seen facts which have been, as it were, unflinchingly filmed. At least, such a rationale could easily be invoked in behalf of *Titicut Follies*, while its ethical justification hardly needs a fresh pleading.* This book's main concern must be with *Titicut's* aesthetic side. Is it or is it not a "beautiful" experience to view an episode in which a naked old man emerges from his cell, is followed along a corridor, gets into a barber's chair to be shaved, then is accompanied back to his cell, where he proceeds to "perform" with a kind of rhythmic stamping on the floor?

It is certainly more moving to see than 95 percent of official Underground films, brimming as the latter are with juvenile low jinks, often of a calculatedly sleazy kind. The inmate just mentioned, after being rebuked for messing up his cell, is baited with humorous sarcasms by the guard attending him. As is true of certain sorts of lunatic, the old man is entirely nude (he uses his hand as a figleaf when seemingly aware of the camera) because, doubtless, he would tear up any clothes he might be forced to wear. His cell is empty because he would destroy any furniture it might contain. Not even a bed is visible; literally the only article in the room (which does have a

* Another—it seems to me much more controversial—film of this kind, *Warrendale*, reveals in great detail a new method for handling emotionally disturbed children; it was also shown at the Fifth New York Film Festival.

window) is a slop pail evidently used as a toilet. Inmates who wish to be naughty decline to use the pail properly; this is what is meant by the guards' rebukes to inmates for "messing up."

In other words, this human individual exists day in, day out, in the ultimate state of physical and mental nudity; he is experiencing the final economy possible to a human organism that is still alive. With horror, one realizes that some criminal act has brought to being circumstances that make "messing up his room" the only possible expression of individuality left to this old man. His condition acquires another dimension, another horror, by our further realization that automatic excretion, along with eating and howling, is the infant's first assertion of its organic existence. The infant's next assertion is also this old man's: a rhythmic beating associated with masturbation, which in babies takes the form of jumping up and down while holding to the side of the crib.

There are formally irrefutable arguments why this old man's treatment is "necessary." Any other logic would imply a drastic revision of the social economy and a totally new moral attitude on the part of society. Let *this* sleeping dog lie for the sake of the argument in hand. In theory, I agree completely with the sentiments of Underground advocates who speak of beauty and poetry, of the imaginative product as against the documentary report. A look of this prejudiced kind would emphasize the fact that at Bridgewater the doleful inmates, typically sullen, taciturn, and withdrawn, can express themselves in communication terms in the "Titicut Follies"—the old-fashioned vaudeville or nightclub turns threading the film. Some of them may have been actual stage performers; others may have yearned to be. Perhaps "Titicut"—a *folie de grandeur*—has offered amateurs an illusion of professionalism which otherwise they would have altogether missed. The most unfortunate, oppressed by isolation and degradation, have no chance to participate directly in the beauties of life except through witnessing or performing in the "Follies" stage show. Thus, aesthetically, the film presents the most drastic of scarcity economies. The inmates otherwise are reduced to the ingenuities of a child alone in a quite empty "playroom" and menaced by supervisors who look most critically upon "ingenuities."

Whatever the general public or Underground filmmakers themselves may think of *Titicut Follies,* a good percentage might well agree that here the camera has been the agent of rather outrageous invasions of privacy. Some doubtless think that everyone should know more of "the horrible truth," wherever it be found. At any rate, without invasions of privacy there would not be the voyeuristic thrill which is organically inseparable from that Underground aesthetic mutually practiced by filmmaker and film audience.

Very well, some of the Underground may say, but isn't there a further consideration? Why align those who portray the misfortunes and embarrassments of the criminally insane with the ranks of quite rational and serious filmmakers whose only desire is to portray certain lyric or orgiastic aspects of life that in themselves don't break any laws—any, perhaps incidentally, but the narcotics law? Some Undergrounders maintain, in film and out, that infringements of the narcotics law (especially as to marijuana) are both rational and righteous. Others, the victims of court injunctions restraining the exhibition of their films because they are "pornographic," or "obscene," are joined by colleagues and sympathizers in denouncing and fighting such legal prohibitions. In any case, even the most "offending" filmmaker is not to be called psychopathic or criminally guilty.

By no means! I readily grant the point to partisans of the Underground cause. And yet on a deeper level it remains a debatable aesthetic, if not legal, issue whether pathological infantilism is not a leading theme in Underground films and how proper it may be to align Undergrounders with drug addicts and lunatics. Aside from the studious prattling of the Dadaists, a more serious tradition has arisen in this century which, so far as I can see, Underground Film has not abandoned or repudiated but evolved: this is *crime and insanity as sources of poetic inspiration.* Antonin Artaud (1896–1948), actor and poet, was an underground demigod of his time who went insane and regarded the theater as a place where the ultimate function of actors is to attack the audience. Also there is the modern play by Peter Weiss, *Marat/Sade,* an indisputably great work of theater; here the inmates of the Charenton asylum, enacting a play under the direction of the Marquis de Sade (himself an inmate), end their performance by assaulting the director of Charenton and his family, who have witnessed the play on stage. So it is not at all un-hip to take the stand that the true difference between lunacy and the Underground may lie only in variant qualities of aim, imagination, and technique.

All will become clear enough when we discuss *The Cabinet of Dr. Caligari* and a precursor, *La Folie de Docteur Tube,* which presents a scientist (not unconventionally) as a loony eccentric. Yet a certain contemporary Underground exhibit offers abundant evidence here and now. *Blonde Cobra,* one of the most popular films circulated by the Film-Makers' Co-operative, may be called a Jack Smith film the way one used to say a Bette Davis film or a Mae West film. It was concocted as early as 1958 by two young men, Bob Fleishner and Ken Jacobs, who evidently had their noses to the wind regarding trends of the evolving avant-garde. Not that Jacobs, as an individual filmmaker, did not pursue a very serious course from the latter fifties onward. Working about the time Brakhage came on the scene, 1955, and later, when the pivotal *Pull My*

Daisy set a definite pattern for the beat-into-hippie transition, Jacobs had anticipated *Blonde Cobra* with a long film called *Star-Spangled to Death,* worked on sporadically for several years and bearing strong marks of the Oldenburg Happenings that were to be filmed in the sixties. *Star-Spangled to Death* is a grimly poetic camp phrase expressing the antipatriotic radical socialism which, Jacobs believes, was the true impetus of the emergent Underground as distinct from the elder avant-garde. The film shows two beat characters, Jack Smith and a male crony, struggling with a life style; Smith represents an ambiguous joie-de-vivre with manic-depressive roots: wild clowning *(en travesti)* amid slum surroundings; his friend shows the utterly dour side, withdrawn and "speechless," lacking any of the grotesque theater which makes Smith an "acting personality."

Yet the use of the trash pile as a source of costume and décor, and the infantile-neurotic style of Smith and minor characters in this film, stem from classic avant-garde painting (that of Schwitters, for example) and especially the step from the object-collagist, Robert Rauschenberg, to the Happening-inventor, Allan Kaprow. Pop Art came later; *sculpture trouvée* and *assemblage* preceded. Antecedents for the Underground development, existing in the domain of film, were, from Jacobs' viewpoint, rather artificial and precious. Examples: Broughton's *Mother's Day* and the slummish milieu of the Maas-Moore *Narcissus* as well as the life style of the latter film's infantile hero. This Narcissus stemmed from Cocteau's aesthetic of the "poor artist," whether or not the artist was, artistically, a success. The whole style of *Blonde Cobra,* like that of *Star-Spangled to Death,* shows the Aesthetic Attitude dumped along with the cast-off clothes, the trash-pile objects used as props, and the kindergarten invention of costume. Here the true hippie life style is still inchoate: it had not reached its "fashion" stage, its poise, its implements (such as drugs), its conscious philosophy of love and flowers, or its sense of self-sufficiency.

Dada and Surrealism had retained a measure of formal invention and playful wit which obeyed a certain economy, a neat lucidity of idea. The Underground note was less intellectual, more existential. The new life style, in other words, began crowding out all the pointed parody and dandified scoffing such as the anti-artist Duchamp had come to typify. Existing quite for its own sake, the Underground motif is rough-hewn, shapeless and diffused instead of epigrammatic and satiric. By no means did it wish to *épater la bourgeoisie;* that, after all, was *déjà vu* by the fifties. It wished to provide a documentary showcase for the underdog's spontaneous, uncontrolled fantasy. By the middle sixties Jacobs for his part had turned to a philosophy of form and content and to strict laboratory devices. But in this respect he simply showed a certain evolution parallel with that of a number of colleagues, such as Brakhage, whose *Desistfilm* was premièred at Cinema 16 in 1955.

Blonde Cobra, twenty-eight minutes long, had all the sacred improprieties of the upcoming Underground several years before Andy Warhol decided to make films. In the strictest sense, the Fleishner-Jacobs film is a documentary of a way of life—that same childish, violent and sincere way of life we have identified partly on the authority of Alberto Moravia. Wildly fantastic in one aspect, the film is simply a candid portrait of an offbeat personality, Jack Smith, the same Jack Smith who later made the banned film *Flaming Creatures.* It belongs in the same general class as the more recent *Portrait of Jason. Blonde Cobra,* whose sound track is an improvised monologue by Smith, has all the traits of Underground Film's most candid camera work: off-center shots, in-and-out-of-focus photography, a way of lurching about and a total look of odds and ends put *performing children, performing madmen*

together. In other words, it has the casual empiricism of technique that may come from inexperience but may be also, as here, deliberately affected by the Underground because it imparts to the most extravagant and grotesque material the air of being literally true. From this point of view the clumsiness of the film's technique is a tour de force.

A flip critic has said of *Titicut Follies* that it "makes *Marat/Sade* look like *Holiday on Ice.*" It seems to me that *Blonde Cobra* makes *Titicut Follies* look like *Holiday on Ice* frozen out. *Blonde Cobra* shows blithe, uncompromising impudence in making a film wholly out of one character's transvestite camp act (it is an act with an assistant, a presumed lover). The footage does not hesitate to go blank while sections of the monologue create an invisible fantasy with words. The material is the seemingly at-home and very grubby life of an adult male given to spasms of female impersonation during which he does routines of his life story from early childhood on. One episode involves a "Riverview Nursing Home," where the subject apparently was a patient. In *Blonde Cobra* what is cheerfully known as the Laughing Academy makes a rather specific—though by no means the only—appearance in Underground films. As another example, in *The Flower Thief* a voice coming from nowhere on the sound track briefly sings the refrain, "We're all mad here," while the action on screen looks like a Happening invented by put-on lunatics.

The closing scenes of *Blonde Cobra* show the hero disguised as a baby in a bonnet, enacting with the audience his first role as a flirt; suddenly he grabs a hammer and aims it at some radio tubes. We see the child's inevitable impulse-to-destroy that can so quickly turn into aggression against his elders. Considered in these terms, *Blonde Cobra* (not much as a *film*) is brilliantly archetypal. Its camera has the true voyeuristic slant and all it records is camp-queen madness: hysterical exhibitionism, falsetto raving, infantile sadism, a drag act presented as a clown act. It is very far from being a put-on: some of it is genuinely funny in the camp-queen way.

To speak of art, any art, in connection with *Blonde Cobra* would seem a real ineptitude. Its authenticity lies utterly in its way of life, and here the way of life, or life style, is less a made-up farce than in *The Queen of Sheba Meets the Atom Man*. *Cobra* is the less figurative and the more existential of the two. As denudation it is shocking enough, but the bare substance it gets at seems more essential than that of the Atom Man film: more of the true pith.

As gross and grotesque as *Blonde Cobra* is, I would say that it does not entirely lack a poetry of pathos and even some bumbling subtlety. Excellent close-ups of Smith's face, when without comic feminine make-up, reveal glimpses of wistful sadness. His is a sensitive face: something oddly sweet lurks in it. All in all, his character seems to betoken a sexuality that is profoundly but philosophically dislocated; his own films help attest to this. At one point here he says (and one is tempted to think that now of all times he's *not* kidding), "Sex is a pain in the ass—sex is *the* pain in the ass!" The image we see then is that of nude buttocks from whose cleavage a large knife is being withdrawn. At another moment he exclaims suddenly, "Why shave when I can't think of a reason for living?" All the same, he goes on living—camping, mugging, shrieking, and in some fashion or other (one can guess) suffering that pain in the ass. The follies called Titicut, the follies of Drs. Tube and Caligari, and the follies that explode in grotesque drag acts aren't really far apart from each other. At least the Underground as a modern film movement puts them into a singe related order.

the paranoiac-critical kick

Salvador Dali's classic idea of paranoiac-critical activity is brought up to date with developments in the filmic avant-garde. It was in 1929, the year of his collaboration with Luis Buñuel on *Un Chien Andalou*, that Dali started exhibiting his paintings in Paris. He called them "SNAPSHOT PHOTOGRAPHS IN COLOR of subconscious images, surrealist, extravagant, hypnogogical, extrapictorial, phenomenal, super-abundant, super-sensitive, et cetera . . . of CONCRETE IRRATIONALITY." In other words, Dali put the paranoiac's delusion of grandeur into painting with a definite pictorial method. It looked like color photography of distorted, melted, and fragmented objects. Julien Levy, in his book *Surrealism*, explained about Dali's ideas: "What he terms the *paranoiac-critical activity* is an attempt to simulate the process of insane *rationalization*—unbelievably energetic and a '*source of splendid and delirious images.*' If a paranoiac, suffering from a persecution complex, for example, sees two men talking together on the street, he is liable to suspect them of plotting against him, and to prove his conviction he will invent the most extraordinary reasoning, false sequence of events, energetic hallucinations, all in order to transform reality to conform with the inner necessities of his obsession." Basically this is nothing but the mechanism of compulsive fantasy, adjudged "insane" only because the fantasist rejects what is known as reality for the sake of his own fictions.

The modern Undergrounder can hardly do less and deserve his title as a filmmaker. It is clear that paranoiac-critical activity is simply a compulsive explosion of imagery whose interest can be measured by two norms: art and insanity. Neither of these necessarily excludes or guarantees the other. Everything depends on what the specific ingredients are and how they are put together; after all, if Dali did not know how to draw and had a paltry imagination, his conceptual formulations might well have gone unnoticed. Paranoiac-critical activity is simply one road (a twentieth-century road) to art. It can either fail or succeed on it. Of course, if criticism of the result is suspended, or the cards of criticism are stacked, the only remaining measure of success with paranoiac-critical activity is that automatic transformation of the world through the human senses to be accomplished by drug taking. I have said "paranoiac-critical kick," but why not also "paranoiac-critical trip"?

It would be an error to make too little of the use of drugs through the ages in magic and in religious rituals. The antique sibyls chewed laurel leaves before going into their "swoons" and uttering prophecies. Initiates in the Eleusinian Mysteries are suspected of having been given (in disguised form) a sacred mushroom to eat in order to enjoy their ultimate transports. Kenneth Anger, in a new (1966) version of his film of 1954, *Inauguration of the Pleasure Dome*, undoubtedly had these things in mind when he subtitled the reissue "The Sacred Mushroom Edition." The entire film is an ornate fantasy of voluptuousness in which a bizarrely garbed cast, representing a mixed suite of mythological deities, finally drink from great goblets a mysterious liquid which brings on an orgy of hilarity and erotic contortions. Anger's film, although too long, has an ingratiating air of being highly sophisticated home movies: a superior kind of camp. Note that the Hollywood film we have discussed, *The Trip*, reflects the hippie cult of drug taking as a source of fantasy; the same cult is reflected in various forms in Warhol's films, and the Drug Attitude has already been imputed here to Underground *filmmaking* and *film taking*.

However, while "trip" does very well to denote the sort of bang mutually sought by makers and takers of Underground films, the Dada-Surrealist origins of painting and film aesthetics did not stress drugs as auxiliary to their various methods of "simulating" extreme states of emotion, such as hysteria. Julien Levy attributes to Dali as a young boy a "frantic repressed energy, equal to the energy of madness." And he directly quotes a statement made by Dali as an adult: "The only difference between myself and a madman is that I am not mad." Dali was the most intellectualizing of the Surrealists, who finally disowned him only because he started "simulating" publicity mania.* But here is the kernel of the modern avant-garde tradition: Art is created by getting into a certain state in which emotions, acts, words are not "real," not actually "meant," but only adopted for the occasion, as an actor, adopting a character as well as a costume, does it for effect and a passing sense of innerness; tries, in brief, to *be* that character. One might put it like this: A Surrealist is one who likes all the advantages of mad hallucination without suffering any of its often serious side effects, such as fatally losing touch with the sane world and being shut up in an asylum or a hospital.

Technically, however, the Dadaists and their direct heirs, the Surrealists, desired to come as close as possible to the real

* A malicious anagram was made of his name, Avida Dollars—that is "avid of dollars."

thing by the actor's device of "simulation." They *lived* a kind of theater just as we find André Breton's fictional heroine, Nadja, living a theater of surreality in the midst of reality. Brilliant precedents have been provided by men such as the composer Erik Satie and the poet Alfred Jarry, who lived, acted, and talked as way-out eccentrics.

Jarry, who died of habitual self-neglect, had a high, rapid, staccato manner of speech that made his conversation hard to understand. One is reminded that Jack Smith of today's Underground is also something of an eccentric and ordinarily speaks in a strange, high, childish little voice. The relation of all this to the childish, violent and sincere way of life is inescapable. It is a token of the Underground life style. Taylor Mead, hero of *The Queen of Sheba Meets the Atom Man*, cannot be mistaken for anyone but a far-out bohemian of whose natural eccentricity *The Flower Thief* is as veracious a picture as Jason's in *Portrait of Jason* or Smith's in *Blonde Cobra*. Not for a moment do I attribute the interesting authenticity of these men to the conceivable fact that they may take drugs. Quite the contrary: they and their Underground legends are more complex than anything mere drug taking could explain. This is also true of Ondine, a superstar of *The Chelsea Girls*.

The term addiction would seem to demand a broader definition than one covering simply habituation to an illegal drug and automatic withdrawal from normal life. Opium, the drug which seemed so dire and fatal in the nineteenth century, earned its artistic prestige through De Quincey's *Confessions* and a single poem by Samuel Taylor Coleridge, *Kublai Khan*, which purported to be the recollection of a dream. What happened to dream literature when the Surrealists formulated their creed was that the risk of addiction was unnecessary, apparently, since the mind and sensibility could be trained to simulate the fantasies induced by either drugs or madness. Thus the Surrealists essayed what they called the "experimental dream" and relied upon automatic inspiration and chance ("objective hazard"). In effect, the mechanism of the dream had been analyzed as free association and a passivity toward irrationally connected images, whose stream could be started, theoretically, by pressing a certain button in the mind. As soon as this significant change occurred (it had already been formulated by Freud) the road was open for art to create a whole new dream literature as well as dream painting and dream film. The method was consciously put into practice with *Un Chien Andalou*, according to Buñuel's explicit testimony.

Today we live in an age not simply of major drugs but of minor drugs, the stimulants and tranquillizers whose use is so widespread by grace of medical prescription. The most formidable of the stimulants, amphetamine, makes a dramatic appearance in Warhol's *The Chelsea Girls*. Thus we live technically in an era of controllable, if not always controlled, drug addiction. As the life of Jean Cocteau proved, even opium addiction is controllable, at least under favorable circumstances: when the addict can be regularly hospitalized for disintoxication. LSD,* mescaline, and marijuana are chemical agents which can transform the sensibility and the perceptive faculties without inevitably causing incidental dangers or perennial harm. Like sleeping pills or tranquillizers, they may cause dependency in the taker, a "moderate" addiction, but this does not necessarily mean an exclusively chemical alteration in him. It may be, rather, a moral alteration assisted by drugs. The point is ambiguous if only because the medical world cannot yet determine whether there is an inevitable long-range effect of habituation to LSD. Yet it is significant that the immediate effect of such a drug is variable and thus at least momentarily risky. LSD currently is to be assayed according to the consequences of its immediate effects combined with its immediate aftereffects.

---

* Of course, effects of this drug are still being investigated and some medical authorities condemn it outright.

The fact is that the use of drugs for the purpose of achieving imaginative works, in whatever medium, has always been itself an ambiguous matter and much dependent (like the short-term effects of LSD or marijuana today) on the individual taker. Actually, art too is, or should be, an addiction—which is only to say, a permanent discipline of the mind and the emotions according to given modes. As for danger, every artist who attempts something very big or very original subjects himself to considerable risk. Practical failure in his project (self-judged or other-judged) may have serious consequences.

Everything I have proposed as part of the Underground creed can be understood in the light of these observations. For Underground filmmakers in general, the "very big" or the "very original" consists in giving up those high intellectual and formal standards to which art has traditionally clung. It means (to many, though not to all, Undergrounders) accepting instead disorder and amateurishness; accepting, above all, *boredom*, with its repetitions, its passive narcissism, its inevitable outbursts of naïve frenzy. It means giving up all poetry except the kind inherent in the spontaneous practices of children and madmen. The relation of Dada and Surrealism to madness is a borderline realm and must always be an experimental issue. But one only has to register Taylor Mead's childlike, touching irrationality of character in *The Flower Thief* to know that the peculiar domain of the current Underground has very little to do with intellectual discipline; it tends to come direct from nature.

Behind most Underground films is the orthodox hippie attitude that life must be lived along the line of least resistance— the surrender of everything but the privilege of the playroom, where one may pass with equal ease into a drug swoon, going to bed for sex, or exulting in vague daydreams such as that symbolized by the slogan Flower Power. Flower Power was predicted by the title of the Underground film of 1960, *Pull My Daisy*, winner of the Second Independent Film Award. The metaphor involved is of course erotic. There is also a piquant, consciously disrespectful reference to the romantic cliché of pulling off a daisy's petals to learn whether one is loved. Yet *Pull My Daisy* is significantly pre-hippie; it is beatnik. It is beatnik mainly because it shows a life style germinating among beatnik poets. Whatever else Allen Ginsberg and Peter Orlov-sky did, or do, they wrote poetry; they had a métier besides their own fantasized private lives. So did their collaborators on this film, the painter Alfred Leslie, the novelist Jack Kerouac, and the filmmaker Robert Frank. Métiers are now rather out-moded in the Underground, as if they must seem affectations; painting, for instance, tends to be replaced by Happenings, and Pop artists themselves turn their paintings and sculptures into Happenings and Environments. As a filmmaker Frank turned out to be inept and imitative, but his development does not affect the authenticity of *Pull My Daisy*—which is *in*authentic from the newer viewpoint only because it shows bohemian life as the *artist's* life, and has an obvious debt (of which it seems naïvely unaware) to the erstwhile literary Establishment of Eliot, Stein, and Hemingway.

Such literary debts have now almost totally disappeared from Underground films. Gregory Markopoulos, one of the most active and style-dedicated of Undergrounders, habitually derives inspiration, by his own claim, from classic myths and literary works of the past, yet these appear in his films as themes for the freest variation. There is sometimes an awkward lack of resemblance to the source work. Moreover, insofar as the artist is not himself an actor, a "performer," he too has largely disappeared. Theoretically an Underground filmmaker is an *auteur* in the sense recently adopted by fashionable film criticism as spearheaded by the Cahiers du Cinéma School of Paris. But practically he is frequently no more than a stage manager of the daily lives of Underground bohemia. Andy Warhol, as an archexample, astutely stage manages the more or less private-life fantasies of his superstars. Warhol may get a scenario of sorts from someone of talent like Ronald Tavel but it is tailored (see *Screen Test I* and *Screen Test II*) to the personalities of given performers. What turns up on film is a little charade, not expressing the scenarist's idea so much as translating it freely into superstarmania. The film camera therefore turns out to be the chief *auteur*—that camera which has such a wonderful faculty of being Narcissus' pool.

Take the Warhol film *Horse*, which supposedly is a parody Western for which Tavel wrote one of his scripts full of pungent campiness. One of the Warhol superstars, Gerard Malanga, reports that Andy wanted to do an "abstract" film on cowboys, but what he really meant of course, as Malanga agrees, was a camp-charade film. A real horse—a large stallion was delivered rather than the requested pony—was rented for it, and one of the young men playing in this freakout charade sits on it, virtually nude, during the typical one-scene action. The main event is a strip-poker game in which an outlaw, his sheriff captor, and a pal join. It ends with the outlaw (played by Tosh Carrillo) getting beaten up by the others for cheating. Tavel relates that, his idea being for the thing to be a sex charade (a psychoanalyzing of Hollywood Westerns), he dutifully stood beyond camera range instructing the actors to use the beating as an excuse to "feel up" the supposed outlaw. The performers, however, got carried away with their sadomasochistic stint and (deaf to Tavel's pleas) continued being outright rough instead of slyly erotic with their victim. . . . *Auteur! Auteur!* Where is the *auteur*? Only the stationary, faithfully grinding camera really remained in charge of affairs on this occasion at the Factory. Its grist here, as often elsewhere, was a childishly violent group psychodrama invented chiefly by the performers. It is now, irresistibly, that Dr. Caligari, manipulator of the somnambulist Cesare, demands his historic moment. We must proceed with the Underground and its phenomenal reforms of the avant-garde from the point marked by that crucial film.

the pad's predecessor: an archetype

It would be absurd to think that *The Cabinet of Dr. Caligari* (1919) is only a definitely datable museum curio, or, to speak strictly filmically, something to mark a stage in the art film's development. This would be an antiquarian view of the film art, and something for academicians who are research scholars to exploit (film criticism does not lack these, although often they disguise themselves as film buffs). To be sure, *Caligari* grew out of the Expressionist theater, with its wild cubistic sets. From the standpoint of literature it is parallel with the tales of E. T. A. Hoffmann and Edgar Allen Poe. This is not irrelevant, though it may seem to be just another antiquarian concern. Baudelaire and other serious artists did not admire Poe for trivial external reasons. Poe's stories (as even commercial movie makers have become vaguely aware) were cradles of surrealism and even of camp. What could have been more prophetic of straight Dada camp than the dental motif of *Berenice*? The only way for the puritanical society in which

Poe wrote to take such a story was as grotesque fantasy, which (as that same society logically decided) was the plausible preoccupation of an alcoholic drug addict and near-madman.

The Cabinet of Dr. Caligari, directed by Robert Wiene, has far more explicit modernity of form than any Poe fantasy. By its careful structure it suggests a much more objective and plausible human situation than anything in Poe, who had to rely on an ultraexotic "simulation of hysteria"; otherwise contemporary society might have been so frightened as to clap him in an asylum. The "surprise ending" of *Caligari,* in which it is discovered that the narrator and his fair listener are inmates of an insane asylum (not just a pair of romantic lovers), is actually a framework of reason. The fantasy here is so powerful, however, that the ending does not spoil the film's imaginative dimension. Rather, it italicizes the fantasy by rendering even this rational explanation of the main action part of a basic ambiguity that preserves the film's mesmeric mysteriousness. A psychoanalytic explanation of the whole is not only inferrable from the setting of the asylum, but may also be drawn from the curious confusion among planes of reality which forms the literal plot. Far from being artificial or stagy (as its unsympathetic critics have said), *Caligari* has an inevitable form which film is the best adapted of all art media to interpret, having exactly the technique for a fluent passage from one mental dimension to another which stamps the most complex—and thus the most realistic—fantasies.

Technically, in *Caligari* we are seeing in visual form a sensational story imparted by a gentleman situated romantically with a lovely blank-faced lady in a garden. His story could be a covert way of exciting her erotically. It concerns the way tragedy enters the lives of a young couple engaged to be married; the lady seated in the garden seems to be the fiancée of the unfolding story, which, of course, since dialogue had not arrived in film, is told visually. The lady's fiancé and a male friend (apparently the narrator) visit a fair where they behold the weird-looking, aged Dr. Caligari, a hypnotist who exhibits his somnambulist, Cesare, as the usual peepshow attraction. Opening the lid of what seems an upright coffin, Caligari reveals a gaunt, dead-looking man in black tights (Conrad Veidt) whom he claims to have under permanent hypnosis. Because a series of unsolved murder cases have appeared in the vicinity, the presence of Caligari and his somnambulist arouses the suspicion of the fiancé and his friend. But when police investigate the traveling home-on-wheels shared by Caligari and Cesare, the former shows Cesare "asleep" in his cabinet. However, Caligari soon releases Cesare and he invades the house of the beauteous engaged lady and abducts her from her bed. Interfered with by her lover, Cesare kills him and attempts to flee with his limp burden. Closely pursued then, he drops her and tries to stagger home. But the jig is up. With Cesare dead, Caligari's grief and frustration send him off the deep end of paranoiac madness. The police corner him and he is put into a strait-jacket.

Though the lady herself is alive, her trauma has been so great that she is committed to an asylum. And now the plot's ingenuity is quickly revealed. The blank-faced lady who has patiently listened to the story rises and leaves the narrator, who follows her back to the social room of an asylum, instantly identified as such by the behavior of the lady (who imagines herself an untouchable virgin queen sitting on a throne) and of other inmates. The chief doctor soon appears; pretty evidently, he is the actor who has played Caligari (Werner Kraus), now without his grotesque make-up. It is rather funny, incidentally, that in the contemporary film *Chappaqua* the one-time drug addict, novelist William Burroughs, was engaged to play a psychiatric doctor. This echo of *Caligari* is another of that Underground film's cross-references.

The narrator of the film now instantly professes to recognize Caligari in the doctor himself. In seconds, as attendants collar the narrator and put him in a strait-jacket, we realize that he too has been committed to the asylum, suggesting the possibility that the whole story he has told is simply his own fantasy. Exactly through this ambiguity of fantasy-enclosing-reality-enclosing-fantasy the film realizes its peculiar power and charm. The ambiguity would not have such power if each step in the story, each emotion, were not itself clear and definite. To the thoughtful, the dénouement cannot fail to suggest that Cesare is the tool of an erotic demon of which Caligari is only the mythological personification, that the somnambulist signifies the released libido of the young friend of the lady's fiancé (the narrator), who presumably has had a hidden impulse to assault her and kill his friend. Once this psychoanalytic-mythic postulate is accepted, we may think of the film as a fantastic modern exploitation of the black forces of sex: that "black" erotic magic traditionally emanating from Satan. We think too of the black-clad phantoms pursuing the hero of *The Trip* and of Maya Deren's black nun, mirror-faced, in her film *Meshes of the Afternoon*: all are erotic figures. Indeed, the black nun's habit hides a lover of whom the heroine has tired.

Cesare the somnambulist (also black-clad) incarnates everything the Surrealists came to revere in their rituals: madness, hysteria, *humeur noire* (black bile), automatism, the dream, chance. The line-up is complete. Though the magician, from his name, is presumably Italian, the story itself is North European and especially, in its stark confrontation between reason and insanity as good and evil forces, typically German. We are reminded that Satan as a creator of illusions is embodied in the Faust legend and that the novelist Thomas Mann would sound, during the two decades after *Caligari*, those modern notes which conceive the artist's fate as tragic because he deceives people with illusions and may end by destroying himself and perhaps others. Ten years after *Caligari*'s appearance Mann created his own Caligari in a stage magician, Cipolla, who is shot to death by a young man he has hypnotized into thinking him a beautiful girl and kissing him. The setting of the story, *Mario and the Magician,* is Italian and so is the magician. Mann's climactic work was *Dr. Faustus* (1947), and in it the composer André Leverkühn, with Satan as his double, wields over his admirers and lovers a hypnotic sort of power that leads to an actual crime of passion.

In the Faust legend man falls in love with the artistry of magic illusion, hoping to regain his vital powers, including sex, in all their youthful flush. In this respect the generations of man never learn the lessons of reason supposedly taught by the advance of civilization. Even this century demonstrates that magic can never be painted so black that it does not attract disciples, worshipers, and practitioners.* The Surrealists endorsed magic by viewing it existentially. Modern thinking has isolated the sexual factor as the sly libido which will sacrifice anything, even sanity, in its own cause, while to accomplish its ends it exerts a kind of magic. With Freud and other philosophers of sex, one may argue that part of the libido's power lies in a profound death wish within human beings. There is a curious way in which, backed by ancient ritual, supreme erotic ecstasies have been linked with sudden death. Insanity is simply an alternative to death as the result of a traumatic, usually ambivalent, sexual experience.

In the eighteenth and nineteenth centuries the heroines of novels were constantly being abducted and/or ravished, with the standard result that they died of grief or went insane; at the very best the dishonored woman immured herself in a convent. This atmosphere is perfectly created in *The Mysteries of Udolpho,* by Mrs. Radclyffe, and in Horace Walpole's novels, which fascinated André Breton. The theme of insanity-inducing

* At least two Underground filmmakers, Storm De Hirsch and Harry Smith, are self-declared magicians.

and death-inducing sexual ravishment also occurs in a novel of a very different style and tone, *Les Liaisons Dangereuses,* cleverly modernized by Roger Vadim in 1954 as a commercial movie. Under a perfect surface of eighteenth-century manners and morals the demonic powers of sex are displayed in all their timeless glory.

Putting the Underground Film in our present perspective, we find in its avant-garde predecessors ample tributes to the sustained dynamic relation between love on one side and death and madness on the other. A scene in one of the rooms viewed by the Poet through keyholes, in Cocteau's *Le Sang d'un Poète,* specifically concerns love and death; in the same film the Poet's suicide takes place as a parable of the artist's immortality and thus is an optimistic anticlimax. Maya Deren's *Meshes of the Afternoon,* whose black nun was mentioned above, is part of her most important film work, an essentially autobiographical trilogy: *Meshes of the Afternoon, At Land,* and *Ritual in Transfigured Time.* We find here the multiple personality used as counterparts to different objects of sexual desire. The heroine's violent death (symbolic because it means only the death of an identity) ends both the first and third works of the trilogy. Maya Deren always displayed a somnambulistic heroine (played by herself) acting as in a dream or some elaborate ritual, always under the spell of mysterious urges somewhere between great desire and great fear, but self-evidently erotic.

Also to be numbered among these pre-Underground avant-garde works is a film by Curtis Harrington, *Fragment of Seeking,* in which the birth of a homosexual identity is signified at the climax by the female's turning into a skull with a blond wig. The form of Harrington's film is shaped by the labyrinth and the search; plot action, as in many avant-garde films (including *Le Sang d'un Poète*), takes its character from antique ritual, in which the initiate is as if blindfolded, or in the dark, and must find his way to light and ultimate revelation.

the pad's predecessor: an archetype

The optical distortion in the stagelike sets of *Caligari* is important because of its link to the psychedelic environments which Underground films play with as a simple result of drug taking or from the orgiastic desire to create an "unreal" setting in which the libidinal desires are free to release themselves in some ritual form, such as dancing. Rhythmic gyrating in fantastic circumstances (a sort of echo of dancing in a stage set) is a permeative trait of Underground films. *Caligari*'s bold black-and-white sets, based on geometric abstractionism, dramatized a serious struggle of the passions and in effect showed the triumph of magic as satanic. In Wiene's film the libido is still the dangerously violent thing which survived into the late twenties and was climaxed with the compulsive and sadistic acts we find in *Un Chien Andalou* and *L'Age d'Or*.

Notice that Dr. Caligari goes through none of the familiar hypnotic operations with his somnambulist, Cesare. On the other hand, he does feed him by way of a spoon holding liquid. What is this mysterious gruel or beverage? A logical inference is that it contains a drug, if only because Cesare seems to be in a permanent trance from which he is awakened specifically to accomplish his criminal acts. Both drug taking itself and the Drug Attitude are species of self-administered magic. The same is true of the spirit of euphoria that is so much a part of the contemporary Youth Attitude and on which so many Underground films are based. That magic has its frightening and malign side, leading to death or insanity, is the explicit thesis of *Caligari*. And here it is an *adult* thesis. So is that of Buñuel in *L'Age d'Or* adult, insofar as its destructive hero, possessed by an infantile neurosis, sees social behavior not as fun but as mayhem.

Despite this, the prime effort of the modern sensibility (duly prevailing in Underground Film) is magically to dissociate itself from the serious aspects of violence by setting the limits of violence as the mock-reality of messing up the play-

97

room, the pad. Raymond Saroff's film *Happening I*, made of Happenings arranged by Claes Oldenburg, is a perfect example of this effort by adults to purge violent behavior of all serious significance. As shown there, a Happening is an ambiguous sort of Halloween prank, involving playing dead, wearing impromptu masks, harmless mauling, and in general that prodigal dislocation of given order which children, from time immemorial, have found so fascinating a pursuit.

From the viewpoint of film craft, Saroff's film is one of the least significant Underground works. The relation of its crude documentation to the "art" of the film is nil, since it has even less connection with art than do Happenings themselves. Yet *Happening I* demands comment in this section for a particular reason. An oddly inert man, we see, has been wrapped thickly in newspapers and people start unwrapping him without bringing him back to consciousness. Later, however, like Caligari's somnambulist, he carries about the seemingly unconscious forms of women. After being set down the women revive and start running away, whereupon the man tries to recapture them. The movements are uniformly trancelike and all takes place in a remarkably limited space. Lacking all plot motivation or semblance of organic fantasy, this Happening incident looks like deliberate deadpan mummery: all emotions, especially the "fright" emotions on which *Caligari* works its variations, are avoided.

We must understand that right here is the great difference between avant-garde film prior to the late fifties and the Underground of the sixties. Why has it been so comparatively easy for the Underground to surface? Because the evil side of magic has widened and insidiously softened its appeal by turning into the benignity of Flower Power. After all, most drugs originate in plants; besides, the intoxicating effect of such "innocent" plants as the banana (and this is by no means camp symbolism) has been discovered. It is Flower Power psychology which

the pad's predecessor: an archetype

governs the universal-tolerance creed of organized Underground Film and shapes the vocabulary of Underground Film criticism. Jonas Mekas goes so far in praising an Underground film by Barbara Rubin, *Christmas on Earth*, as (waggishly?) to offer a childishly false syllogism about it: "Barbara Rubin has no shame; angels have no shame; Barbara Rubin is an angel."* The juxtaposition of Christmas and angels to the stark erotic subject matter of the film (an anatomic fantasy with the sexual organs as the dominant motifs) is patently a deliberate effort to replace black magic with white, to saturate adult sexuality with a "childlike" innocence. Mekas' recognition seems to fit a quite new category: Underground Corn.

Certainly the real and psychological dimensions of Dr. Caligari's pad have survived in Underground films and so has the generic nature of its subject matter: love as a great dream action. Still, the Underground has made an effort to completely reverse the prevalent mood of its avant-garde predecessors. From horror and tragedy it has moved to ecstasy and happiness. For the moment let us ignore the perennial and subtle claims of sadomasochism and all the aesthetics of evil that, for his part, Baudelaire symbolized by *flowers*. There is nothing undesirable about ecstasy and happiness as such, or their legitimate place in the arts. Yet it happens that 95 percent of such manifestations in Underground films embody not an apt and subtle *art* of ecstasy and happiness so much as a crude, inept *propaganda* of ecstasy and happiness—something that is very close to publicizing certain personality cults that have emerged from beatnik and hippie milieus. And the truth is that, with the ecstasy often childishly feigned or grotesquely aped, and the happiness presented as euphoria, the propaganda itself is to be suspected.

We have only to look briefly at the avant-garde forties to notice that outstanding experimental filmmakers of that period,

* From the Film-Makers' Cooperative catalogue.

such as Sidney Peterson and James Broughton, had a much more objective grasp of the same themes that the Underground handles today. Take the theme of infantilism and the child-man comedian. Broughton's *Looney Tom* is a fabulously accurate reconstruction of the style of popular screen comedy in the teens of the century. Turning to something more creative, in *Mother's Day* the same filmmaker used the pictorial plan of the family photograph album to work animate and amusing variations on common human themes: mother's stately courtship and marriage as against the naughty erotic rebellion of the new generation. Adult infantilism emerges here too, but it is held in neat perspective by the mother's effort to keep eternally young by imagining the teenagers as still babies. Again, Sidney Peterson, in his quasi-Surrealist film *The Petrified Dog*, recreates the world as a sort of holiday spent by Alice in Wonderland. His Alice transmutes her parents and people they meet on their picnic in the park in a way corresponding to her own experiences in the movie house. The obvious film trickery in these works is justified by the light comic satire. The scale and the touch here are "right." Under tutelage of the Underground style, the same things were to grow pretentious. That the satiric edge was to turn into self-indulgent camp was already apparent in a later film by Broughton, *Pleasure Garden*, which is a precursor of Underground works that good-humoredly revive pop stereotypes of the movies and conceive the world as, by right, a layman's paradise in which adult life is confined to making love and having fun: a pursuit frustrated only by official puritan morals.* Already, in *Pleasure Garden*, the seeds of euphoric megalomania are growing. Its mood exactly chimes with Flower Power.

How did these shifts in the avant-garde film come about? A year or so before he died, Marcel Duchamp, known today

* Compare *Pleasure Garden* with *Hallelujah the Hills* as conscious parodies of the old commercial films.

as the grandfather of Pop Art, expressed himself in an interview in a way that sheds much light on its extensions as seen
in Underground Film. The new art, Duchamp asserted, was to
be "loved, not judged." Duchamp (who gave up art as a pro-
fession in 1923) was a true intellectual of cheerfully abysmal
ironies. One thing is surely to be inferred from the statement
just quoted. As it would be fatal to the new art to judge it,
the kindest thing possible is to love it. But, speaking seriously,
love itself is necessarily a judgment. All art, assuredly, asks
to be loved. But so do all people ask to be loved. In Underground films it is most apt to be people, not art or artists, who
ask to be loved. I think that is what Duchamp meant.

underground film is primitive film

Here Underground films have already been technically associated with primitive art as various forms of beginning. I have just proposed the idea that the Underground is very close to the psychological dimension of the playroom, where a let's-pretend attitude purges violence of its basic drive. Some psychologists say, for example, that children ought to play at war games, Wild West stuff, and so on, because in obeying the conditions of fighting and killing as a sport—in practicing a sort of childish sadism—male children in particular, it is supposed, purge themselves of the humors that would lead to serious violence and actual killing.

One of the independently produced commercial films that have sidestepped Hollywood formulas through the decades (and can be called demi-Underground) was Morris Engel's *Little Fugitive* (1953). This was about a seven- or eight-year-old boy who, playing at killing with his older brother and some friends, is told by the older boys, purely as a prank, that he has actually killed his brother. Stunned and frightened, he runs away and boards a subway train that ends up in Coney Island, itself a sort of never-never land of mock-deadly games. Its diversions manage to distract the boy from his panic and all ends benignly as the little fugitive is safely recovered and returned home. There he joins his brother at the TV set, where make-believe killing is really make-believe killing. The moral implications are rather skillfully confused: the boy is absolved from killing because his action has been make-believe and only make-believe. The filmed cowboys watched on TV are also playing a game. Their noise and their roughhouse are real enough (so is football), but their bullets are not real. Now what should this prototypic little boy, living as a little boy today, think when he sees a new or old war film on TV? Yes, it's make-believe as a film. But does it imply that Vietnam is a myth and that the President is acting in a Hollywood movie?

We need hardly pause to remark how silly propositions like the one implied by *Little Fugitive* are, in any realistic educational sense. My own opinion is that, like the combat training of army draftees, a fighting "sport" is nothing but a preparation for the serious business of killing in international and gang wars. The fact remains that education is not the only medium for the notion that violence can be symbolized into harmlessness: art has the same notion. And this idea, I think, is one which Underground filmmakers have intuitively come to repudiate because art has steadily lost, in this century, its prestige as an imaginative adventure, an end in *itself*, and come to be regarded as actually, like "war games," one of the programs for turning fantasy into reality.

There is some question about the ambiguous violence of man's deeds on the planet from day to day, but there is no question about the downright violence of his thoughts and their faculty for evoking an as-if reality. "If thoughts could kill," we say. One need add nothing to this except the contemporary

103

saw about the hypothetical person who would, if he could, push a hypothetical button that would destroy the world in a twinkling. Sensible people have remarked that if such a deed were possible, the world would cease to exist most abruptly. The nonchalance with which the hypothetical grounds for *hesitation* in such a case have been ignored by commentators on it, is an alarming note in itself. The most obsessive thought in the world, I take it, is push-button imagination—the same button that the Surrealists relied on to produce mad dreams. The Surrealists isolated this push-button power of the mind. Tributes rendered by the Surrealists to ordinary behavior, to the principle of common possibility, the scientist has always rendered to his dreams of invention, of the discovery of great hidden principles and their possible function in the aggrandizement or decimation of mankind.

Outside the scientific realm, traditionally, the Devil has been assumed to have charge of all such magical secrets and their appropriate weapons. One such weapon was unquestionably, from very ancient times, drugs. The desire to transform the world did not always trouble itself with effecting total material and external change, but settled for the internal, purely subjective conversion of groups and individuals. An allusion to Marx's "opiate of the people" seems perfectly relevant here. For individuals, drugs make the already existent look novel and far more agreeable than it is. Also, even in the form of ordinary liquor, intoxicants tend to let down the bars of taboo and to homogenize the sexes. It is interesting that homogenized sex, rather than homosexuality, is so often the "deviate" note struck in Underground films; consider *Flaming Creatures*. Palpably, drugs induce the otherwise "sane" to indulge in a limited freedom of violent physical as well as mental actions.

The classic vehicle by which man plunged into such sensations was the orgiastic rite. As the cult of the witches' Sabbath, this rite survived the Christian church in Europe for at least sixteen centuries. All such survivals meant no more than that the cheated human libido was in serious and permanent revolt. The revolutionists of Underground films think that the elementary happiness of the libido is of more importance than the art of the film, and that programmatically film should discourage the subtle equilibrium created by successful art among the savage human appetites (including killing) and make itself, at any cost to technical brilliance and artistic maturity, into a propaganda for the peaceable, notably passive emotions.

where the rub is

Among the subjects of archaic film (circa 1900 in Europe) was Aladdin's lamp, which, when rubbed, could produce a slave of the passions out of thin air. It was not necessary, in the time of George Méliès, to make that *Trip to the Moon* on film in order to see the moon and stars impersonated by shapely ladies in alluring attitudes. One could have one's trip among draped or almost draped nudes by attending performances at any classy or unclassy variety house in Paris. Archaic film, primitive film, was nevertheless obsessed with the tacit spatial proclivities of the medium, which were "magic carpet" in kind. Through the primordial faculty of magic, man decided that the sun should be persuaded to rise. Film soon proved itself able to show the sun rising with the speed of an Olympic champion and to portray a rosebud blossoming with an efficiency that put nature's pace to shame. All such illusions have one important symbolic function if no other. They express man's sovereign impatience, the fierce immediacy lying at the root of his inborn, irrepressible desires. Surely that sovereign impatience contributed to Stan Brakhage's creation of his later film style and the co-ordinate creation of his children.

Yet archaic film trickery, becoming the order of cinema in film's first decade, cannot rightly be considered avant-garde or Underground except as, at that time, film was part of the discovery of scientific method. As a new communication medium, film primarily was not active and creative, but passive and documentary. Arabian Nights fantasy, so closely associated with traditional theater, was decidedly not avant-garde, nor was the accelerated action of the film chase that was to become a classic in the Westerns and the Keystone Kop comedies of American films. These film types expressed popular taste from the very beginning. What appealed to the Surrealists about the Keystone Kops, and the bathing beauties with whom they were usually involved, was precisely what was violent, childish and sincere about the idea of militant manhood and the struggle to gain the favors of Venus. The Surrealists made film avant-garde by a perverse and retrospective manifestation of taste: by a revision of what was pop as well as old-hat. It was the caprice of a new artistic elite. To the world of the twenties and early thirties filmic stereotypes began appearing in primitive nudity, as if they were projections of some far-out playroom imagination. What is more reminiscent of another sort of pad, the film fan's den beplastered with photos, than the parody of Valentino by the hero of *Le Sang d'un Poète*? Accordingly we find Underground films carrying film-star portraits on their walls—as in *Guns of the Trees*, and in *Scorpio Rising*, with its evocation of Marlon Brando and the deified James Dean.

The Surrealists were also much attracted to the criminal mystery films produced in Europe and the United States. It was essential that such films be serials, as if the sinister struggles in them were part of life's daily round. The Surrealist favorites were French: *Fantomas* (the name of an archcriminal) and

Les Vampires, shown in virtually its entirety (six hours) at the Fourth New York Film Festival as a Retrospective Choice. Breton himself pronounced the opinion that, as an image of pure evil, the female principal of *Les Vampires* seemed to him supreme in the history of art. The opinion is highly instructive as to the precious status of the absurd in Surrealist aesthetics.

This film's very name suggests the first "serious" heroine archetype of American films, the Vampire, the one who nowadays arouses giggles. The Vampire of the first three decades of film is now a legitimate camp and little else. Actually, the heroine of *Les Vampires* is a supernaturally dynamic (the heroines of serials were always *that*) gangster's moll who functions as a sort of right-hand woman to the gang leaders, and is clearly, like the archetype, an erotic demon. Although the various gang leaders of the Vampires (the name of a gang just as today we have the Skulls, the Red Devils, and so on) successively perish in internecine strife for the control of Paris criminal activity, the prodigious queen-moll survives in all her beauty and energy till a climactic disaster arrives.

The acting style in *Les Vampires* is itself archaic and moreover had to be simplified for the pop audience of which filmgoers were then, supposedly, exclusively composed. This ghoulishly implausible serial, hilarious from beginning to end, is comparable to some of our own time's far-out comic strips. Its high moments of action could provoke, at the Film Festival, only salvos of camp laughter mixed with camp applause. The valid question comes up as to why the Surrealists, as recently as the twenties, took its criminal aspect, its moral evil, so seriously.

To understand the adulation of Breton and his colleagues, one must invoke what is aggressively and radically "anti" in the dogmas of the group. The whole action of *Les Vampires*, in which death lurks beyond every doorway and the sole occupation is to steal and kill, is anarchic and anti-Establishment.

108

Crime is the sole raison d'être of these rival gangs, just as for the Marquis de Sade crime became the sole raison d'être of sex. Only at the very end of the serial does the erotic orgy occur; then the action comes close to a parody of ritual because the apparently victorious Vampires, imagining themselves free to celebrate with a great drinking party, are really the victims of a trap set by the police and perish ignobly or are captured. It is like the mass sacrifice of victims to some pagan deity which permitted an orgy of the condemned to precede their death.

At the New York Film Festival *Les Vampires* was offered as a gourmet's delicacy of antiquarian avant-garde; was offered, that is, as camp. A contingent of film buffs was willing to admire it solemnly for its forthright action and downright tone—to admire it as pure style. But this is as much an abstraction as the penchant of the Surrealists for admiring it as anti-Establishment evil. *Les Vampires* has no more importance to philosophical or ethical evil as such than does gangster crime in any era. The Marquis de Sade, after all, was not a gangster with a sneaky bedroom vice. The Surrealist aesthetic of evil was only partly Baudelairean and Poësque and was expressed largely through *humeur noire.* In regard to sadism, this black bile meant a systematic cruelty, an infantile addiction to cruelty, which Baudelaire would have considered arbitrary and ultimately barren. But Sade's criminal philosophy of sex, though on a grand scale, is precisely violent, childish and sincere; so is the black bile that, to the Surrealists, saturates the compulsive daily activities of the Vampires. Hence we have a pure aesthetics, not an ethics, with which to deal. In the childish imagination nothing is too absurd, too implausible, to enable the Vampires to gain their illegal, gratuitous, violent ends, the satisfaction of their evil desire for power. This is why the gang's preposterous maneuvers so often provoke laughter; we are really present, not at actual crime, but at the child's naïve gluttonous parody of actual crime. Theft and homicide for the

Vampires, sex for Sade, have the same monolithic abstractness: at once a sensual ecstasy and an absolute raison d'être.
It is a self-vindicating, rationally conducted insanity. And thus
the monotonous capers of the Vampires are definitely not
"reality." They are sheer fantasy—the life of the ideal in
terms of the most primitive and lawless lusts. This is another
(deliberately sinister) rub of Aladdin's lamp. But not more
than that.

the abstractness of avant-gardes

The Vampires, when engaged in their criminal work, wear a uniform. No one will be surprised to learn that it is exactly the uniform of Cesare, Caligari's somnambulist: black tights. In addition, the Vampires always shield their faces with black hoods having eye slits. The heroine duly appears in this garb, identifying her sex only by certain curves. The Vampires' whole tactic, like that of the black erotic figures of *The Trip*, is to look like anonymous phantoms. As Cesare represents the criminal agent of the libido, the Paris gang represents the criminal agents of the id.

The libido as the erotic member of the love-insanity-death triumvirate emerges in the filmic present as less macabre than it is psychedelic. We shall find that in the transplantation of the European avant-garde to the United States this became increasingly true. Despite the serious aims of the old avant-garde, the Underground innovation has come to reflect the Love People, who are young, young, *young*! Whenever serious violence such as murder or attempted murder actually takes place in hippieland, an ominous note is sounded that embarrasses the ingenuous, passive, peaceful fantasists of Underground beatnik-into-hippie filmmaking.

The latitude of the avant-garde film, permitting it to stretch from the severity of Cocteau, Buñuel, Dali through the expatriated Hans Richter, Maya Deren, and a few predecessors to the current free-form fantasy and antitechnical filmmaking of the Underground, is determined by the whole abstract nature of mythological thought that has animated the avant-garde from its beginnings. The antique concept of the love-death, for instance, means a radical joining of extremes that naturally suggests myth and seeks a ritual form of expression, a form lending itself easily to fantasy and symbolism. Cocteau has been a positive influence in this respect, being the animating genius of one of the most technically responsible and incidentally stylish Underground films, *Narcissus* (1956), by Willard Maas and Ben Moore. Though the film has weaknesses, it it a paragon of structural filmmaking when compared with many of today's Underground productions.*

Maya Deren's film trilogy is one continuous love-death ritual. Cocteau's *Le Sang d'un Poète* is a ritualistic parable of the artist's sacrifice of his libido, beginning with the fantasy sex of masturbation (the palm of his hand becomes a mouth asking for air) and ending in two phases of his symbolic death. Stan Brakhage's masturbation film, *Flesh of Morning*, has the same fantasy sex in a realistic, everyday pattern: the young hero's sexual obsession makes it possible for him to sacrifice marriage and possible children. Very interesting, in the last three works mentioned, is the repeated use of a wholly black figure to symbolize a malign form of Cupid. More light is shed on Caligari's somnambulist if we recall that, in the classic myth of Cupid and Psyche, the young love god first

* See later discussion of this film, page 219.

appears shrouded in darkness and is reputed to be a monster of whom Psyche is afraid. An early film by Gregory Markopoulos, *Psyche*, was a free adaptation of Pierre Louÿs' modern version of the legend in which a woman seems to dread a naked confrontation with love.

In *Flesh of Morning* the filmmaker himself as the naked masturbating hero is suddenly seen in negative (that is, in "black flesh") at the moment of achieving orgasm. Brakhage uses negative similarly in the tragic dénouement of his somewhat juvenile *The Way to Shadow Garden*. At the end of *Ritual in Transfigured Time*, Maya Deren, when the frightened, fleeing heroine (herself) enters the water and drowns, shows the positive film suddenly turning negative: the modern nymph is fleeing from a modern satyr. Both devices may well echo, perhaps subconsciously, Cocteau's device of the Angel of Death, representing in *Le Sang d'un Poète* the death of a boyhood passion. While a Negro dancer actually performs this role, there is a moment of apotheosis when the entire film becomes negative, turning black to white and white to black.

Some people laugh or sneer at the Abstract-Expressionist style of *Caligari*—its artistic as well as filmic datedness—just as others (or the same people) laugh or sneer at the archaic pop fantasy of *Les Vampires*. In the crudest sense laughter is a way not only of recognizing incongruity and absurdity but also of escaping moral responsibility or imaginative participation in the serious implications of a film or a theater piece. The most trivial and absurd popular film, comedy or drama, may become important through the techniques of psychoanalysis—just as an animal on whom scientific experiments are made becomes more than just another dog, mouse, or guinea pig. Since the aims of avant-garde film are different from those of scientific method and experiment, we cannot look there to help fortify the Surrealist position. Yet intrinsically there is no more reason to giggle or sneer over *Caligari* than there is to giggle or sneer over *Titicut Follies*. It means only one audience response among many.

By the concepts of the absurd and of black bile the Surrealists did not signify "laughing matters" in any usual sense. Their code was to embrace the fearless freedom of the mind, to accept any extravagance of imagination (no matter if conventionally insane) because the reward would always be great: the recognition and enjoyment of primordial desire—primordial desire which has passed unmodified and integral from childhood to adulthood. André Breton called it "the marvelous." This is why the childishly exhibitionistic, violent, antisocial adult hero of *L'Age d'Or*, conventionally so laughable, in this perspective becomes a hero as serious and significant as Siegfried or Galahad.

A mythic hero is simply one who converts his wildest dreams into practical action. And that is why Breton created the heroine of his novelette named after her, *Nadja*, who lives a life of pure mental fantasy, as if "reality" were simply the raw material for hour-by-hour, minute-by-minute imaginative fictions. The narrator of the story falls in love with her while perceiving that his love cannot be satisfactorily consummated in the ordinary way. The relation of Nadja's temperament to insanity becomes clear when finally she goes technically insane and enters an asylum. What Breton accomplished with the story was simple enough: he showed that the Surrealist invention— its plausibility, all its connections with the ordinary world— does not differ technically from the usual fantasies of lunatics.

Today we constantly hear of black humor and black comedy without relating them to their Surrealist origin. Usually the things meant are something converted from Surrealism to existentialism. From pure, or "abstract," fantasy we take the step to existential fantasy, and we now find, on stage or in film, people acting out semifictitious psychodramas, those "charades" which, like puzzles, are supposed to have solutions. The parallel comes in aptly because this conversion is just what has turned the official avant-garde into the official Underground. With relaxing severity, a relaxing sense of form and discipline, the avant-garde evolved from the Surrealist sphere, its heritage from Europe, which it occupied in this country till the late fifties.

The decline of the phantom of dreams and his replacement by the social types known as beatniks and hippies is one vastly important symptom of this change. I have mentioned that in a filmed Oldenburg Happening the criminal rape action in *Caligari* is echoed by adults doing a childish, seemingly unconscious, at-home parody of it. This is a concrete Underground emblem of the new anti-aesthetics, the deformalized fantasy of the avant-garde tradition. It no longer proceeds from an "idea," which is abstract and theoretical, but from playroom fantasy, which (whatever else it may be) is always concrete.

the avant-garde laboratory

As Poësque fiction *The Cabinet of Dr. Caligari* harks back to the romantic satanism of the nineteenth century. As a bold fantasy of involuted violence it has the actual focus of the sensibility that was about to formulate the ideal of nonsense—i.e., insane gibberish—as serious and meaningful (Dada) and to promulgate as aesthetic postulates the simulation of hysteria, the absurd, black bile, and so on (Surrealism). What before was the realm of the nightmare and the insane asylum became, in the 1920's, *the laboratory of the artist who practiced the experimental dream*. This was the original ideal of the American avant-garde film that was radical and ambitious enough to emulate Europe's best examples. With obviously faked and toylike sets and actors like comic marionettes, *The Life and Death of a Hollywood Extra* was exactly a parlor charade derived from the style of *Metropolis*, Fritz Lang's Expressionist satire on modern industrial civilization. In the United States Melville Webber and J. S. Watson treated the biblical legend of Sodom and Gomorrah, in their film *Lot in Sodom* (1933), as if it were an "experimental dream" of applicable film devices. Without having the Surrealist bite, it has many Surrealist technical postulates.

These earlier ideals were anti-aesthetic only insofar as they were anticonventional, as they pointed to a drastic revision of artistic form. The important shift from the standpoint of the imaginative creator was taken, strangely enough, from Cesare the criminal somnambulist, incarnation of the libido, to Caligari himself, the mad magician who (as it were) invented Cesare as his creature and tool in the way that Mephistopheles produced Helen of Troy in Marlowe's *Dr. Faustus*. The Dada and Surrealist focus was on the *author*, who disciplined himself, like a monk or a priest, in order to experience "the marvelous."

Hans Richter's feature-length avant-garde film, *Dreams That Money Can Buy* (1946), was an elaborate salesroom display of the wares of fashionable modern painters, with the accent on Surrealist art manners. Much of its episodic action seemed to be "live illustrations" of the themes of the involved artists (Duchamp, Calder, Max Ernst, Léger) and it verged signally on the pop style to come. Richter rerpesented one of the theoretical cornerstones of what, in the American twenties, were known as cinepoems—productions based on a theory of the film as pure poetry. His ideas were taken up by *Film Culture* when it first appeared in 1955, before the official birth of the Underground, but were tacitly dropped a few years later, except in that very perfunctory way in which the epithet "poetic" has survived in Underground vocabulary.

Caligari, the "alchemic" hypnotist, cherished Cesare as a divine principle just as Satan, as personified, cherishes the "satanic," the sacred essence that saturates and explains him. The film finds it easier than the stage to create a sense of unreality in the use of human beings; after all, the person is not himself present, only his reflection. Cesare was primarily a

117

mental projection; so were Cocteau's Poet and Buñuel's in-fantile erotic giant (that rampageous hero of *L'Age d'Or*), and so were the multiple personae of Maya Deren's own image in her films. The magician as hero or villain is far from being a fresh theme in art. In the old Faust legend the hero aspires to be a magician by grace of Mephistopheles, who is the villain and who ultimately ruins Faust after playing with him. In Thomas Mann's version the artist is hero-villain by grace of in-nate magic powers. Mann's novel displayed, just as clearly as the Surrealists did, that the moral ambivalence of the creative artist has a supernatural stature. In the artist good and evil are subsumed by the same immensity of nature. Even crime (as in Sade's works and films like *Les Vampires*) is permitted the artist's nature as part of its supernaturalism; not actual crime, that is, but the aesthetically projected crimes of the imagina-tion. Hence we have the function of a figure such as Cesare, whose master, Caligari, it finally appears, is no less fictitious than his somnambulist.

Henri Langlois, director of the Cinémathèque Francaise,* told an illuminating story when he introduced the screenings of an Abel Gance retrospective at the Fifth New York Film Festi-val. Speaking of the earliest film on the program, *La Folie de Docteur Tube* (1915), Langlois informed his audience that the reason this film long ago gained its reputation as a Surreal-ist precursor was that at first the "framing story" footage was missing from the print in the Cinémathèque's possession; only some years later was it discovered and added to the version now shown.

The first scenes of *La Folie* show us an eccentric scientist portrayed in the fantastic style of early films as old and "mad,"

---

* M. Langlois was dismissed in 1968 and, owing to pressure by the student uprising in Paris, was reinstated the same year. He is now said to be successfully running the Cinémathèque by daily showings from the film archives, including avant-garde works.

wholly alien to sobriety of mood. As if by accident, he discovers a chemical combination that completely distorts the given anatomical proportions and scale of objects (including people) when it is sprinkled over them as a powder. The fact that the backgrounds also become ambiguously distorted suggests the element of optical hallucination.

Of course the idea was inspired in Gance by the existence of anamorphic (distortive) lenses, which are as adaptable to motion-picture use as to still photography. First the old scientist plays the trick (fortunately he provides himself with a prompt antidote to the chemical's effect) on his little Negro assistant, then on two pairs of sweethearts who visit him, one of the young ladies apparently being a relative. It is the old situation comedy of farcical mischance and misunderstanding. First the ladies get the chemical sprinkled on them; then, while they are ranting about in despair and bewilderment, their lovers join them, are horrified at the sight, and instantly get sprinkled themselves. At the peak of the resulting hysteria, the old scientist, laughing heartily, is dragged forth and induced to reverse the chemical transformer. All the characters promptly return to their normal shapes and in great relief manage to consider it all a huge joke.

What happened with the film at the Cinémathèque was that at first only the anamorphic sequences were found. It seemed to the viewer, without knowledge of the supposed chemical trick, that a total world of anatomical absurdity had been invented, in line with the world as seen by Cubism and Expressionism. The wild, desperate gestures of the smartly dressed young ladies and gentlemen make them resemble a parody of the most extravagant style in the tragic theater. The lenses Gance used have exactly the effect of the distorting mirrors at old-fashioned amusement halls. At the same time, because the gestures and postures of the actors are those of wild despair, the anamorphic images resemble persons dressed in the costumes of some grotesque ritual, intended perhaps to be majestic but appearing absurd, instead, through the costumer's insane imagination. Without the laboratory of the "mad" old scientist (in the footage discovered later) the film would be a perfect Surrealist joke giving vent to a lunatic plastic imagination. Not to question the absolute veracity of Langlois' story, this losing and finding of film footage was also a perfect example of doing and undoing by the operation of "objective hazard."

Why is *The Cabinet of Dr. Caligari* not a pure Surrealist work? Principally because of the "framing story" in which one discovers that the narrator and his female listener are inmates of an insane asylum. Without the nuance of the asylum doctor's resemblance to the mad magician, Caligari, there would be no interesting involution to the film. It is easy to grasp, then, how Caligari would be the figure for the surreal artist who ritually works himself into a state of hallucination in which fiction automatically changes places with reality. Sometimes it is a matter of logical dispute as to how "conscious" the behavior of a madman is and thus, from the legal standpoint, how morally responsible he is for the criminal act of which he has been legally convicted. As a recent example, when Sirhan B. Sirhan was tried for the murder of Robert F. Kennedy, his attorney defended him by claiming that he killed while in a state of trance. Apparently drugs had no role in promoting Sirhan's "trance life," but that killing Kennedy was for long an obsessive hallucination for him was shown by evidence offered in the trial. Kennedy's confessed killer became violently hysterical in the courtroom and himself asked to be killed summarily.

Limiting the application of such an argument to art, it becomes clear that the artist-madman asserted his right in the nineteenth century to "go mad" on hallucinations (whether drug-induced or not) and freely to commit "crimes of the imagination." The only general vindication for this doctrine, perfected by the Surrealists, is that the artist's den or studio is

120

a laboratory parallel with the scientist's *but not to be confused with it*. The Surrealists finally divined and formulated the secrets of what may be called the atomic imagination. This realm has no more to do with the fantasies of technically certified madmen who commit crimes than the discovery of atomic fission has to do with the composition and use of the atomic bomb—no more, that is, and no less. We have only to allow for the ambiguous margin of reality that is attached to all art.

Sometime ago the judges of the annual Pepsi-Cola art competition awarded first prize to a little-known painter whose idea was, plainly, that the use of the atomic bomb would actually convert human anatomy to proportions resembling those of figures from Picasso. The only subtle point about the disgusting vulgarity of such a notion is that the figures in the winning work *looked like* figures from Picasso paintings but *were* nothing of the kind. The difference lay entirely in the degree of art employed by the two painters respectively and had nothing whatever to do with nuclear explosions. In our psychedelic age it is possible that people (including filmmakers) depend too much upon the optical "explosions" occasioned by drugs, too little upon the parallel explosions of the creative imagination.

dotting the eyes of distortion

Some austerity-minded filmmakers consider anamorphic lenses too mechanical and transparent a device to use as a strong filmic style. Surely, if the overall result is monotonous, the whole screen design overschematized, the objection is justifiable. However, there is more than one kind of anamorphic lens and much depends on whether anamorphism of image is used for a special effect, for a single sequence, for a brief film or a feature-length film. The success of Sidney Peterson's *The Lead Shoes* (1949), made at Workshop 20 in the California School of Fine Arts and using a lens that mostly compresses images horizontally,* leads me to believe that according to the type of story, its intrinsic interest and treatment, there *is* artistic aptness in anamorphic vision for film.

Naturally, anamorphism is a bit shocking to those who overvalue realism and who are unfamiliar with the good results ob-

* Compression from right and left *elongates* images; from top and bottom, *flattens* them.

underground motifs

plastic cosmos

Right: Song 14 (*Stan Brakhage*); *mold-growth, paint, chemicals, and scratches. Opposite, left: Hedy Lamarr in* Ecstasy (*Gustav Machaty*). *Opposite, right:* Portrait of Jason (*Shirley Clarke*).

physical sensation

personality portrait

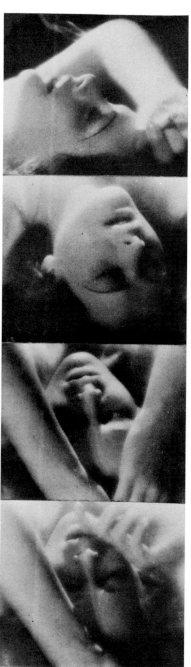

from concrete abstraction…

Mood Contrasts (*Mary Ellen Bute—Ted Nemeth*).

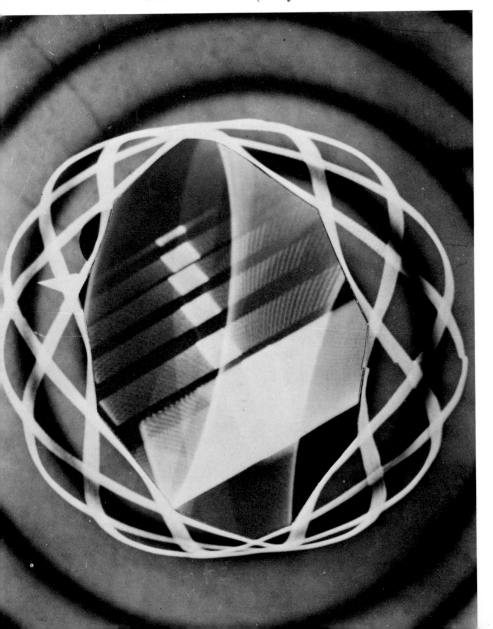

to dream concretion

Scene from Finnegans Wake (Mary Ellen Bute).

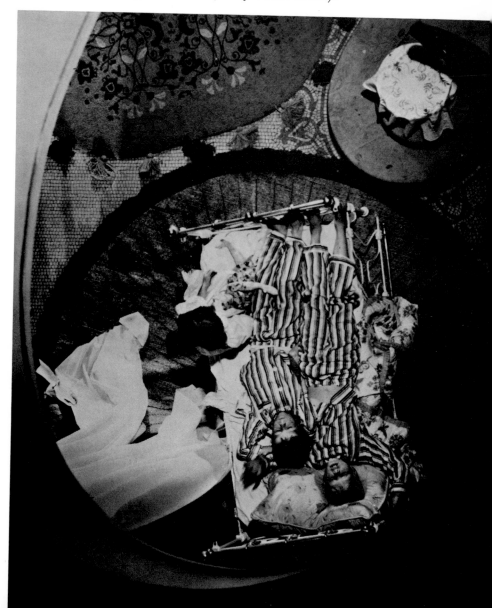

voyeurism

Top left: Open-air sex. Scene from L'Age d'Or (Salvador Dali–Luis Buñuel). Top right: Naked transvestite in The Queen (Frank Simon). Bottom: Turned-off eyewitnesses. Jackie Curtis, Candy Darling, and Joe Dallesandro in Flesh (Paul Morrissey–Andy Warhol).

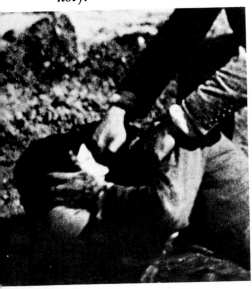

aesthetics of sadism

Top left: Optical rape. Scene from Un Chien Andalou *(Salvador Dali–Luis Buñuel).* Top right: Agonic masturbation. *Stan Brakhage in his own* Flesh of Morning. *Bottom: Glorious mutilation. Falconetti in* The Passion of Joan of Arc *(Carl Dreyer).*

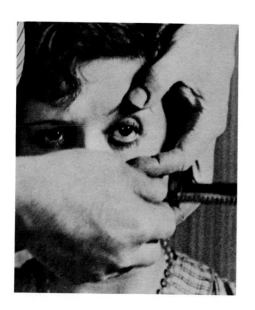

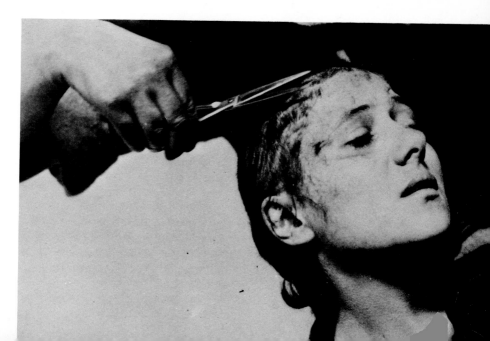

infantile eroticism

Top left: Nikos Koulizakis in Johnny Minotaur *(Charles Henri Ford). Top right: Scene from* Desistfilm *(Brakhage). Center left: Scene from* Hallelujah the Hills *(Adolfas Mekas). Center right: Scene from* L'Age d'Or *(Dali–Buñuel). Bottom left: Taylor Mead in* Lonesome Cowboys *(Andy Warhol). Bottom right: Scene from* L'Age d'Or *(Dali–Buñuel).*

transvestite phases

Top left: Unisex Apollo: Michael McClure in Beyond the Law *(Norman Mailer). Top right: Glamor-girl drag: Mario Montez in* Screen Test *(Andy Warhol). Bottom left: Pop sex-twist: bathing beauty from* The Queen *(Simon). Bottom right: Flaming creatures: filmmaker Jack Smith with transvestite Francis Francine.*

aesthetic nudes and naked realists

Top: Scene from The Rite of Love and Death (*Yukio Mishima*).
Bottom: Scene from Love Making (*Brakhage*).

Top: Larry Latrae, Tosh Carrillo, Gregory Battcock (back of head visible), and Dan Cassidy in Horse (Warhol). Bottom: Joe Dallesandro, Patti D'Arbinville, and Geraldine Smith in Flesh (Morrissey–Warhol).

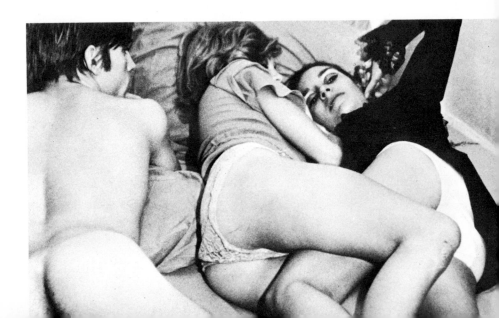

Top: Scene from the collage film Black and White Burlesque *(Richard Preston). Bottom: Scene from* Hallucinations *(Peter Weiss).*

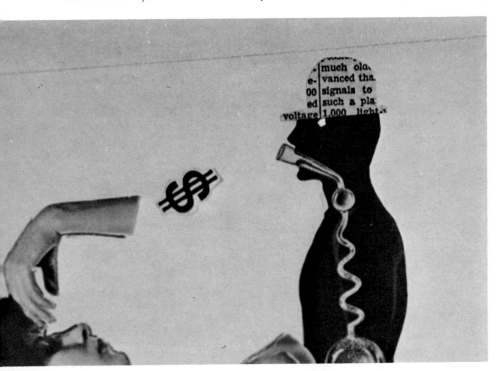

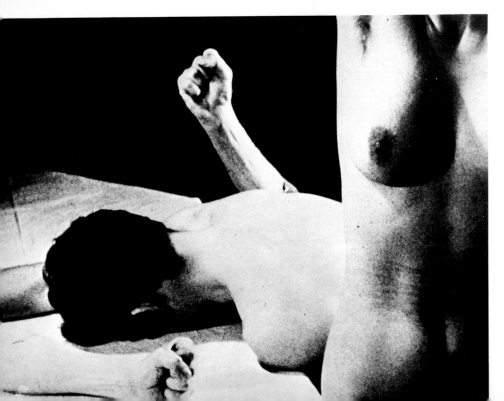

Top: Louis Falco double-exposed in Dionysius *(Charles Boulten-house). Bottom: Scene from* The Mirage *(Peter Weiss).*

narcissus in focus

Top left: Gregory Markopoulos in Winged Dialogue (Robert Beavers). Top right: Kenneth Anger as his own Leather Boy in his own Scorpio Rising. Bottom: Paul America in My Hustler (Warhol).

Top left: Luis Buñuel himself in Un Chien Andalou *(Dali–Buñuel).*
Top right: Ben Moore as Narcissus in Narcissus *(Willard Maas –Ben*
Moore). Bottom: Two Maya Derens in Meshes of the Afternoon
(Maya Deren).

tribal moods

Left: Marxist love-pile in Po-
temkin (Sergei Eisenstein).
Opposite, bottom: Samson de
Brier (right) in turned-on
camp masquerade from Inau-
guration of the Pleasure Dome
(Kenneth Anger). Bottom:
Put-on psychiatry. Ingrid Su-
perstar and Ondine in The
Chelsea Girls *(Warhol).*

Top: Ungroovy love-hunger. Scene from Echoes of Silence *(Peter Goldman). Bottom: Family spat à la Chelsea flat: Marie Menken and Gerard Malanga in* The Chelsea Girls *(Warhol).*

Top: Ronald Tavel (script in hand) and his consortium in his dialogue-charade, The Life of Juanita Castro (*Warhol*). *Bottom: Allegoric alienation. Scene from* No More Fleeing (*Herbert Vesely*).

transmutation of the human: mystery,

Right: Section shot from Peyote Queen (*Storm De Hirsch*). Bottom: Shot from Psyche (*Gregory Markopoulos*). Opposite, top: Shot from Metanoia (*Ilya Bolotowsky*). Opposite, bottom: Shot from The Art of Vision (*Brakhage*).

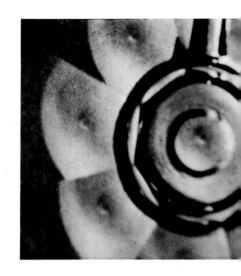

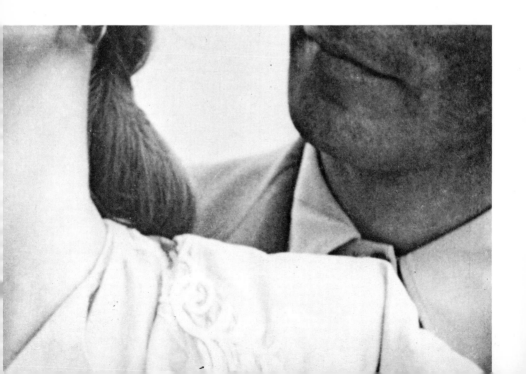

abstraction, and pattern

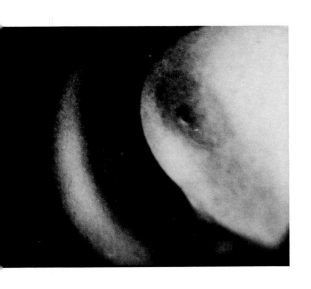

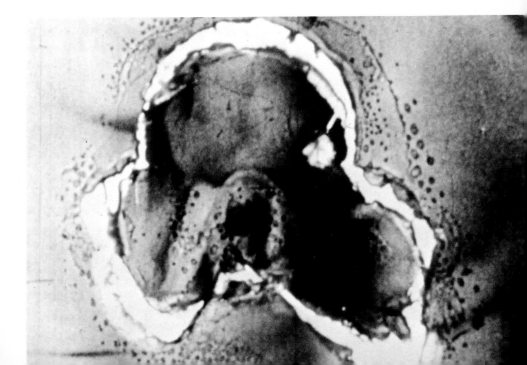

Top: Shot from Le Sang d'un Poète *(Jean Cocteau). Bottom: Stan VanDerBeek with his mixed media.*

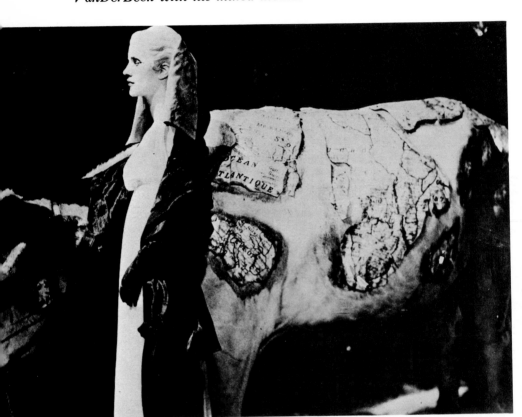

Top: Shot from Dance Chromatic (*Ed Emshwiller*). *Bottom: Shot from* The Jetty (*Chris Marker*).

Top: Anamorphosis of viewpoint from Un Chien Andalou *(Dali–Buñuel). Bottom: Anamorphosis of lens from* The Lead Shoes *(Sidney Peterson).*

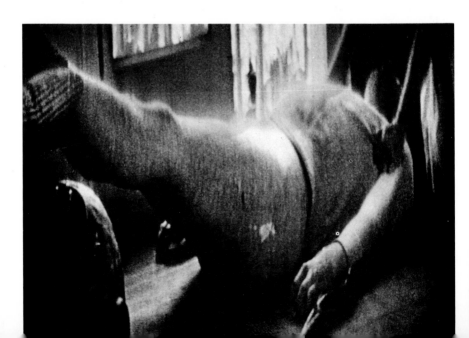

Top: Shot from The Cabinet of Dr. Caligari *(Robert Wiene). Bottom: Animated wig from* Dom *(Borowczyk–Lenica).*

rape by charade

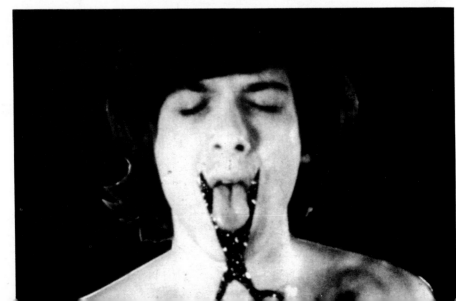

Opposite, top: Wild West spoof. Viva and Eric Emerson in Lonesome Cowboys (*Warhol*). *Opposite, bottom: Avant-garde ecstasy from* Touching (*Paul Sharits*). *Top: Hollywood comedy spoof from* Hallelujah the Hills (*A. Mekas*). *Bottom: Junkie hysteria. Scene from* The Connection (*Clarke*).

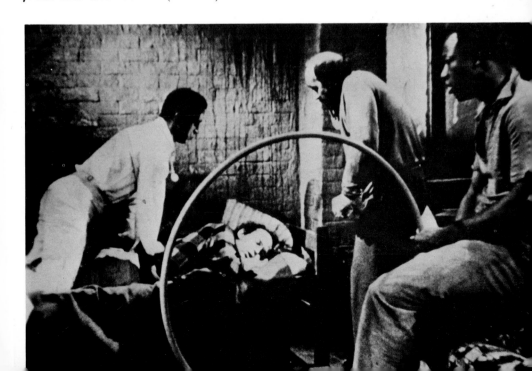

pre-happening and happenings

Right: Scene from Zéro de Conduite (Jean Vigo). Bottom: Scene from Fotodeath (Kouzel–Oldenburg). Opposite, top: Scene from 8x8 (Hans Richter). Opposite, bottom: Scene from Mothers' Day (James Broughton).

*the underground hero evolves
from laurel-crowned poet...*

to neckerchiefed hustler...

Left: Shot from Le Sang d'un Poète *(Cocteau).*
Below: Shot from Flesh *(Morrissey–Warhol).*

from the face in the cocktail table to the cocktail table in the face

Top: Charles Boultenhouse in his own Handwritten. *Bottom: Willard Maas in his own* Orgia.

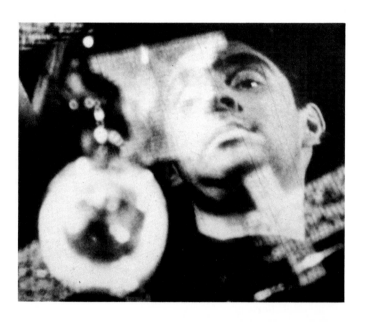

tained by distorting lenses. But after an era of victory by "significant form" in the visual arts, it seems unsophisticated to dismiss anamorphism out of hand, and as an eye-dazzling technical novelty, anamorphic optics seems a "natural" for film. Its effective use in the brief comedy *La Folie de Docteur Tube* made that point as long ago as 1915. There it is clear that the anamorphism, while supposedly a chemical mutation and suspiciously optical, nevertheless appears "surrealistically" as a mode of magical existence—that is, those on whom the trick mutation is worked temporarily cannot account for it and believe it "real." Thus, as in the style of Expressionism, it is a *way of seeing* wedded to, and supposedly expressing, a *way of feeling*. It is not a question of cause and effect, ultimately, even though, in a comedy of misunderstanding, it provokes hilarious woe (when worked on the unknowing), then pure hilarity. Curiously enough, this emotional pattern follows the euphoria-cum-paranoia motif of Underground films.

Among the pictorial arts there is the relevant case of Aubrey Beardsley, whose works are having a pop revival in our current period of psychedelic vision. This is due to the general preference for Art Nouveau because it seems twining, yielding, elastically feminine: to capture one by its serpentine allure and thus by "pacific" ingratiation. Think of the Vampire's body undulations! Yet there is more than that to Beardsley's popular prestige as part of the blow-up poster rage. The truth is, without abandoning the formalized natural curve, and without being an Expressionist, he anticipated the Cubist-Expressionist style that disregarded nature's proportions and normal anatomic sequence and relations. Since Beardsley's art is not one of color, its present popularity is all the more striking: maybe it reminds people of the traditional black and white of the movies. Glancing at his comic illustrations for *Lysistrata*, in which the exaggerations pivot on the phallic, we are reminded that one of the most natural sensual impulses in the world is to exaggerate, in the strict psychological sense, one part of the body at the expense of another. Psychoanalytically this sort of distortion is called overestimation or underestimation, but aesthetically or "expressionistically" it merely expresses the strength or weakness of a located feeling. Of course Beardsley was not always phallic in his interest; he tended to make both male and female thighs and buttocks especially voluptuous—and in the *Salome* suite there is the heroine's great oval belly. There is an anamorphism of erogenous zones that is not necessarily expressed by graphic emphasis. Yet if we also notice how Beardsley created the same eloquent and imposing rondures with costume *bouffantes* and regal trains, we may isolate an anamorphism of the eye expressing sensuality and—reverting to the filmic theme— grasp a key to the luxurious comic irony of the transformed figures of Gance's film comedy, which makes the ladies' long dresses melt along the ground in gorgeously decorative patterns; their bodies, underneath, are also tacitly "melting."

"Crazy" is a charged word of modern slang. In hipster language it can mean okay in the sense of wonderful. In the wider sense it means something lunatic or simply odd, offbeat. By a mere optical trick, anamorphism converts ordinary things into looking crazy in a heavily charged sense. To some, it is crazy to go on a psychedelic trip—meaning the sort of madness that is both benign and wonderful. In this state one tends to see outside usual focus, through a sort of anamorphic mental lens that operates on the location and size of objects, and on their stability. Hence we find the saturative play of colored lights in discothèques transforming figures into re-emphasized and dislocated, abstract-seeming parts.

The late Weegee begins his film *New York* with scenes of the city converting straight lines into abrupt curves and (since the film is color) defining boundaries by wide, fiery, jumpy prisms. The optical novelty appeals "psychedelically" even to those not under the influence of a drug. However, Weegee put together the whole film in an essentially rhythmless, documentary manner, so that on one hand the viewer is tired of the anamorphism before it is over, and on the other (during the long, crowded, nonanamorphic beach scenes) must rely on peephole sensation to enjoy the lovemaking couples whom Weegee has sneak-shot in bright sunlight. A much more carefully planned and interestingly shaped film, *New York New York,* was made some years later by Francis Thompson. This is the city mostly in broad daylight and broad color. Shot after shot, we see fantastic scenes of buildings pulled out of whack, at times mirror-doubled like pseudo organisms floating in space. This means that Thompson used a variety of lenses, including prisms, which he aimed in a variety of ways. Watching the film becomes a kind of guessing game in which identifying an automobile beyond doubt seems a triumph of one's own optical skill.

Technically very expert, Thompson's film (which has a splashy jazz score) is daring enough to belong to the Underground canon. Yet there is something boring about it, even though, to the board of directors of the Creative Film Foundation, it seemed impressive enough in 1957 to gain an annual award. For the ceremony at Cinema 16, where the winning films were always shown, Salvador Dali presented certificates to the filmmakers. Privately, there, both Dali and his wife remarked that *New York New York,* despite its amazingly gyrated objects, seemed flat in dimension, essentially tiresome. True Surrealists, they were right! The idea, divertingly optical as it is, remains altogether formal: one's feelings are not involved, there is almost no human or narrative shape to it, no interesting development; it ends by being an acrobatic stunt.

The same is by no means true of Peterson's *The Lead Shoes,* although for the main action it uses one lens, elongating the figures vertically throughout. The film's success is due entirely to the rightness of anamorphosis in relation to the theme. It begins in a high key which it maintains to the end. This might prove monotonous except that there is also a story action based on a classic version of incest and murder. A Negro jazz band supplies the music score in the form of a ballad sung to swing with the incessant, wailing revival-meeting throb. This dimension is made more ingenious by the nature of the ballad: a cross between versions of two traditional ballads, *Edward* and *The Three Ravens*. The device imparts a choral, fluently repetitive inflection to the visual story, which is shot in dramatic alternations of slow and fast motion. High-pitched "dark" voices fill out the screen action of a mother whose heart is torn by her love of two sons, one of whom has murdered the other.

What we first see.is a mature woman in brassière and petticoat, suddenly seized with a tragic intuition (or she may have heard the ballad's voice) of the tragedy, frantically leaving her house to rush down to a beach, where she finds the murdered son in a great old-fashioned diving suit that makes him look buried —again a "crazy" play on love, birth, death and insanity. Since the action here is essentially dream action, we see mother and son dancing on the beach, then the mother striving to dig up her encumbered son from the sand. Succeeding, she drags him home in a cart, and at last, imploring passers-by to help her, manages to hoist him up on a rope, as if he were a piano, to a room where she divests him of the diving suit and falls lamenting on his dead body. The time sequence as well as the choral repetitions are circular, but by the end we have seen the murdering son walking away in kilts and thrusting a knife in a loaf of bread, which spills out blood. The climactic image is thus of castration as consistent with the classic tragedy of incest.

Peterson's film is an Underground precursor whose seriousness and artistic verve have been almost lost in the current avant-garde efflorescence. The inevitably grotesque effect of the anamorphosis is both funny and macabre—indeed, what have we in this work but an authentic "simulation of hysteria" that is entirely surreal? Part of its structure is the rhythmic counterpoint and complication offered by the steady beat of the chorus and the slowed-down and speeded-up sequences of action. The artificiality of the elongated images (like prolonged, high screams) is perfectly adapted to the relentless high pitch of the frantic action, whose slowed-down sequences make the involved emotions all the more strangely urgent. Slow motion, in fact, is a temporal expansion parallel with the expanded parts of ana-morphized objects. An especially exciting touch is produced by the diver-suited son's prostrate form: now that he is horizontal, the anamorphosis makes him squat and fat instead of tall and exiguous.

This film belongs to the best part of the avant-garde canon accumulated by the American Underground. Before 1950 only Maya Deren's trilogy and some half-dozen other avant-garde films could compare with it for filmic style and concentration of form and subject matter. Peterson's somewhat more ambitious *Mr. Frenhofer and the Minotaur* is based on Balzac's prophetic tale of abstract action painting, *Le Chef-d'Oeuvre Inconnu*, and Picasso's *Minotauromachy*. The "action painting" which obliter-ates the human figure in Balzac's tale is the obsession of an artist who goes insane through frustrated love for his model and burns up the painting and himself. Peterson's treatment has little to do with this theme. The film, moreover, has a rather capricious use of anamorphism and modulated speed. Presented as the stream of consciousness of a modern female art student (heard on the sound track), it emerges somewhat vague and too oblique. Peterson is surer of his aims in *The Lead Shoes* as well as in *The Petrified Dog*, mentioned above as the daydream of a modern Alice in Wonderland. A key to the distortion of Alice's fantasies is furnished when she stoops to look in the rounded metal hub of an automobile wheel, where she sees herself and the world schematically distorted.

When considering the merits and demerits of anamorphosis as a potential of film style, we must realize that it is not merely

an objective mechanism, but also, as a reality-distorting phenomenon, may originate in the behavior of human vision and in
the mediation of atmospheric conditions between objects and
human eyesight. Our view of both the color and size of the moon
and the sun changes according to points in their ascent and de-
scent; waves of heat can be seen to make inert objects "ripple."
An effect like the last was used in an interesting feature-length
avant-garde film, *No More Fleeing* (1957), by Herbert Vesely,
to help characterize man's symbolic last stand in the desert
before his extinction by the atom bomb: existence becomes
a mirage. Further, by the conscious maneuvering of our
eyes objects can be seen to divide themselves and coalesce
as their volumes stretch, contract, and momentarily overlap.
Photography, still or moving, dramatizes the optical law of
foreshortening by making certain parts of an object (consider
the act of making love with open eyes) much out of given
proportion with other parts. Pavel Tchelitchew's great painting, *Phenomena,* plays on the emotional irony of fragmented
anamorphic vision by juxtaposing foreshortened anatomy
with the anatomies of freaks of nature. The point is that
visual mechanisms (including photographic lenses) collaborate
with human passions and human repulsions to produce that
world of significant form on which modern aesthetics (especially
Expressionism and Surrealism) is based. There is a perceptible
line of anamorphic tradition from *La Folie de Docteur Tube* to
the most recent avant-garde usage, including, along the way,
the "psychedelic" waves of distortion that distinguish a dreamlike sequence in a recent Hollywood adaptation of *The Fall of
the House of Usher.*

psychedelic anamorphosis and its lesson

A curious thing about the simple anamorphic phenomenon as produced by photography is that, whether a figure is flattened and fattened (vertical compression) or flattened and elongated (horizontal compression), we feel the quality of *gain* rather than *loss* in either case; that is, the figure has gained either height or bulk: the corresponding loss is overlooked. It is a plus phenomenon. This can be due only to the psychology of consciousness by which an object's faculty of changing its appearance is a trait belonging to it, as a chameleon can change its coloring; that is, it can alter itself, and then, returning to its original state, prove it has really been the same all along, has lost nothing; though its form has changed, its content has been the same. This is classic magic psychology. For example, Aladdin's lamp itself, on being rubbed, supposedly caused the geni to appear; rubbed again, it could cause him to vanish. The geni is only an extension of the lamp's innate faculties. If a room in which people are dancing, or just lounging or standing about, is drenched with moving color patterns (as in the Electric Circus or Warhol's Velvet Underground), the figure is momentarily swallowed up or altered, or fluidly disguised like the chameleon itself. The principle of illusory dislocation or fragmentation illustrated here is equivalent to the proportional revision of anamorphosis. It tends to seem a human attribute, rather than something imposed on the human from outside. What color-pattern psychedelism achieves, in other words, is the illusion of an inner state extending from the drugged spectator to a spectacle or environment. It is, and pretends to be, an environmental aid to the enjoyment of consciousness-expanding drugs. What it may lose *may exist* but is quite invisible.

Expressionistic stage sets, as used in *Caligari,* were a type of anamorphosis insofar as human figures seemed to blend and unblend with their abstractly stylized black-and-white patterns, only partly based, as they were, on nature and architecture. The effect is of blown-up stylized chiaroscuro, of which Caligari himself and his somnambulist are the abiding spirits of the dark parts, of night and evil as symbolically identical. In *The Chelsea Girls* Warhol (or someone) created for the psychedelic sequence, suddenly appearing in color after black and white, a montage of female dream figures seen with (and presumably by) the male subject who sits at the screen's lower right. Psychedelism, technically drug-induced, is psychic anamorphosis in that it implies that the image-carrying mind, like self-reproducing organisms, can detach part of itself and allow it to become (or seem) a separate individual but without breaking a basic tie with it. In classic psychology this is known as projection. It is what enables artists to paint pictures, write poems and novels, and call them "theirs": consciousness has expanded to the final point of illusorily objectifying itself. Here we have the origin of what, in analogy with human birth, are called brain children.

Thus whenever the world is in any way transformed from

psychedelic anamorphosis—and its lesson

what it seems normally, from what can be scientifically verified (let us say) by an accurate photographic lens, it is identified with the action, the will, the wish *of the spectator*. This is the illusion we call art—and the visual compact to accept it as real arises from the spectator's collusion with the artist. The trouble with the Underground evolution of avant-garde film and its one-time radical transformation of reality is that current filmmakers regard such "magic" as easier than it is, as basically "inexpensive" (it isn't), as only a matter of instant psychedelism . . . a lump of doctored sugar in your coffee and you virtually have a film, or if not, you have a trip, which to some is just as good as a film. This insidious attitude—the Drug Attitude, as I call it—does not depend upon actual narcotics but is a psychological idea with a moral force. I believe it a great continuing error and trust that somehow the Underground will work out of it by growing up and realizing the responsibilities of art. The artistic history of the avant-garde has very real models to offer the Underground filmmaker, if he will only understand both their do's and their don't's. As it is, the New American Cinema notwithstanding, he has to overcome much infantile self-indulgence and fashionable camp hauteur. A thing may well be groovy and yet far from great.

dotting the eye of history

The trouble with dotting the eye of history is that history has more than one eye (many more), and if it be thought to have only one mouth, that mouth gives infinitely variegated evidence. The history of Underground Film, no less than the history of the world, is complicated by conflicting evidence—not so much as to whether this or that took place, whether this or that film exists as a dynamic survival or only as a filed document, but of just what some individual film is composed and what, accordingly, its "reasons" were, its aims in conjunction with how it is, and was, interpreted. Here abides the power of the documentary view that all film is information; it reports this or that as something which, at the moment of shooting the film (if not now), had its integral existence and survives as evidence of some sort.

As I have said, the film camera as voyeur is the particular emphasis which avant-garde, experimental, and Underground film, as phases of one activity, have always held as a constant if film is conceived functionally as an investigator of reality.

132

dotting the eye of history

What inflected all film toward the avant-garde was an interest in investigating the "surreal"—the possible in distinction to the given; the imagined as against the literal. Undergrounders, while sacrificing a number of qualities introduced to the avant-garde by Surrealism, have kept one thing: the desire to use film as an instrument going beyond the real, in that it goes beyond surfaces and penetrates reality *especially* where protective conventions frustrate the eye. Its weakness is in lack of true invention and shaping by the individual filmmaker, who is often too passive and casual toward his findings.

In going beyond the given and the usual, Underground Film has more or less automatically rejected the traditional theories for doing so. There was, of course, a consistency in the Dada-Surrealist theory of inconsistency. The surreal—as is well recorded—is inconsistent with the real because it tends to transcend and replace it. It is not simply a "dream," because dreams coexist with the real and are governed only by symbolic systems —psychoanalysis and so on—which interpret their images back into terms of the given ("life," "reality," etc.). Hence the infantilism to be found in both Surrealist and Underground films has a broad spectrum involving everything from crude curiosity and self-indulgent egotism to set exhibitionism and bold aggression. All Underground infantilism denotes no more than the very first state of rebellion against the "real," a rebellion quickly becoming passive and compromising because of the playroom-pad's let's-pretend. The Surrealists were far more serious and truly aggressive. Buñuel's adult hero in *L'Age d'Or*, by falling back on "infantile" aggression and rebellion, becomes a satiric counter of the filmmaker, who desired to show that bourgeois-capitalist civilization has been a systematic cheat where the human instincts are concerned, that true passion has been historically bottled up by the various inhibitions of polite morality.

The main drive in *L'Age d'Or* is, as I have emphasized, sexual. Buñuel was an extraordinarily pure Surrealist in 1930:

133

he disdained camera tricks, "magic carpetry," any of the distortions and artificial stylizations we have talked about in previous sections. Here we come upon the factor still to be reckoned with in Surrealism: it broke away even from the most modern art styles. *Un Chien Andalou* and *L'Age d'Or* are surreal mixtures of very literal elements: hence their peculiar affinity with photography are mere record. We should remind ourselves again that Dali called his first truly surreal paintings "snapshot photographs." As remarkable as the juxtapositions of these two Buñuel films are, they hold no magic or dreamlike atmosphere achieved through "filmic" trickery. Nothing in them is "impossible"; there are no "magic transformations" like those in *La Folie de Docteur Tube* and *Le Sang d'un Poète*. The man separated from his mistress in *L'Age d'Or* reacts to the barriers between himself and her in the most naked, impulsive ways; for example, he kicks a blind man coming between him and a taxi and furiously knocks him down. The film's opening shots have prepared for this. There is a charade allegory, very macabre, of the founding of imperial Rome (the religious ceremony of the first scenes) and shots of fighting scorpions who proceed to kill a rat. This is far-out but orthodox montage of Eisenstein and Pudovkin. The idea would seem to be that individuals may as well take advantage of the sheer brutality of animals and the politic brutality of civilization itself to gain the fulfillment of desire.

The destructive violence of the early ideals of the avant-garde film cannot be overemphasized. I said above that the apparent slicing of a woman's eye by a razor, the only "film trick" in *Un Chien Andalou,* was a symbol of the film's optical assault. The true direction of the Surrealists and their precursors was to revolt against Symbolism in behalf of the Surrealist act. Also I have made something here of Underground *propaganda* as distinct from Underground *art.* Yet it is a difficult problem to see just where Surrealist violence against reality locates itself if it be abstracted from the fantasy life of the mind to the actual arena of life. Is something utopian, an "earthly paradise," also behind the Surrealist system? When, for instance, in an article titled *En Avant Dada* (1921), Richard Huelsenbeck (a Dada founder) says that literature "should be made with a gun in hand," it is impossible to decide whether he means people should be casually shot in the process of literature (and presumably filmmaking) or whether the phrase implies the dictatorship of culture which forces people, under threat of punishment, to accept certain canons and reject all others.

About ten years later, in the Second Surrealist Manifesto, André Breton seemed to think that such a remark was a *program for action*—that is, surreal activity in the real world—for he formulated (in a "utopian" mood?) the "perfect Surrealist act": to fire a revolver at random into a street crowded with people. This would be Russian roulette on a mass scale and without consent of the participants. Surrealists of course have a cavalier way of being ironic as part of their black bile. On the other hand, Artaud's idea of the theater as ultimately an assault on the audience easily comes to mind. Is Surrealism, first and last, a program of revolution in the practical political sense? Its formal expressions in art media would then be a mere prelude to total social and political revolution, in which obviously the "art" status of pre-existing Surrealist works would vanish, since after a successful revolution of this kind the social conditions under which revolutionary acts are required would have vanished.

Historically this ambiguity saturates the Surrealist attitude and affects its changes. Surrealism in retrospect proffers the special varieties of irony which we have been exploring here in avant-garde and Underground films. Buñuel's *L'Age d'Or* hero would be an anachronism if seen in the perspective of a society in which formal repressions had ceased to operate. This is important because it throws light on the Surrealists' rejection of dream *as* dream and magic *as* magic. Buñuel states of *Un Chien Andalou* that it was the "result of conscious psychic automatism and to that extent it does not recount a dream although it profits from a mechanism analogous to dream." This is a precise qualification. The only value of making the dream mechanism into an abstract one, with potentially deliberate applications, was to dissociate Surrealism from the totally unreal which dream, technically, represents—dream, that is, as a spontaneous, unsupervised phenomenon. Film tricks, to the Surrealists, were like the tricks of the mind which make fantasy sufficient to mere formal ends. The dream per se, according to the Surrealists, is not surreal activity, not reality's other function, but as much an illusion as the stage tricks of prestidigitators.

In a sense the dream must imitate—but not as illusion imitates reality. Here lies the reason for the official Surrealist rejection of Cocteau. The latter's *Le Sang d'un Poète* seems rightly to be an allegory filled with demonstrations of "dream magic," a work that could be interpreted as exclusively symbolic of mental processes. It does nothing to change everyday reality, to supplant it; rather, it is a very deep interpretation of given things—*given* things though they be *great* things, too. When Breton created his surreal heroine, Nadja, he was expressing the Surrealist platform of fantasy, but as a feminine and passive occupation. Literally, Nadja gives herself not to reality but to daydreaming about real elements which she arbitrarily juxtaposes. The realistic order is not optically disturbed or even morally attacked; this is not even the hysteria of the paranoid, only an insistent subjectivity marking off its difference from objectivity. This much is elementary and has nothing of the masculine violence of Buñuel and Artaud . . . it has no hint of "guns."

Perhaps Breton was so much impressed by the relation of the archaic serial's female vampire to deadly weapons that he valued her even above Nadja. Indeed, in *Nadja*, supposedly being the diary of the heroine's lover, Breton recounts seeing "the only dramatic work which I choose to recall." It happens to be a Grand Guignol sort of play about a cult of gory murder in a girls' school in which the school's principal and a mysterious female friend seem to conspire. The point is that in this play women have utilized the surreal act of murder as an aggressive weapon. They have not, "femininely," relied on mere fantasies, however violent. The Love People of today, with whom the Underground is infiltrated, rely mainly on passive fantasy as aided by drugs. Therefore, from the angle of Surrealist activity in its radical programmatic sense, it seems right to term Flower Power a classic "opiate of the people." Naturally, there are arguments for the desirability of this Power. But they are neither precisely Marxist nor precisely Surrealist.

So long as we think only in the dimensions of fantasy, and a fantasy-bred art, so long will all the terminology of film as based on dialectic have the creative implications of sex and birth rather then the destructive implications of sex and death —I mean aside from the matter of literal themes. The physical child, like the brain child, is a dialectic product and primarily it is optimistic: the positive result of a peaceable dialectic and in itself an untarnished gain. Undoubtedly this is the rosy Underground emphasis of the present. The same lyric note was the first emphasis given the world movement by the American avant-garde as initiated in the late twenties. In mood, therefore, Clair's Dadaist *Entr'acte* was soon more influential in America than the villainous nightmare of *Caligari* and the sadistic violence of *L'Age d'Or*.

The Poësque fantasy, brief and starkly romantic, attracted filmmakers not simply because it was macabre but because it was lyric and impressionistic. As a boy, Curtis Harrington did an eight-millimeter version of *The Fall of the House of Usher*, and versions were made later in the United States (by the

137

French experimentalist Jean Epstein) and abroad. Sadism as such—that is, cruelty of fate as inspired by the libido—took longer to appear in other than romantic form. It definitely surfaced, however, in a pivotal year, 1947, in Kenneth Anger's *Fireworks*, which Cinema 16 first brought to New York audiences for the avant-garde. Reseen today, it holds up remarkably well as a film made while its author was still in high school. It is a film to be shown wherever the question of the validity of the *auteur* theory comes up in discussion of pre-Underground American filmmaking.

Boldly, Anger undertook to project a homosexual fantasy in the form of a visual poem. The movement from shot to shot does not have the suavity of a well-done poem and yet the elements and the innerness emerge secure. Here is the type street adventure of a homosexual cruising sailors, taking one or more home, and getting beaten up. This is the material, but it is magically converted from the prosaic and merely sordid. The whole has a home-studio look (and even a urinal scene), but the inventions of a hallucinated evisceration of the young victim by the sailors, the parody of a *Pietà* with a sailor holding the boy's body, the seminal stream turning into the milk first orally desired by the infant, the Roman candle from a sailor's opened fly and in apotheosis the flame-tipped Christmas tree that celebrates the martyrdom by being worn ritually on the victim's head, all exist in surreal immediacy and leave their imprint on the memory.

The whole point about what may be called the *surplot* of the Surrealists was that life, as the product of human relations and human relation with objects, should never appear logically in terms of conscious cause and effect. This would rule out the fairy-tale fantasy of *Caligari* as well as the allegorical fantasy of *Le Sang d'un Poète*; Cocteau's rejection by orthodox Surrealism, as I have mentioned, had concrete canonic reasons. No matter how extravagant or elliptic or symbolist the narrative methods of these two avant-garde films, not only could the action be followed in terms of rational cause and effect (once the key of Cocteau's film was grasped), but in the purely formal sense each also held a suggestive analogy with life as lived every day. *Caligari* is about pathological crime, *Le Sang d'un Poète* is about a poet's struggle with creation (the *mise en scène* is an elaborate poet's pad equipped with hallucinogenic devices) and with the idea of real and symbolic suicide. Generalizing or summarizing Surrealist films, as I have attempted to do in this book, has the air of being only tentatively successful, however much the Surrealist surplot runs parallel with conventional human behavior.

When in *Un Chien Andalou* someone contemplates a detached artificial hand lying in the street and draws a crowd, or when in the same film two grand pianos, each loaded with a dead donkey, are dragged by two men toward a woman cowering against the wall of a room, the action does not agree with any plausible scheme of cause and effect, even far-fetched; it is entirely the "plot" of the irrational and it defies traditional dramatic sense. Even in *L'Age d'Or*, which might be interpreted as the story of a real satyromaniac, the hero's specific actions, together with their settings, are arbitrary, come to us as utter surprises. Surrealism is a glorification of the unexpected by virtue of the gratuitous. In *Fireworks* the evisceration of the youth and the apparitional Christmas tree have the same status as the action in *L'Age d'Or* if they are isolated from the framing homosexual adventure. Surrealism, in film or elsewhere, indicates human behavior and the use of objects *either partly or wholly dislocated from normal motives and realistic context.*

It is conceivable that an adult male, frustrated in climaxing a sex passion, might slap the face of a lady who accidentally spilled wine on him, and then go haywire, as happens in *L'Age d'Or*. Yet it doesn't make what one calls dramatic or moral sense, it is gratuitous with a sadistic vengeance. The man's

139

literal behavior can be explained only by the assumption of lunacy, just as Caligari's behavior, to be "explained," has to be characterized as that of a hopeless madman. Surrealism proposes its behavioral patterns *totally without explanations or reasons*. It was perfectly apposite for Dali to say, "The only difference between myself and a madman is that I am not mad." And yet on reflection we find that the truth is that, were it not for purely formal explorations of the abstract sort in world avant-garde film, cherished by devoted workers from the twenties till now, we would be much less likely to accept the Surrealist postulate (so influential in Underground filmmaking) of socially irrational action. As laboratory procedures, pure Abstract and Abstract-Expressionist painting are fully as "surreal" as Surrealism.

film aesthetics: rampant and purist

Hans Richter, writing on film as an original art form in the January 1955 issue of *Film Culture* (the magazine had just started) insisted on the world-wide importance of the film theories of the early Russian directors, Sergei Eisenstein and Vladimir Pudovkin, which appeared in the twenties. In Russia itself, ironically, it was only a few years after Eisenstein did ·his world-famous *Potemkin* (1925) that his theory of montage, known as "collision," * was accused of being formalist by the Soviet film bureaucracy, apparently on the grounds that such a theory meant (as evidently it did mean!) the widest practical application; that is, "pure film" could be created out of any subject matter whatever, regardless of the immediate external and internal political interests of the Soviet Union. The U.S.S.R.

* Image A directly juxtaposed to Image B, Eisenstein believed, resulted in a totally new image, or idea, C. Pudovkin proposed "linkage," a gradual building up, as the correct method of montage. In practice the supposed theoretical opposition could lead to no more than differences of style and a question of aesthetics, not science.

was then engaged in an internal economic struggle and sub-
sisted intellectually on the theory that every possible medium
must be utilized as a propaganda of optimism.

Actually, as Richter makes clear in his article, the Russian
practicing theorists were committed to the position that no true
art would be attained by film which considered the camera a
mere recording instrument. "Reproduction" of given reality, the
passive documentary view, was exactly what these men opposed.
This much is clear and simple. The first command of filmic invention was to edit reality, to give it form by expressing an idea
about it. Basically this is what Surrealism too proposed as
formal practice. The difference was in the type of invention explored—*in the divergence of the ideas themselves.* Say that a
"plot" may be called a conventional or formal idea expressing
typical human relations. Surrealism *explodes* such a thing; an
allegory or a charade *symbolizes* it. An extravagant fantasy or a
nightmare performs symbolic functions through violent dislocation. But for filmmakers in the Soviet Union during the twenties
there was only one archetypal plot; whatever filmic method
Eisenstein or Pudovkin or Donskoy employed, it had to obey the
favored Marxist assumptions about the 1917 Revolution in
Russia.

Richter's statement in his *Film Culture* article that the film
poem, so far as technique was concerned, should not have a
"traditional form," simply means that style of statement in
film must have a strictly visual nature. But it also implies that
the pure film style is such that, when essaying anything like the
traditional story form, it wrongly detours to resemble literature
and thus seems dependent on it. Omitting consideration of
sound dialogue, which had not yet arrived in the period Richter
was discussing, the only point here was that, in the radical
sense, film should differentiate itself from the other arts. The
banner of the practicing theorist, Richter, was nothing if not
Aestheticism.

the plot thickens—but seriously

It is easy to see how film could eliminate an air of being "prose narrative," yet it is hard to see the adequacy of such reasoning. The fact is that, unless one applies Surrealist canons to film-making, a "film poem" is very close in technical procedure to the literary tradition of the lyric poem. This is exactly what was brought out in the earliest avant-garde forms essayed during the twenties in the United States: the cinepoem and the city symphony. The latter was well represented by Robert Flaherty's *Twenty-four Dollar Island* (1925), a loosely impressionistic poem about Manhattan. Ruttmann's *Berlin: the Symphony of a Great City* (1927) was a more formal model for this kind of film, and American variations on it, of which *New York New York* is one, have appeared ever since. The Berlin film does much with repetition patterns (for example, pedestrians identified by moving legs) that verge on decorative collage. Inevitably the geometric character of architecture lent infinite opportunities for framing shots of clustered skyscrapers that paralleled

143

underground film

hard-line geometric abstraction in painting. Filmically putting
together bits of the modern city was much like what the Imagists
had begun to do in poetry. Indeed, the search for a pure visual
form was carried by filmmakers into themes that were "plastic"
in the painting sense; outstanding instances include Fernand
Léger's film, *Ballet Mécanique*, about the world of mechanical
organisms, and the American Ralph Steiner's H_2O, entirely of
water patterns. It is obvious how these and much more recent
films (many of them "animated") relate to Duchamp's *Anemic
Cinema*, with its delicate play on the the role of optical illusion.

Well might all such films be accused of "formalism" and
"aestheticism"! Turning to nature as a picture-postcard scene,
with seasonal moods, was fairly inevitable as a branch of cine-
poetry. A number of films made before 1940 can be admitted to
this canon, among them the film historian Herman G. Wein-
berg's *Autumn Fire*. At times a thread of plot, or at least hints
of a plot situation, made the cinepoem into a classic sort of love
idyl. The pioneering films of the American Emlen Etting belong to this class and so does the later, somewhat inflated
Markopoulos trilogy, *Psyche, Lysis, Charmides*. There survives
today a school of such filmmaking—tender, imaginative—
which unfortunately verges on the arty despite its seriousness
and its broad implications. Even its "masters" are not exempt
from a fascinated, tenuous brooding upon the undefined erotic
dilemmas of often lovely, more and more denuded people. Entranced gazes and postures, gestures, encounters, passings imply
plot situations that remain unarticulated and tantalizing: an abstracted series of tableaux vivants. Many of these films have
more variety, it is true, than Warhol's fixated camera, and at
times they show real photographic ability. But this nondynamic
sort of filmmaking places too much demand on optical ingenuity (not always forthcoming in the film) and on the film
tricks and mannerisms tabooed by the Surrealists. The fact that
the nude is often beautifully used (at least in the still-photo-

144

graphic sense) lends excitement to the film pulse, but little strength to the advance of the film art. Far from denoting what has successfully surfaced, the "underground" in the avant-garde sense seems to mean suppressed opportunities, suppressed realizations—sometimes gracefully, sometimes ungracefully indicated.

It is interesting to note that fitting into the same historical category is an independently produced commercial film by the Czech Gustav Machaty, *Ecstasy* (1933), famous partly because it introduced Hedy Lamarr in the nude to the world film public. While this rather clumsy film has a rudimentary plot, it is built like an expanded cinepoem in which a nude woman, nymphlike, is discovered undressing and then moving through the countryside to enter a stream and swim; finally she is seduced by a voyeur who has glimpsed and followed her. One sequence of *Ecstasy* is composed entirely of shots of Miss Lamarr's face showing supreme erotic pleasure; this should be compared, in fact, with Warhol's *Blow Job*. *Ecstasy* remains as one of the very first "sex films" that were to be vulgarized by the modern nudie film; actually, however, it is sincere and therefore escapes, if narrowly, the dishonesty which has spoiled many a commercial effort in the same direction.

Style in film, based on the Russian montage theory (which had, as it were, isolated and polarized D. W. Griffith's narrative method), emerged as "avant-garde" simply because it pointed to the fact that film was not merely a visual (later audio-visual) translation of a novel, depending on a more or less complex plot, but could build itself frame by frame, shot by shot, as a poem builds itself word by word, line by line. Metaphor is a visual unit which may be as adaptable to film as to poetry. An arresting episode took place in 1953 at Cinema 16, then under the direction of the alert and pioneering Amos Vogel, when a symposium titled "Poetry and Film" was held with Maya Deren, Dylan Thomas, Arthur Miller, and the present writer participating and Willard Maas as moderator. Most of the text of the long exchange among the diverse-minded participants was printed ten years later in *Film Culture*. The earnest Miss Deren heroically raised the standard of formal method by proposing that "film poetry" has a *vertical* development and "film prose," equivalent to literary narrative or a stage play, a *horizontal* development. Dylan Thomas reacted facetiously and Miller professionally, so that the argument, injured by the audience's hilarity at Thomas's wisecracks, was quickly thrown into chaos, where it remained for the duration.

Beyond doubt, there is a large grain of sense in Maya Deren's rather academic formulation. What she meant, of course, is familiar to all serious critics whether their field is literature or the film. To a great extent narrative is defined by time lapse; that is, the events of a complex action, with the modern novel as a norm, require both literal space and literal time in which to move and develop themselves. Examining Miss Deren's brief, rather dreamlike films, we see that space there is magical; while a variety of scenes is shown, their relation to each other is not that of real (geographic) space; they are built in the vertical dimension of dream and become complicated metaphors; in a more radical sense, they become (however much modulated) an ideogram, or word structured by an aggregate of images: an ideogram, literally, is "picture language." I say "dreamlike" and the "dimension of dream" because Miss Deren's films are precise in continuity of development whereas dreams tend to be hazy and discontinuous.

The time dimension of the ideogram is vertical because it can be apprehended all at once: its elements live (one might say "revolve") in one place and simultaneously. Certain brief dreams or fragments of dreams have this faculty of seeming not to occupy clock time, not to be "narrative," but even those that are "sequential" are more like narrative paintings which show two, three, or four phases of one continuous action by repeating a key figure at different geographic points. Such paintings always suggest ritual journeys, and so do Maya Deren's films. In this sense they are "plotted" to a certain extent, but exist in a more or less symbolic space—a magic-carpet space like that explored by the Poet in Cocteau's *Le Sang d'un Poète*, laid out exactly like a prototypic initiation rite. Avant-garde dance films, like ballets themselves, tend to be laid out like rituals; for example, compare Boultenhouse's *Dionysius*, Emshwiller's *Totem*, Peterson's *Horror Dream*, and Shirley Clarke's *Moment of Love* (a kind of cinepoem) with the Frederick Ashton ballet, *Illuminations*, a symbolic biography of Arthur Rimbaud. It is also profitable to compare Maya Deren's trilogy with the scenario of *Le Sacre du Printemps*.

The fact is that geographic space—the space of the everyday, literal world—is ellipsized by poetry into symbolic space. This is exactly the *vertical* development of film space, whereas real space, as partially ellipsized by prose narrative, is simply an editing of literal action to show its significant or "high" points, which would be the *horizontal* development of film space. Horizontal edited space, the spatial aspect of edited narrative action, must be held distinct from vertical symbolic space, since such space is meant to substitute metaphoric narrative for literal narrative (however much the latter be edited). If this terminology seems rather dense, the concept is nevertheless, as Miss Deren protested on that memorable evening, a perfectly logical thing. However, we can come to grips with it in still other ways. Like painting, film is a plastic apprehension of visible things. The reportorial function of the camera on one hand, and the "translation" aspect of film plot as a version of prose narrative on the other, both militate against the direct plastic approach.*

For this reason the inevitable destiny of the avant-garde was to preserve and perpetuate what is loosely known as the

* See later discussion of *Finnegans Wake*, pages 192-194.

"poetic" aspect of film. A scrupulous and highly knowledgeable craftsman such as Sergei Eisenstein (whatever the bias of his theories) always bore in mind shaping a narrative in conjunction with filmic plasticity. This is as true of *Potemkin* (1925) as of *Alexander Nevsky* (1938). His very term, vertical montage (an exact correlation of word, music, and image in telling a story), expresses kinship with Maya Deren's formula of vertical development in film imagery. It is impressive that in film scripts notations of vertical montage appear *atop* each other; this is the way Eisenstein did it and the way Charles Boultenhouse, with the composer Teiji Ito, worked out the synchronization of music with the words and visuals of *Handwritten*. Stan Brakhage's breakdown of the shot composition in his *Prelude* vividly illustrates the difference between *reading* and *looking;* one "reads" down, line by line, but one "looks" all at once, seeking to grasp a field of imagery simultaneously from side to side and top to bottom.

The incomplete footage of *Que Viva Mexico!*, Eisenstein's ill-fated American film, offers much illumination of vertical development. The epic form is the dramatic or "horizontal" development of lyric poetry based on the primordial chant, being the recited or chanted events in the life of a hero or demigod. Wagner's music dramas are well-known examples. Eisenstein, desiring to present the life of a collective hero, the Mexican people, chose episodes each of which dealt with ritual material: a funeral, a wedding, a bullfighter's preparation for the arena, a scapegoat peasant's martyrdom, a carnival. These episodes, left unintegrated owing to Eisenstein's being forced to abandon the film,* bear something of the aspect of those dream episodes whose discontinuity yet relatedness tantalizes the dreamer.

* The original backers, Upton Sinclair and his wife, withdrew all support when Eisenstein repeatedly neglected to meet deadlines for the finished film. He wished to take his own time, and besides, he was filming much unusable pornographic material.

the plot thickens—but seriously

Anamorphic photography, while one must admit it could easily become overschematic in effect, should suggest to us the kind of dynamic development of film movement meant by the vertical/horizontal concept. The vertically exiguous images of Peterson's actors in *The Lead Shoes,* besides suggesting the height of figures in classic drama, work *against* the natural horizontal movement of organisms on the earth's surface. The result is a dialectic tension which is further sharpened in Peterson's film by the slow motion, in turn working against the fast, insistent pulse of the choral singing. Maya Deren, of course, was also intuitively aware of this purely plastic complication introduced by slow motion: psychic urgency straining under physical slowdown. The tension is finally kinaesthetic; we identify it most easily through reference to dreams, in which the dreamer's headlong movement often seems unaccountably restrained. As we observe of the rush of water in the normal physical world, a barrier in its path will cause it to leap up, that is, become momentarily vertical; this is true of rushing emotions that seem to leap up, frustrated, when encountering, as it were, the barrier of the breastbone. In an aesthetic of film, one must reckon with such things. It is *Underground* aesthetics —whatever the current heresies toward it.

The solid time of Warhol's early films, with its delayed-action stalemate, is a *temporal* anamorphosis; the stretch of what seems a vertical situation, in *Harlot,* for instance, is only abstractly horizontal. According to Ronald Tavel's synopsis, the situation of the four main characters in the film is potentially a design for real dramatic action of a funny or campy sort. The feminine two on the sofa are "Jean Harlow" (a drag queen) and a lesbian; the masculine two leaning on the sofa's back are a "mafia-type lover" of Harlow and an "admirer" of the lesbian. A charade atmosphere is established by the not altogether plausible casting. The supposed lesbian (a plumpishly attractive female) holds a fluffy white cat; Harlow and

149

her lover are in evening clothes. Capsuled, the action of the film's seventy minutes would read like this: Harlow, reclining against her lesbian friend, works herself up by a very leisurely banquet of one banana after another into kneeling on the sofa and giving her lover a prolonged, prodigious kiss. The mafia-type's eyes have usually rested on her while the lesbian and her admirer have stared steadfastly into the camera. The mafia-type makes a friendly gesture of offering the lesbian's admirer a cigarette (repeated "funny business" here), and then, toward the very end, lesbian and admirer pour beer over each other in playful malice. The only other action has been the cat's spasmodic effort to get out of the lesbian's lap—a procedure that probably was not anticipated, but for which one is grateful. With this to go on, any number of "plot actions" and "situation developments," mild or violent or whatnot, might have been thought of to fill out the running time. But, of course, not so: the vague, insinuating situation (fuzzily interpreted by the badly transcribed dialogue of three male watchers) is left, so to speak, hanging vertically before us, a sort of drugged, anamorphized shape, while time stretches the barely animate tableau into horizontal grotesqueness in the spectator's addled optic nerves. Here we have a psychic parody of film's possible plasticity through an abortive distortion of plot.

the plastic pulse ticks on

Warhol's early manner is a kind of decadent primitiveness.
Even now, when ambitiously he essays more and more plot,
more and more movement, more horizontalism, his film movement limps, exults in doldrums, is arbitrarily episodic, as in
the two distinct parts of *My Hustler*.* In the twenties American
avant-gardistes were far more form conscious in the orthodox
sense of film plastics. A film such as Paul Fejoz' *The Last
Moment* (1927) significantly exploits the vertical dimension
by presenting the life-in-retrospect of a drowning man; horizontal narrative is precipitately verticalized: again psychic
anamorphosis. It must be remembered that as soon as the film
camera achieved all its mobilities (panning, dollying, easy
close-ups)—as soon as it matured a broad vocabulary of ways
to represent natural action—movement (including multiple
exposure) became an aesthetic ideal in itself; the old-fashioned
chase was simply the most primitive form of the thrill of head-

* See later discussion of this film, pages 183-184.

long illusive passage through space—the *simplest* form of the horizontal plastique.* Today's space-age films tend to synthesize the vertical and horizontal: this is the plastique of a new era in physical science itself, with both time and space holding strange elisions and expansions—for example, the "magical" shift of magnetic fields.

In regard to Warhol's revival of primitivism, it is remarkable how much his actors suggest an important segment of film's mythological personnel: all the puppetry, the "mechanical man," the "invisible man," and so on. A film mentioned previously has retained its avant-garde fame and is still being circulated in the underground world of film societies, *The Life and Death of a Hollywood Extra,* made in 1928 by Robert Florey and Slavko Vorkapich, who was to have a long career as a Hollywood special-effects expert. The film is a sort of playroom satire on the robotization of people obsessed with getting into the movies, and while playing only "extras," imitating and worshiping the great stars. This is expressed in the rapid doll-like movements of painted-up actors and furnished with children's Mechano sets to suggest the studio-fabricated illusions of scenes shot in miniature but projected in commercial films as if in natural scale. In short, this film has a blown-up miniaturism, a psychically condensed anamorphism. Like the "last moment" of the drowning man whose life is recapitulated in instant form, it has the horizontal compression. The film's rhythm is animated, as if a series of edited still frames had been put together. This technique has made various reappearances in Underground films and is conspicuous in the humorous photo-collage animations of Stan VanDerBeek and Richard Preston, both of whose films essay at times the

---

* Parallel cutting (narrating two spatially distinct but related actions by rhythmically intercutting them) was the classic complication of film narrative, pioneered by Griffith and carried to the present by Hitchcock.

voyeuristic flavor of the naughty-nudie films given a blunt sadistic edge of the surreal. For good measure, a dose of political cartooning is added to such films.

What may be called generically the robot man, implying the basic animation of film as a rapidly run succession of still frames, has long been an object of fascination to movie-goers if only because a "robot" hints of the magic plasticity of all pictorial art, especially that of Surrealist painting. VanDer-Beek's crudely animated female nudes, their anatomy arbitrarily dispersed and put together again, contain a lurking pathos of this kind. They are still photographs to begin with! Bruce Conner's live nude, in his *Cosmic Ray*, is a more humane, tender development of the same anatomic gyration. We might reflect, too, that the fingertip touch between Adam and Jehovah on Michelangelo's Sistine ceiling is a paradigm of the human connection between supernatural creation and artistic creation. Not coincidentally, I think, this fingertip touch is repeated with strange poetry by two grotesque epicene figures in Jack Smith's film in progress, *Normal Love*. In numberless commercial films mechanical men have come to life, dead men been brought back to life, ghosts and zombies and somnambulists walked and immobilized themselves or been immobilized. Hypnotized subjects (think of Caligari's somnambulist) bring up the same drama of life, establishing a vertical circuit like sap in a tree or blood in human veins. Rudimentarily, film dramatizes this movement when it portrays the growth of a plant from root to blossom in one uninterrupted, smooth, kinetic sequence within a few seconds.

Film, in sum, brought rebirth to the lyric "drama" of the act of creation, of filling space with responsive organic life. Exactly by being *artificial*, film animation suggested the power of illusion to simulate reality, and by simulating, to rival. Here was the *original avant-garde function* expressed by the small, independent, noncommercial film; this sort of product explored film form exclusively as a sequence of basically abstract movements, like dance.

One inevitable type, developing from painting, was moving color abstractions, changing, appearing, disappearing, individually and in groups. The principal pioneers in this genre have long been celebrated: the Englishman Len Lye, the Germans Oskar Fischinger and Hans Richter. Lye's *Free Radicals* of 1958 (he had been working, and in the same vein, since 1921) seems a morally motivated pun on the Marxist dialectic as formulated in montage by Eisenstein. Being a mathematical term (the film consists of freely moving, freely drawn lines) does not prevent its also referring to political radicalism and the concept of freedom from oppressive forces. At any rate, a whole film school of plastic formalism developed in various directions from the twenties to the forties, leading to the jazzy, superspeed "action painting" of Norman McLaren in color, the much more severely measured, classic black-and-white abstraction of the Whitney brothers, John and James, and the work of Jordan Belson and Hy Hirsch. McLaren was a native of Canada while the other four men worked on the West Coast of the United States. Mary Ellen Bute (who began as early as 1937 and finally made *Finnegans Wake*) was one of the purest: a choreographer of light and color strictly, a little too strictly, obeying patterns of classical music. Most of this genre was truly abstract, but in the forties Francis Lee began using a start-stop motion for a decorative object such as a bead; he also used ink spilling over a map (this was during the Second World War) to modify the abstraction with a kind of impressionistic symbolism. In the semicommercial field a kind of animated documentary used a "magic map" technique with realistically drawn figures.

In 1923 Jean Epstein announced that film should "become" exclusively cinematography; he expanded the position by saying that it should avoid any connection with historical, educational, romantic, moral or immoral, geographical, or documentary subjects. Despite the ambiguity of Epstein's own film practice, theoretically this ruled out all subject matter as worth filmic-aesthetic attention and made film a pure formalist—that is, plastic—art. It is difficult to see what such an art could be but the filmic variety of pure abstraction—unless, that is to say, in the modern psychedelic sense, whatever phase of identifiably human or natural action he recorded on film, all meaning be expunged from it and it become (under the auspices of the Drug Attitude if not drugs themselves) sheer optical mirage.

Hans Richter, apparently agreeing with Epstein, says in his *Film Culture* article, "Eggeling and I came directly out of the structural problems of abstract art, nolens volens, into the film medium." For whatever reasons, Richter at least did not stay within those structural problems but overflowed into Surrealism. *8X8* (1957), his next film after *Dreams That Money Can Buy*, was based on the structural problems of chess; he was probably inspired by Duchamp's passion for chess and Duchamp is in the film. However, chess is a "structural problem" (i.e., a game) carried out by animated human figures more or less formalized or abstracted; hence the concept of *8X8* was to treat chess as "animated" into a sort of Surrealist surplot and to use real human beings as the counters. The film turns out to be not so brilliantly structured and photographed and is rather like a treasure hunt in masquerade costumes.

In the May-June 1955 issue of *Film Culture*, Jonas Mekas, in a brief historical survey, made an attempt to distinguish between "film poetics" and "cineplastics" as well as "film drama" and "film poem." He tried to qualify Epstein's formula for cineplastics with a system of classifications covering the types of abstract film we have been discussing, including films that make use of objects treated as abstract counters. It is easy to grasp how close this is to Breton's formulation of Surrealist plastique: "The external object has broken away from its habitual environment. Its component parts had liberated themselves from the object in such a way that they could set up new relationships with other elements." This condition, since chess is an abstract game pattern, prevail in Richter's *8X8* except that, as I say, the counters have been "magically" converted into actual human beings. *Cineplastics* has betrayed itself here to *film poetics*. Mekas' classifications, having to do with the general aesthetics of film, simply subsume abstract plastiques in the "underground" interests of maintaining film (whatever its subject matter) as a formal aesthetic governed by the same laws of rhythm and harmony as music or painting. Alas! Mekas and a major part of the present avant-garde cohorts now march under a much modified flag.

If there is one abstract painter whose forms and successive styles suggest best the layout, individual forms, and dynamics of filmic painting-in-motion, it is Wassily Kandinsky. Yet film itself can perfectly reproduce the abstract style of painting. One of the most aesthetically satisfying abstract color films moving to music that I have ever seen is a work by James Whitney, *Lapis,* given a screening at the Fifth New York Film Festival (1967). Here the hypnotic image of a yantra is seen pulsating evenly, to the rhythms of a classical raga, with endlessly contracting and expanding circles of multicolored dots, all moving in complicated counterpoint and seeming as dense as the atoms of the sun. The plastic style corresponds to the pointillism of Post-Impressionist painters. There is a kinaesthetic feeling of constant swelling and subsiding that recalls the motion of respiration, so that the immense yantra on the screen easily becomes an image of the human heart serenely compounding the flow of chemicals throughout the body.

in the pad: plastique versus surplot

After 1920 a whole gamut of technical means was soon in use among the avant-garde (more generally known as experimental) filmmakers. This finally included direct painting and drawing on the film strip (Lye, McLaren, and others). *Free Radicals* is simply marks "etched" freely upon the film surface. Stan Brakhage and Kenneth Anger are among the Undergrounders who, more casually, have used a direct free-form scratching on the film for plastic modulation of straight photography. The literal tactile concern which entered painting with the Cubist mannerism of incorporating things into the paint surface led to Surrealist objects and abstract "constructions" in place of traditional sculpture.

In painting, the neo-Dadaist, pre-pop Robert Rauschenberg showed the paint surface (during the fifties) "exploding" with pictured objects seeking, as it were, a life in three dimensions —and sometimes attaining it in terms of three-dimensional objects, such as a stuffed rooster. That these semipictorial effects were often achieved with photographs marked the era of film plastique that appeared with the stroboscopic (3-D) screen: a universal way of interpreting the sort of illusion achieved in *Anemic Cinema*. The modern sculptor Marisol, placing painted and photographed faces on cubic facets and on semi-cubistic human figures, has worked arresting variations on this same plastique. As to film, there is yet another way of expressing an extra, or third, dimension on the flat film screen.

The Undergrounder Marie Menken was one of the very first to endow the hand-held camera with an elementary sort of dance pulse: a swing and sway to and from the photographed field or back and forth before it. Although a narrow, somewhat schematized modulation of plastique, it has worked particularly well in two of her films, one on a painter, the other on a sculptor: *Mood Mondrian* and *Visual Variations on Noguchi*. Sometimes the technique becomes futile because of a lack of rhythmic tension, but two collaborations by Miss Menken (Mrs. Willard Maas) with the talented Teiji Ito have led to a pair of audiovisual gems, *Arabesque for Kenneth Anger* (visions of decorations on the Alhambra) and *Moonplay* (literally glimpses of the moon used like abstract counters). The former has a rather loose play of restlessly moving camera but Ito has so cleverly synchronized it with his music that it deserves (with *Moonplay*) being labeled a new plastique-in-depth: vision/sound integration. *Moonplay* is entirely of mono-shots of the moon played rapidly over the screen.

All in all, here was a general emulsion of the sensibility that was bound to translate itself at an early point into filmic work of the truly aesthetic sort. Its latest manifestation is the mixed media, which seem to draw the circle of the plastic tangents adopted by easel painting all the way back to the theater itself, combining light-painting (as in Gordon Craig's and Tchelitchew's theater) with painted scenery and of course human actors, and finally (as at Bayreuth for Wagner's operas and on the current ballet stage) with projected film, both abstract and figured.* Black-and-white leaders for special effects and moods have been, for years now, a commonplace in Underground films of varied sorts; so have the numbers tabulating the film rolls themselves (as in Bruce Conner's blackly bilious *A Movie,* which consists of piled up newsreel shots of disasters).

Oddly enough, during this century's teens introducing tangible things was a way of modulating abstraction, while now, in the sixties, the inclusion of geometric tags identifying the physical film strip modulates pictures of human beings with abstractions.

George Landow, working in the sixties, has gone further than anyone else in utilizing multiple exposure, not as is usual by transparent overprinting, but literally by showing duplicate reels running inside one reel (a device adopted by commercial films in special effects for *Grand Prix* and in animated stills in the credits section of *The Knack*). Landow went still another step beyond himself by producing a film showing the film *Fleming Falloon* being projected inside a room with the spectators visible. All of which is mechanical enough and not necessarily expressive. Yet here is an exclusively *plastic* version of the story-within-a-story of literature and the play-within-a-play of the theater, consequently such a film remains a theoretical graph of situations-within-a-situation. Dramatically it is relatively sterile and has, conceivably, only a "psychedelic" power —simply because little or nothing in the plot sense happens in such films. Psychedelism cannot be fully evaluated unless it is understood in part as a force (see *The Chelsea Girls*) paralyzing plot action and concentrating on the monologue with gestures.

Landow also brings into view the film's sprocket holes to modulate, with vibrating fixity, the image of human beings. We are back with the struggle between the human image and plot on one side and all the narcissistic personalism of the self-sufficient poet-filmmaker's pad on the other. Sheldon Renan's generic

* The Joffrey ballet *Astarte* is an example.

159

term for the Underground type film is "personal," with "personal statement" as the logical extension. The term and its extension cover a multitude of sinning home-movie forays, technically hit-or-miss and bringing new disorder into the most cherished traditional poetic disorder; for instance, Baudelaire's name has constantly been taken in vain regarding the "personal statements" in films made by Undergrounders. Yet the word "personal," in regard to animated abstract color, surely has relevance. It indicates a hard-core personalism defiant of commercialism and relying upon playfulness and ingenuity of kinetic movement to compensate for any lack of effectual talent in drawing and painting.

More painting-in-motion filmmakers have had ambitions to paint and actually have been painters than it would be convenient to list in a paragraph. During the fifties the Cinema 16 film showings began featuring the animated painting of Carmen d'Avino, who, because he applied his intricate, brightly colored decorative designs to objects such as stones and furniture and even a statue of the Venus de Milo, added the ordinary three-dimensional world to painting-in-motion. One can easily be reminded of the revolving lights which clothe the dancers in discothèques. In *The Room* d'Avino covers a small room, including walls, ceiling, radiator, and articles of furniture, with his psychedelic-type, rapidly overspreading colors: a complicated though not precious conventional design. Animation makes the solid colors run like pushing rivulets till everything visible is totally tattooed.

Marie Menken's camera had already demonstrated the nervous, somewhat eccentric, rhythmic play of which the camera as itself a moving agent is capable. Brakhage, meeting Miss Menken in New York and seeing her early films, was more influenced by the example of her mobile, playful camera than by Maya Deren's careful surplotting (*surplot* = the arrangement of a "plot" of the sensibility *with* natural action rather than a "plot" *of* natural action as it takes place objectively in the world). On the other hand, the natural world, while still and invisible to the naked human eye, becomes in certain extraordinary aspects (as under the microscope) a nest of visible, more or less rhythmic movement. Menken demonstrated this with a brief film called *Hurry, Hurry,* which is nothing but the action of filaments in seminal fluid filmed microscopically: the tadpole-like bits jump and dive about spasmodically, continuously.

Underground cameras have a characteristic way of imitating this literally underground, quixotic *sexual* rhythm. Brakhage, for one, correctly sensed its relevance. Like musical beats, of course, sexual beats are variable, and variably musical. In the act of copulation there may be rhythmic breakdowns as well as sudden changes of rhythm, anticlimaxed crescendos, postponed climaxes, and so on.* Charles Boultenhouse, in the satyr-play section concluding his *Dionysius,* which at that point shifts to modern dress and a parody of *Last Year at Marienbad,* uses rock rhythms (vocal and instrumental) in which the crescendo is featured. He remarks that the music of both Wagner and Ravel contains mounting rhythms which suggest (primarily in the "Bolero") the drive toward sexual climax. His parody of *Marienbad* is thus consciously orgasmic. Markopoulos' single-frame sublimities and the rhythmic leap-editing of other filmmakers (especially when, as in Kubelka's films, it is cyclic) display the faculty of the camera as a musical instrument of vision.

Recently a kind of atonal, or at least conspicuously dissonant, visual rhythm has been exploited by Storm De Hirsch in *Third Eye Butterfly,* an interesting film requiring double projection (two separate films run contiguously and simultaneously). Miss De Hirsch's film is made up of complicated, notably jumpy rhythms which a modern-music score helps to control; one feels that chance rather than choice has deter-

* Warhol's later film, *Fuck* (released as *Blue Movie*), contains a good version of listless bad sex.

mined most of the visual dissidence. In certain passages the filmmaker divides up her two frames into multiples, at times two in each of them, making a total of four. Butterflies are simply image motifs in a series of semiabstract color patterns that vibrate, jump, and change frequently. Usually the pattern is made by objects sometimes formalized by the use of a flower-shaped prism (center and petals). A female breast becomes one unit of the multiple pattern in *Peyote Queen.*

Such filmmaking corresponds directly with abstract style in painting of the pictograph type; that is, with a set of cubicles each containing a different though perhaps related pattern. The total effect here is exciting and complex in the superficial terms of pure retinal agitation, but it is hard to find in it more than a psychedelic mood. Its tempo is so swift that, along with the actual music accompaniment, an effect of rhythmic blur occurs that both helps and hinders; it glosses over passing crudities, accentuates passing imprecisions. None of Miss De Hirsch's visual effects is exactly new, yet she is both daring and industrious in exploiting the film laboratory's resources.

The sheer technical concentration required by painting-in-motion film (whether produced with objects, light, or actual paint) is immense. This is a formal activity that should constantly provide models of study for avant-garde filmmakers of all kinds. But especially with the Underground moods of today, just these elements of technical precision and concentration on formal structure are deemed of scant account except in very elliptic and contingent ways. For example, the late Ron Rice's last completed film, *Chumlum,* being a home-movie camp dressed up like a Middle Eastern harem (see Maria Montez' old films), is plastically interesting because of the way the camera's nose has been inserted into spaces festooned with multicolored draperies so that the look is that of heavy, perhaps magnified webbing. The movement for much of the film is supplied by seminude or partly costumed creatures of doubtful sex, who swing and conduct rather static flirtations in a

162

great hammock enclosed by draperies. Surely what is meant is a psychedelic mood, although the music is quite heterogeneous —not the pure vulgar-orgiastic of rock, that is, but snatches of classical stuff like *Schéhérazade*. This too manages to be a "Jack Smith film" if only because he is a lead character, here not in drag but as a sort of sultan. A woman, Beverly Grant, taking a lead role blending houri and odalisque, shares honors with Mario Montez, in drag as usual.

The film laboratory in which a color-abstractionist wields his brush and pen is virtually the same as a painter's studio, an intimate and personal place where he works primarily alone. D'Avino's *The Room* is plainly a prototype of the studio especially transformed to be backgrounds and environments for Happenings and Trips where others beside the *auteur* participate. The group strategy of filmed Happenings is therefore easy to detect: the filmmaker is documenting the personal mood which associates a human individual only with things among which abstract color forms come to birth on screens and film strips; this is then converted into social moods in which playing around with paint and other materials, as well as each other's bodies, is the traditional parlor game—here one of filmic modernism smartened up with current visual vogues. All this developed in the sixties. Its genealogy is important because it literally reveals the disintegration of that formal preoccupation which inspired so many filmic animators during the twenties, thirties, and forties. If one had to name a true avant-garde film in the best spirit of our time's Underground aesthetics—that is, one formally preoccupied with converting the pad into some coherent and imaginative film statement solely about the pad's occupant—one could do no better than choose Charles Boultenhouse's *Handwritten*. The fashion, and the danger to film, is to consider *Handwritten* as arty. The film is slightly imperfect in detail; it is not arty. The surplot need not be arty, any more than it need be a garbage pail. Unless you love garbage pails (full).

163

hard-core history

Above all arts, the visual arts are held to be an international medium because the eyesight does not present any "language barriers." Historicizing for *Art in Cinema* (1947), a publication of the California School of Fine Arts, Hans Richter declares that the "avant-garde" developed during the decade 1921-31 and that, besides being "noncommercial and non-representational," it was "international." Indeed, the United States quickly responded to exciting signs from Europe. Richter, then working with Viking Eggeling in Germany, produced some of the very first abstract animated film by using collaged paper squares; the series thus begun he entitled *Rhythmus* (1921, 1923, 1925). Interestingly, the filmic impetus came from figured scrolls which he and Eggeling made and animated even before *Rhythmus*. Then in 1926 Richter's work made abstract forms evolve into objects. Three years earlier Man Ray (an American who was parisianizing himself) had done the opposite by turning ordinary objects into abstractions by revolving them while playing light on them; these were called Rayograms. His female nude (in the Dada-titled *Return to Reason*), writhing rhythmically in front of a window while sunlight makes abstractions on her torso, is an antecedent to similarly inspired visions by Undergrounders Ed Emshwiller and Bruce Conner.

Another, "purely optical" film of Man Ray's, *Emak Bakia* (1926), dramatizes the film camera as though it were a pair of human eyes whose owner ran into hazards (this had been done even earlier by Abel Gance in his commercial epic *Napoléon*). Ray brought out the somnambulistic quality of dream experience by painting false eyes on the eyelids of the famous artist's model, Kiki, and photographing her walking along casually, seeming to see with her artificial eyes and then looking at the spectator with her true ones. This anticipated the quite different effect obtained by Cocteau in *Le Sang d'un Poète* when he painted false eyes on his Poet's Muse, a real woman who was also a statue. It was impossible, as soon as experimentalists began to explore possibilities of filmic illusion, to separate the genesis of avant-garde interest in artistic expression from the interest in dream-fantasy and the supernatural, whether Surrealistically motivated or not.

Freshly discovered film tricks were a standing invitation to explore hallucination as an *inward* life—as that which penetrated outer, "realistic" surfaces, and that which turned a searchlight into the self where desire and memory played their own special tricks, created their own brands of montage. In the forties Maya Deren became the pre-eminent American film-maker to put "trick" vocabulary seriously at the service of the "personal film." Less personally, Emshwiller in *Thanatopsis* utilized visually complex images of a female dancer (together with a man's head) for a melodramatic meditation on death. The First Surrealist Manifesto (1924), with its proclamation of "the marvelous" (chance, automatism, dreams, and so on), unquestionably had a great deal to do with the abandonment of pure abstraction in the pad for hallucinations in the street; a main point about such avant-gardism, however, is that its film space is *pan-personal:* the space of the mind that encompasses the "street" and *all* objectivity.

Commercial film had another formula for "objectivity." Men like Richter were always technically equipped to make "commercial films" and did make some because they paid off and because the filmmaker had the know-how to do them. The early international avant-garde, in this respect, was the opposite of today's American Underground, where on the whole filmic know-how is an object of suspicion or polite tolerance, where indifferent, semiblind naïveté toward matters filmic (and matters adult) is an important criterion of merit.

A good deal has been recorded in these pages about the cause for so strong an Underground distrust of all sorts of sophistication. The European attitude (despite the success of Dada and Surrealism during the same period) was just the opposite; there was nothing "sophisticated" about mastering the technical possibilities of film, about viewing it as a rich, resourceful language. On the contrary, one was learning the rudiments of a new, rather difficult but highly promising craft. Being "playful" about it *could* be a way of being serious about it.

Perhaps the whole alienation atmosphere of our times— from Dada's rejection of high official art, through Surrealism's taboo on reason and the formal plot, to existentialist disillusion with all idealistic morality—has finally led film Undergrounders, two generations later, to repudiate their own technical tradition as artificial and formalist. As we know, there was no such revolt in the middle generation of the American avant-garde or in those Americans who took cues from European filmmakers as fast as they could be found abroad or detected on their way across the Atlantic. Currently, however,

the element of editing to give story shape to a film has suffered
a major loss of prestige in the American Underground; it is
as if shapely film narrative were something on which commercial film had put a curse—even were the "shape" to be
irrational.

Only among young Underground *critics* is there still a cult
for classic film storytelling (for instance, the films of Carl
Dreyer); among the filmmakers themselves, very few hope,
even wistfully, to use as models films with solid plot and
measured story line. Dada and Surrealism have had something
to do with the decline of narrative montage (whether in films
brief or long) but inasmuch as the latest Underground has no
Surrealist discipline or Surrealist ideas, it would seem as if
the apostasy from montage and all technical finish is solely the
result of the traumatic revulsion from commercialism.

When the Russian Dimitri Kirsanov made *Ménilmontant*
in Paris, at the same time (1924) that Clair made *Entr'acte*,
he apparently had no Dada-Surrealist ideas, only the "personal" idea of telling the story of an unfortunate seduced girl
while using the emergent poetic vocabulary and a hand-held
camera. This is also true, incidentally, of Goldman's *Echoes
of Silence*, a much later film. Kirsanov's lead was a beautiful
Russian who evidently bore to him something of the relation
that Brigitte Bardot bore Roger Vadim, Monica Vitti bore
Antonioni, and Anna Karina bore Jean-Luc Godard. Much
sensitive commercial filmmaking today is based on a kind of
woman worship in which film stories are literally the same
kind of technical "vehicles" that have always featured commercial star players, especially in the United States. In special
cases a film may tend to change from a "story" to a "portrait,"
and today there are many European examples of this semi-
disguised personality adoration. It is definitely what happened
to Nadia Sibirskaya, Kirsanov's lead, when he next put her in
Brumes d'Automne (1926), thus establishing a model that may

167

actually have inspired Machaty to do *Ecstasy* with Hedy Lamarr about a decade later.

The love lyric and the love idyl have already been cited as typical avant-garde genres. There are some of these in Underground Film. One wonders, for instance, if the recent portraits of offbeat male personalities (Jack Smith, Taylor Mead, Jason Holliday) aren't the products of strange erotic transferences: a cult of transsexual idolatry which in practice means, at times, turning sex into fixated fetishism. Fetish footage, we find, is inseparable from true Underground habits.

In the twenties Kirsanov went on to make commercial films. So did René Clair—on and on *and on*. The Dada-flavored chase after the runaway hearse in *Entr'acte* became a device in nearly every Clair plot thereafter, just as it was anticipated by his very first film, *Crazy Ray*, in which a scientist's runaway invention stops daily activity in the whole of Paris: a purely comic exploitation of stop-motion. Undoubtedly the temptation to increase one's scope through accepting or applying for commercial offers had a good deal to do with the fortunes of the historic avant-garde. Animated abstract films, such as Richter's earliest work and *Anemic Cinema*, are largely laboratory matters, accomplished with minimal expense in the pad, with paint, light, and film. When a filmmaker tries, however, either four decades ago or now, to expand his personal aims to storytelling, the costs and the difficulties automatically rise. One acquires collaborators, film technicians as well as actors, and thus enters the other, traditional world: the theater with all its human and physical paraphernalia. Yet its traditional scorn of taking just this "commercializing" bent has beset the avant-garde's ranks with fears and helped to create the ambivalent procedures which glorify and degrade the narcissistic art of independent filmmaking.

The truth? There is a law of limitations governing the antics of the pad insofar as they compete with painting. Painting with light, starting with Man Ray's Rayograms, has gone beyond itself into discothèques and art museums. Today it belongs, as we have noted, both to the realm of pictorial abstraction and to the play of colored light in providing psychedelic environments into which real people merge themselves. What seems paramount in the history of avant-garde film is the way in which, without being abstract, without depending on the animation of drawing or painting, color and light can also "paint" people. Regardless of plot design, there is (and always was) a cineplastics of the human being. Possibly Stan VanDerBeek's most interesting film is *Mankinda*, an animated fantasy showing man as an infinitely variable plastic organism that might have been invented by a child, Paleolithic man, or a twentieth-century painter who obliterated the figure the way Balzac's mad artist, Frenhofer, does in *Le Chef-d'Oeuvre Inconnu.*

Much is to be said, I think, for the Surrealists' opposition to film trickery—the stunts on which animation depends to be amusing—as well as their opposition to the classical plot. In this the Surrealist movement is inseparable from the true avant-garde film movement of which the Underground is the current point of evolution. After all, popular animation (one thinks of Disney and the UPA cartoons in America) has furnished as much ingenuity as the animated style can well take. Beyond techniques, of course, there are ideas to be exploited—intellectual wit as interpreted by plastic wit. Robert Breer, for instance, has gained some avant-garde fame by being plastically cute and emulating primitive drawing instead of respecting the sophisticated Disney cartooning style. A great many brief films of dry wit, satire, or just with a cute slant have come out of Europe and done little or nothing to enhance the achievements of the avant-garde or forward the development of film language.

Misguided but alert young filmmakers of the Underground have beat the bushes of inspiration by exaggerating, tightening,

169

and indefinitely prolonging technical procedures that have long been familiar to the avant-garde. As a painter, Norman Mc-Laren made no noticeable dent in the world. When he took to animating simple aggregates of dabs, blots, whirls, and streaks of multicolored paint, making them jump and race, he converted his métier into an avant-garde novelty that soon became popular. At least half the success of his work with art-house audiences is due to his animation's being set to fast jazz scores. Here we are in the marginal domain of the avant-garde. Just as connoisseurs of the commercial admired the best Disney work, serious film fans tended to find McLaren and other jiffy-type animators the sources of "adult entertainment." A true experimentalist like Brakhage, whose incidental inventions can be breathtaking (and breakneck), simply pushes to the extreme and beyond the viewer's tolerance for repetition of quality and extension of effect. His racing abstractions, tending to be "cosmic" in context, are more subliminal than any single frame of McLaren's—that is, they flash on at a seemingly higher rate of speed and collectively go on much longer. For minutes at a time (and without music) we get in Brakhage's later work something looking very much like a literally palpitating rectangle from a Jackson Pollock swirl-and-splatter abstraction.

The issue is as simple as that of take-it-or-leave-it abstractionism in still painting. The point is that many Undergrounders who aren't really using abstractions—but rather, perhaps, animated figure collage, period-film parodies, or the Happening formula—place the same extreme burden of interest on a monolithic and only mechanically varied style, especially when brevity is abandoned and the larger, longer film gesture is taken up. Andy Warhol's early solid-time miniactions simply isolate these elements into one self-evident, already discarded genre. Even Warhol himself has now gotten away from "primitivism."

A quite unexpected reversion to aesthetic ingenuity came on

the scene as early as 1958, at the first international Experimental Film Festival in Brussels, when—to the annoyance of a great many besides competing filmmakers—an entry called *Dom* carried away the grand prize.

Dom was strictly a "pad" film. It was made by two Poles, Walerian Borowczyk and Jan Lenica, as if they had tried to realize a historic *ne plus ultra* of concentrated avant-gardism. Man Ray was fortunately on the prize-giving jury. If he had not been, perhaps this immensely clever film would not have come out so triumphantly. It is ironic (and perhaps the irony was meant deliberately by its makers) that *Dom* should be so aesthetically conscious an experimental film; actually, it is poised avant-garde and its polish alone would irritate, in the sixties, the more aggressive Undergrounders. I wrote of *Dom* in the Spring 1959 *Film Quarterly*, after Cinema 16 had screened the Festival's attention-getting films on one of its programs, as follows:

It [*Dom*] has one vital, governing premise: the mechanical recording of natural movement and the photographic surface of nature (as well as nature's colors) are "out"; movement in film is to be as varied and arbitrary as movement in music, while the image itself can be transformed or distorted in any way suiting the purposes of the film artist . . . actually, the movement is usually equivalent to the earliest cinematographic attempts to record nature, but here paced variously at will. By *Dom*'s courtesy, therefore, we can discern the same sort of movement *as aesthetic value* because (as when we are shown an antique film print of two men fighting and fencing) it is manipulated rhythmically and spatially in whatever way desired; the film's modernist music score italicizes this point. Using film, art, and scientific prints, as well as direct photography of nature, *Dom* provides a consistent feeling of artifice that nowadays may strike us as "puritanical": it is pre-eminently a *laboratory* film, the true creative work being concentrated in the ways that already created drawings and photographs are reused; no laboratory device is actually original (I believe) and yet the ensemble, since a highly conscious idea animates it, is beautifully presented and holds together.

171

Dom uses a basic symbolist method. . . . The symbolist idea in *Dom*, however, could hardly be simpler or stricter. "Dom" means *house, home*. . . .* A woman waits for either husband or lover, whose footsteps she hears on the street outside (the fighting sequence indicates he may be away having a duel); he comes in, places his hat on an old-fashioned hatrack, and appears to her as a handsome clothes-dummy's head, which she caresses only to see it disintegrate under her eyes (perhaps signifying the wounds he has suffered in the fight).

. . . The film's central idea has been communicated, I imagine, by a sequence dealing with a primitive graphic concept of the brain's mechanical structure: man's true "home" is his brain, which forms all his notions of the outside world. This theme has been presented in terms of an old house front, old prints, and old-fashioned props, including a very lovely "vamp type" lady; as still images, many shots are close to the Dada collages of Max Ernst and Francis Picabia's paintings. The strictly controlled rhythms and repeated image-sequences build up suspense and tension. Someone is coming; someone waits; what will happen? A green wig is animated as though it were a spider or an octopus; it moves in minimal jumps the way the woman's head is made to move as she opens her eyes on hearing the man's footsteps. Time is cyclic because—as psychology has long known—the anxiety of waiting, in the mind of the one who waits, anticipates and reanticipates an event over and over before it happens.

. . . The distinction of *Dom* lies in an asset which a great majority of the films seen at the Festival, for one reason or another, may have seriously neglected, and whose presence in *Dom* may account for its gaining the Grand Prix. This is a careful, sensuously beautiful surface: a continuously designed and appealing area of vision whose clean, dramatic composition is never allowed to lapse. If any fault at all were to be found with it technically, one could observe that it is sometimes a little on the smart magazine "layout" side and resembles the advertising décor influenced by the Bauhaus as well as by Surrealism . . . all the more surprising, then, its true inspiration.

Since this was written the Underground has exploded— but the essential filmic situation, artistic and technical, remains much the same despite the psychedelic and voyeuristic novelties that now absorb attention. For voyeurism to quite lose its edge,

* Also, of course, "master of the house."

its "novel" thrill, both nudity and exposed sex acts would have to become much more customary public spectacles. Meanwhile, psychedelically dressed novelties have an explosive charge with an undefined destruction potential.

The neuroticism of modern life, with its new and unusually morbid accent on youth, has chosen Underground Film as one of its more violent instruments. The international festival at Knokke-le-Zoute, Belgium, which took place almost a decade later, in December of 1967, represented all that has been cooking, stewing, sizzling, and otherwise reacting to flame since *Dom* triumphed to the discomfort of so many. In this latest festival Walerian Borowczyk, one of the makers of *Dom*, was on the prize-awarding jury (composed entirely of filmmakers, including the American Shirley Clarke), and the grand prize of $4,000 went to *Wave-length*, a film by a new American filmmaker, Michael Snow. It is very instructive to compare this much longer film to its winning predecessor, *Dom*.

Wave-length is one uninterrupted zoom taking forty-five minutes to traverse the length of the filmmaker's loft and approach its row of front windows, which overlook the street. Thus it is another "pad" film. While all this delayed-action time is being consumed, certain incidents take place, all very fragmentary; a couple walks in and eventually a woman telephones the police that a corpse is in the room. In other words, another pitched battle is staged between spectator interest and a time vacuum created within a very small area—another quasi-ritual struggle with boredom. Here there is a special suspense based on expectation (when and how human beings will materialize) that is similar to *Dom*'s but is extended far beyond the breaking point. The zoom, by now, is a familiar filmic device. Its effect is usually achieved by the sudden swiftness with which it devours the space between us and a distant point of interest that becomes clear at the zoom's climactic halt. Obviously Snow wished to turn this standard effect inside

173

out, titillating one's bored suspense by introducing the few fleeting incidents.

Perhaps the fact that *Dom* also has to do with someone who waits in suspense provoked a note of sympathy in Borowczyk as a judge. But whereas nowadays a courted Underground value is boredom unlimited, in 1958 it was a state of tension produced not only by waiting but also by desire—by waiting for something expected, a climax at the end of the suspense. Long before the end of *Wave-length* one guesses that the "climax" will be the camera eye's arrival at the windows and perhaps a view from them. Yet despite certain optical variations during its zoom, there is no true visual climax, no revelation, only the breaking of sustained tension like the snapping of a cord. Instead there is a sonal climax alone: all along an electronic sound grows louder and louder till, at the end, it reaches an unendurable pitch. I don't think the *Wave-length* sound can be called in any way *musical*, although there is a certain musicality in such effects as the continuous electronic screech accompanying Emshwiller's *Thanatopsis*, in which a dancer seems to fragment herself in superspeed movement.

Other prize winners at the Belgian festival included one that had to do with a nude girl who photographed herself in a mirror (narcissistic voyeurism); a psychedelic collage about a rock-'n'-roll band; an animated film made with computer and microfilm plotter attached to a camera (robot filmmaking in which the mixed media are indisputably the message); and a film called *Self-Obliteration*, which ends with, as described by Amos Vogel in his report for the *New York Times*, "a free-for-all body-painting sex-orgy"—in short, an erotic Happening. All these films are American with the exception of the narcissistic-voyeuse item, which is German. One need only add that a Japanese filmmaker, Yoko Ono, had a ninety-minute entry called *Number 4*, composed entirely of twenty-second-each exposures of 365 pairs of buttocks belonging to London artists and intellectuals. Clearly avant-garde film has become fashion-mad. It is inventing all sorts of ways to be free of art and its formal aims, the chief way being to exploit the medium at the expense of the message, and not even chiefly to exploit the medium but rather to *under*exploit it.

One of the overadvertised traits of the Underground is, oddly enough, this technical underexploitation. If, on the contrary, there are cases that seem like overexploitation, that is only because the message, or content, has been deliberately reduced, correspondingly, to a minimum. Vogel and other intelligent observers at Knokke-le-Zoute noticed a definite decline of quality, of imagination and daring, in the avant-garde film movement. The great accumulation of technical effects (especially multiple exposure and arbitrary speeds) had produced an overloaded technique that looked as lopsided, at times, as the vacuousness of no-technique.

The 1958 prize winner, *Dom*, gauging its technical devices to a given content, an *idea*, justified its entire form as *expressive* and therefore is not boring. It is not merely that, colloquially speaking, "things happen" in *Dom* but that these things are humanly coherent and put together in an interesting as well as economical way. In *Dom* the whole history of avant-garde film can be traced, up to the anarchic disintegration that set in with, so to speak, the "Underground wave-length." I would recommend the close study of *Dom* to Underground film animators, as I would recommend Maya Deren's trilogy and Sidney Peterson's *The Lead Shoes* to would-be Underground storytellers and idyl painters. Especially the Polish film and Miss Deren's best work provide archetypal models of form whose deep influence would be very healthy. Again I emphasize the importance of having not only feelings (who hasn't *some* feelings?) but also *filmic ideas about feelings*. If so significant a qualification is to be ignored, why bother with a "medium" at all? One might argue that the strategic, perhaps unconscious, aim of the newer

175

avant-garde is to create conditions in which art simply withers away (e.g., even media wither away), as capitalism was supposed to wither away after the revolution that produced the Soviet Union. Ultrapermissiveness (part of the Underground creed) is a sort of socialist ideal, but when it becomes ultraper*mess*iveness its ideal desirability is put in serious question.

the ethics of film history

We might consult the record from the side of theater exhibition. I have already suggested that the Underground is made largely of commotion and that a good part of the commotion is promotion. The sixteen-year existence of Cinema 16 as a film society—as well as a distribution organization—considerably softened up the more serious-minded film public in New York by acquainting it with the existence of non-Establishment film. Meanwhile so-called experimental films were being distributed to colleges, museums, and film societies many years before the Film-Makers' Cooperative went into business. Then, in 1955, when the magazine *Film Culture* appeared as an "underground" organ of the independent film movement, the interested film public was reminded that theories and a history lay behind the activity of small, non-Establishment filmmakers whose works might look arty to some, but which on the whole, if seen in the proper perspective, made sense. I have more than hinted what the proper perspective was and is—but again, just what is it?

It is the moral preservation of the film as a noncommercial exploration of technical and aesthetic possibilities. As usual, however, the human race here as in other fields has erred on the side of technique, believing that by tinkering around with the sheer technical possibilities of the medium of moving photography, the proper historic aims of independent filmmaking are being fulfilled. This is a reactionary rather than a progressive attitude. It is an error of cultism, snobbery, and inferiority compensation in which the collaboration of a part of the audience with the filmmaker is functional. This complex of moral feelings probably has more than a little political coloration, which is where the anti-Establishment trend asserts itself and where the *art* of film becomes confused with the *social protest* of film.

Looking carefully at the record of the avant-garde's development before the *Film Culture* era, we see that Europeans or adoptive Europeans such as Duchamp, Léger, Man Ray, Richter, and Jean Epstein clearly wished to bring the plastic sensibility of painting into filmmaking, with the idea of film as a *nonrepresentational* medium; this would exclude social protest *as such*. When this aesthetic message crossed the ocean and occasioned the birth of the international avant-garde, men such as Lewis Jacobs (also a film historian), Ralph Steiner, Robert Florey, Paul Strand, and Robert Flaherty all used facilities and themes in this country to cultivate the international sensibility formulated by the Russians and exploited in tricky ways by the Dadaists.

As predecessor of the Film-Makers' Cinémathèque in New York, Cinema 16 actually had a more open-minded policy than the later organization toward documentaries of unusual caliber; for example, it showed films of advanced experiments in education and psychology, usually involving therapy. Cinema 16 also imported foreign films and had an international spirit. Occasionally the Cinémathèque has done likewise, as

when (in 1967) it imported avant-garde Japanese erotica—
most of which, however, being in the Happening mode, was
very disappointing.

The great importance of an *ethics* of film history is to dis-
count the latest informal and disintegrative trends as the least
meaningful of the continuing avant-garde. We have only to
consider Sergei Eisenstein's case to realize that, however truly
anti-Establishment the Dada-Surrealist canon was in relation
to film, there existed a huge domain of endeavor which might
be called the *epic*—a domain which, in comparison with the
corresponding forms of the novel and the drama, was super-
dramatic, supernovelistic, and, one might say, super-Establish-
ment rather than anti-Establishment. True, disinterested, noncommercial filmmaking of all varieties has always had a gamut
of possibilities before it, and it is not fair to these possibilities
to assert that true avant-garde art ought to limit its concern to
the filmic equivalent of the lyric poem, simply because it is
economically convenient to do so. What, then, about the ex-
clusion of social protest, considering that Eisenstein and the
other Russians belonged to a nation oriented to social-revolu-
tionary ideology? Answer: *the epic form absorbs and tran-
scends mere social protest.*

Consider that what Abel Gance did in his pioneering epic,
Napoléon (whose very projection cost too much in 1925 to
allow it to be presented theatrically, as Gance wished), Andy
Warhol did in *The Chelsea Girls* through a fluke dictated by
practical convenience. When the episodes of *The Chelsea Girls*
were shot, Warhol did not have the idea of counterpointing
two scenes by projecting them simultaneously side by side as
one dualistic image. Doing that was thought up as a way of
reducing the showing time by half and stimulating vision by a
simple contradiction. Not so with the Gance who invented the
film triptych for his epic statement of Napoleon's career. His
triptych corresponded to the horizontally extended mural in

painting. It also corresponded to the present-day cyclorama, but went beyond it in plastic ingenuity by proposing to combine scenes to make, not merely one huge "partitioned" scene, but a great collage of plastically different scenes related by idea as well as by certain "musical" repetitions of form. At times Gance achieved effects by extending a scene to right and left with the repetitive butterfly pattern; at other times he flanked an allegorical scene—a personified female France urging on French soldiers—with reversed views, to right and left, of a realistic scene of marching soldiers. Such effects have a choral and balletic character.

Here was an abstract plastics as venturesome as the uses of animation; indeed, its principle is the same as that used to-day which reduces whole-frame film units in order to include several of them in one normal-sized screen. It is also a variation on the multiple exposure of superimposition. In any case it has always meant expanding and complicating the field of vision and modulating its textures.

"Pure film," as the concept announced by the pioneering theorist-filmmaker Hans Richter, would seem to exclude anything like storytelling, such as *Napoléon* or elements in Richter's own later films, for that would involve the "romantic," the "moral," and even (since Gance was reconstructing history) the "documentary." Only the irrational formula of Dada-Surrealism seemed to invent ways by which human action could be shown as divorced from, uninterested in, emotional values that could be termed moral or romantic, historical or political. Of course, personally, I think that, as fertile as some of the Surrealist formulations remain to this day, their practice cannot avoid positive moral implications; that is, to take the much cited *L'Age d'Or* once more, being anti-Establishment, this Dali-Buñuel film is a way of asserting neglected and primitive human concern with the human, and is therefore moral—moral just as ideas of social anarchy propose a new moral order of human existence, or as the nonpsychological, objectivist novels of Robbe-Grillet propose still another order, however fragmentary and arid.

This novelist's later development as an independent filmmaker has offered a very instructive spectacle. All the implications of his literary practice are against the psychological plot, against metaphors and aesthetic metaphysics. Yet his own exploitation of the film medium, *L'Immortelle*, not only employs filmic technique of a conspicuously avant-garde type but also essays the "personal" film, the film of fantasy and fetishism, in a perfectly deliberate way. He has a surrogate self-hero (unattractively and self-consciously acted by his critic friend, Doniol-Valcroze) but, obviously, the mysterious heroine with whom this protagonist falls in love is a source of erotic fantasy, so that mainly the film is an *hommage* to obsessive states of desire (sometimes ambiguously hallucinative) induced by this attractive woman—a veritable *femme fatale* in the classic sense. As filmically sensitive as the elaborate, feature-length film is, its story development simply does not sustain interest throughout.

The beguilement of the eye through lovely atmospheric shots and magically appearing and disappearing mirages (so easy in the film medium) is here limited by content and inflated by repetition. The element of time is as ambiguous as it was in the *Marienbad* film done by Robbe-Grillet with Alain Resnais, but here (even as with dull Underground films with much less finesse of touch) the interest of both technique and subject is overburdened with the stubbornly static quality of the erotic obsession. As in many Underground works of the sixties (Markopoulos' films, for instance), there are long promenades through picturesque landscape whose content is no more than a mild sex flirtation or a monotonous erotic "chase." Obsessive filmmakers often don't care that spectators do not share their actual obsession with the particular actress or actor being pursued or courted, however charming this actor or actress may be. The result, for Robbe-Grillet as for others, is an animated album of uneven interest that is mostly dependent on decorative variety: the various shots with their special composition and chiaroscuro.

L'Immortelle unquestionably belongs in the respectable library of modern poetic films, bravely done in defiance of commercial considerations—done, in fact, for the filmmaker's pleasure. As such, it deserves a passing mark. Yet in a truly enlightened perspective, as more than a talented man's fetish footage, it is oddly banal and· eventually boring, despite some rather pyrotechnic (though not original) effects which the filmmaker has invented to end this legend of a great erotic frustration. The heroine, drenched in overmuch glamor, slips forever from her lover's presence. Severely scrutinized, character, situation, and device in this film suffer from both romantic and filmic triteness. After all, the school of personal film poetry has its own clichés, and with the latter-day growth of the Underground Film, we have seen these clichés played with, tossed around, turned inside out and upside down, so that we are as familiar with them as with the rhetoric of nineteenth-century romantic verse. The bulk of this same verse needs genius to survive the historic burden of cliché and the ennui of standardized vocabulary. Why should the realm of film poetry have escaped the same dilemma? The fact is that Robbe-Grillet's *L'Immortelle* (despite its poetic sensibility) is a bible of the clichés of romantic/Surrealist film poetry.

The last resort of modern Underground films accused of formlessness, triviality, messiness, and amateurishness is that they are important *private* matters: they assert the individual's sacred personality. Assuming this argument's validity, in Robbe-Grillet's case as in others', it still cannot guarantee that a given personality is interesting or vital enough to have something unforgettable to contribute to human sensibility through film. Maya Deren's film trilogy is efficient proof that, if film is free to present a personality pattern, rawly, in the rough, by direct social confrontation, film is also free to express personality pattern in conjunction with plastic pattern, so that we have, at best, something beyond an interesting document, something that can really be called artistic. Let us return to the matter of the cult of personality for personality's sake, which casually represents aesthetics without any conscious standards: so free-form that it's naturally slack and by rule beyond criticism because it is "documentary." This is the trend lately taken by Warhol's films, which duly came to have both Broadway and Greenwich Village runs—outstandingly *My Hustler* and *Bike Boy*. In its new, augmented form *My Hustler* is virtually a personality study of an individual (played by Paul America). One cannot know how "true to life" this study is but at least Mr. America's role is acted with unfaltering plausibility, and as for the others, the *camping* is assuredly authentic.

The fiction is that a tall, good-looking young blond is being initiated into the business of hustling sugar daddies. As an employee of Dial-a-Hustler, he is now fulfilling an engagement with a male client at a beach cottage. What happens is that two women and two men, including his host, all make serious plays for him and offer various lures. Oddly and insinuatingly enough, the offer "most likely to succeed" seems the one in which he will have to do some teamwork with an older hustler who knows the game, rather than become the spoiled gigolo of either his host or one of the two women. The action has no pretense of being smooth or shapely, although, for a Warhol film, it has a startling visual variety, including startling use of a panoramic zoom. As a home movie it is brilliant and inspired. The coveted neophyte seems cavalierly, for the moment, to leave everyone in suspense; the new version ends with a screen-filling close-up of his face (in a position to indicate he is reclining) in alternate states of trying to look serious and being forced to break out in a pretty smile; this continues in perpetual motion till, as usual with Warhol films, time drops dead.

Bike Boy, laid out (like *I, a Man*) as a series of sexual encounters, begins in a Mod men's-wear shop with a lot of nudie posing by young customers trying on pants and swim trunks; here some nelly clerks flirt with a Leather Boy (or rather Bike Boy, as the newer sobriquet is). The action then shifts to a flower shop, where Bike Boy takes a female customer on his knee, and resolves into several seduction scenes in the haunts of four very offbeat ladies of bohemia. The last, longest, and only successful one ends with man and woman completely nude and restrained profile visibility of the man. Apparently the dialogue is altogether ad-libbed and sometimes, especially in Bike Boy's lines, it is quite funny, though in general "realistically" prolonged and halting. Bike Boy, as if playing "himself," gives a brilliantly candid and convincing performance of a free-lance, penniless, nature-boy sort of male whose morality of the bedroom (once he likes a girl) is determined and animal-simple. As a personality-portrait, the film seems a hundred percent cinéma vérité. Beyond that, its relation to the art of the film is nil.

the population explosion and the remedy

With its policy of admittance to anybody with a printed film reel, the Film-Makers' Cooperative has become, in the past decade, a very crowded affair, with a catalogue whose every new printing tends to double the number of films listed. There is a population explosion among the brain children of Underground Film. Having seen hundreds of such films, I have concluded that, while both technical and story ideas are apt to recur in them, twenty-four out of twenty-five seem made by a person who feels free to ignore the organic sense of form possessed by the best avant-garde films of the past, even when those same films are not quite successful. For example, *Lot in Sodom* and Richter's *Dreams That Money Can Buy* and *8X8* are integral conceptions, whatever their defects of imagination and technical execution. The same is true of two distinguished feature-length films from abroad, imported by Cinema 16 in the fifties: *No More Fleeing*, by a German, Herbert Vesely, and *The Mirage*, by Peter Weiss, author of the play *Marat/Sade*.

185

Both films use fantasy and both are basically allegories of modern life with social-protest implications. *No More Fleeing* is laid in the desert, where the atom-bomb experiments are made; it pictures the civilized world's last stand with a very economical cast of characters: a stylish woman of the world, a young driver-mechanic who takes her to the scene in a dump truck, a tavern owner still "in business" in a desert outpost that is now a ghost town, and the local idiot girl as well as a mentally retarded little boy. Debilitated society, reduced to penury and sordid lust, makes a poor show girding itself for the zero hour of the world's self-destruction. Before the last count-down, we get a view of a fascist-like militaristic government persecuting its citizens to the very end in this desert setting. Scenically very well designed, with many good shots, the film is neither very rich in conception and execution nor quite satisfying in pace and style. Still, it is an effort in the right direction for the avant-garde: it aims sincerely at cinematic style and originates in an idea uniquely suited to film.

The same is true of *The Mirage.* It too is panoramic, using urban perspectives and architectural features as *No More Fleeing* uses the open vistas of the desert "invaded" by remnants of a vanishing civilization. The Kafkaesque young protagonist of *The Mirage* himself invades the modern city as an outcast and remains hopelessly alienated despite meeting with some human kindness and finally a girl whose comradeship is like that of Chaplin's girls with Charlie the tramp. Actually, Weiss's hero is as much a fugitive as a criminal would be. Spending the night in a large trash bin, he and the girl are unceremoniously transferred at dawn to a garbage truck, and the film ends. It is like a long initiation rite turned inside out in conformance with the pessimistic alienation mood of our times. Again, the style here is not really sharp or vivid enough; its inventions are a bit stale and unoriginal. Yet it has some excellent scenes, is densely cinematic (with dialogue much sparser than in the other film), and, like *No More Fleeing*, states an authentic view of life.

Such films are related to Surrealism through their assertion of dream fantasy as the dominant imaginative rule. All the elements are real and modern enough; it is the way they are put together that creates their surreality—their surplot.

The surplot might be defined as a pattern of action which approximates but does not reproduce human events as they take place in reality. As in Proust (and of course in symbolist poetry), the mental dimension operates along with and basically determines the physical dimension. It is the opposite of the slice-of-life realism which, strictly speaking, depends on what people actually do and say to establish the reality of the mental dimension and in which psychology and motive, though perhaps implied or stated, are secondary. Classic supernatural plots release reality altogether into the keeping of mystic forces and the power of a god or gods, so that people become more or less helpless pawns. Richter's chess film, *8X8*, uses the mechanical convention of supernaturalism to create a surplot: who are the real movers? The human chessmen themselves are only apparently in control. *Lot in Sodom*, starting with a supernatural biblical story, uses rather thin means, at times ingeniously, at times transparently, in faithfully reflecting the main events. The handling and acting are a little amateurish but of a sincerely uncompromising imaginative spirit. The Watson-Webber film must be added to the major statements of the avant-garde movement, through which its historic development may be traced.

Such films, already mentioned in these pages, are due an exemplary massing—for in their indications, and only there, lies the desirable future of the avant-garde. *La Folie de Docteur Tube, Entr'acte, Ballet Mécanique, Anemic Cinema, Berlin: the Symphony of a Great City, Ménilmontant*; Richter's *Rhythmus* series, his Dada film *Ghosts before Breakfast*, and the later

187

underground film

Dreams That Money Can Buy and *8X8*; Man Ray's Rayograms;
the early abstract-animation school up to Norman McLaren,
Jordan Belson, and the Whitney brothers; *Un Chien Andalou,
L'Age d'Or, The Cabinet of Dr. Caligari, Potemkin, Le Sang
d'un Poète, Lot in Sodom*; Maya Deren's trilogy and her *Study
in Choreography for Camera*; Peterson's *The Lead Shoes* and
The Petrified Dog; Harrington's *Fragment of Seeking* and *On
the Edge*; Broughton's *Mother's Day*; Anger's *Fireworks, Inauguration of the Pleasure Dome,* and *Scorpio Rising*; Brakhage's *Desistfilm, Reflections on Black, Flesh of Morning* and
The Dead (to which can be added, with reservations, his *Anticipation of the Night* and passages from *The Art of Vision;*
the Maas-Moore *Narcissus* (influenced by the Cocteau of *Orpheus* and *Beauty and the Beast*) ; the international festival
prize winner *Dom*; Genet's *Un Chant d'Amour*; a set of Marie
Menken's brief films; Cassavetes' *Shadows*; Storm De Hirsch's
Third Eye Butterfly; Emshwiller's dance films and his *Relativity;* Warhol's *Harlot, Lonesome Cowboys, My Hustler,* and
The Chelsea Girls; Morrissey's *Flesh*; Rice's *The Flower Thief*;
Bruce Connor's *Cosmic Ray*; *Blonde Cobra, Flaming Creatures,*
and *No President*; Boultenhouse's *Handwritten* and *Dionysius*;
Markopoulos' *Twice a Man* and *The Illiac Passion*; Chris
Marker's *The Jetty*; Shirley Clarke's *The Connection* and *Portrait of Jason*; Bruce Baillie's haiku film, *Mr. Hayashi*; the
abstract painter Bolotowsky's *Metanoia* (a very pure essay in
magical photography and ritual movement by human figures) ;
Touching, Tom Tom, Star-Spangled to Death; Jonas Mekas'
filming of the play, *The Brig* (which shows it as more than ever
a harsh gymnastic ballet) ; and *Echoes of Silence*—with *The
Mirage* and *No More Fleeing*—all these form the central canon
of avant-garde into Underground that is essential for study
by young filmmakers, or indeed by any critic interested in
comprehending the history of serious independent filmmaking.
The chronology, from about 1920 to the present, is covered by

188

this archive of relevant films; I have not mentioned *all* relevant films, simply those that seem to me *mainly* relevant.

We must imagine a rather complicated dynamic situation provided by the canon as I have just constituted it. There are, in effect, two dynamic movements: toward and away from the idea of film as essentially a formal craft taking its place along with the tradition of the elder arts. A centripetal movement may be imagined in opposition to a centrifugal movement. There is a group of recent films which are "sound" in obeying the centripetal movement—for example, films by Lloyd Williams—which show a laudable sense of craftsmanship and readily embark on fantasy yet do not reveal any one really distinguished manifestation. Williams' "major statement" film, *Line of Apogee*, shown at the 1967 international festival in Belgium, is a generic avant-garde film, pure in intention, conscientious in execution, and yet lacking high spark, sure touch, and a personal film style. In this case the filmmaker's dreams have been copied as literally as possible, the result being the history of a neurosis that amounts to a symbolic self-portrait going from early childhood to young manhood.

On the other hand, to select a typical case from the opposite trend, Paul Morrissey (currently Warhol's chief assistant) made some early films with interesting story ideas but cast in a lean, straightforward narrative convention like old-fashioned commercial film, and with nonprofessional actors not up to their parts. The only exception in Morrissey's early, more ambitious films is one thrillingly photogenic young actor with a personality of his own. The better of the two films in which this actor appears, however, is no more than a series of incidents parallel with those in *The Flower Thief*—that is, designed to express a single character—and on the whole this Morrissey film, *Civilization and Its Discontents*, has neither the drive nor the conclusive form of Ron Rice's work.

The chief handicap of the Underground school of centrifugal movement—*away from* integrative form and style—is that its virtues are random and fragmentary, mixed irresponsibly with all kinds of defacements and embarrassing letdowns. Alas for all adult and fine-art values, these same defacements and letdowns have become sacred to some Underground cultists. To separate formal virtues from vices in any degree commensurate with the number of films involved would not be worthwhile because such a listing would become intolerably repetitious. If the worst fault of the tacit Underground creed is lack of form and true filmic esprit, it is because far too many young filmmakers start out with the smug assumption that any form of anti-art is per se interesting and significant so long as it has the look of self-expression—especially that collective self-expression typical of the pad crowded with one's fun-loving friends. Underground Film has informally taken over an old vice of commercial films, the Star Vehicle, but in collective as well as individual senses. It doesn't matter what "happens" in a film: the Underground spirit is expressed in the group star and in super-starmania. The only "form" discovered by this still active school of film is the Happening, and the cruelly objective fact is that the Happening is fact becoming a cliché (as parlor games always become). By now a filmed Happening is usually just a fashion-mad cliché in cold storage.

With this summation of the opposition to the avant-garde in the Underground—the school that equates anti-Establishment with anti-art—we may proceed to a look at what it means to make a significant filmic statement; that is, a *major* statement regardless of how "personal" or up-to-the-minute its conscious intention may be.

basic film forms

It is not the revolutionary politics of *Potemkin*, either local or universal, that makes it a great film, but the plastic intelligence of Eisenstein which understood it, and could project it, *as an epic form*. One would be mistaken to think that the epic, the myth, and the lyric (simply because literature and the dramatic stage preceded the film) are necessarily *literary* forms. The myth as literature implies a brief story from the lives of the gods; doubtless its most ancient form was a chant, or words declaimed to musical measure. If film, no matter what the theme, is not to be considered a cleverly animated photograph album, then (quite aside from its frequent use of speech) it exists in time sequence just as the novel does. To refer back to the aesthetic formulation of horizontal and vertical develop-ment, the proper distinction between a lyric film and a narrative film has nothing necessarily to do with words, either spoken or printed. Within literary terms, at the same time, the novel and the lyric have differences corresponding to those between the narrative (horizontal) and the lyric film (vertical). In the film of ritual or mythic pattern, as we have seen in discussing *The Lead Shoes, Dionysius,* and the Deren trilogy, a story may also be involved, though without having novelistic complexity.

Hence all distinguishable general forms, in literature or film, come under the one head of statements *meaningful in terms of a complete action.* These forms are not static and wholly exclusive of each other but represent typical and flexible concepts of human behavior and consciousness. Ever since Joyce's *Ulysses* it has been rumored that "historically" the novel is dead. It is true that Proust and Joyce, early in the century, broke the rules of the novel's conventional structure and especially, in *Ulysses,* the convention of a unified and even prose style. We find in *Ulysses* uniformity of style turned into an eclecticism of language compassing straight dialogue and the interior monologue and at times high parody of journalistic reporting, scientific terminology, the sentimental novel, and even the antique principle of the dramatic unities (the time span of *Ulysses* is one day and the action is in one city). All the same the basic idea of *Ulysses* is the *epic*: the lifetime adventure of a great hero. It would be more accurate to say of this work, rather than that it announced the novel's death, that it revealed its resurrection.

Following *Ulysses,* however, came Joyce's last revolutionary contribution to literary form: *Finnegans Wake.* This is the apotheosis of a hero's dream life, a revision of consciousness and therefore a revision of style. While the generic Common Man is technically its hero, it remains epic in just the sense that a great ritual poem such as *The Divine Comedy* remains epic. Radically, Joyce chose the portmanteau word as the pivot of his language and made it, moreover, polylingual, so that *Finnegans Wake* is an invented palimpsest of meanings whose layers have to be carefully analyzed to even begin being intelligible.

We must notice how *Finnegans Wake* has been converted into filmic terms by the independent filmmaker Mary Ellen Bute. Called, in its finally edited form, *Passages from Finnegans Wake* (1967), it is a set of visual illustrations which are, rightly speaking, *inferred* from the complex façade of the work's portmanteau or multidimensional style; that is, the physical action tightly interwoven with the difficult tapestry of Joyce's prose has been abstracted by photographing some of its main story features. What has happened is that Miss Bute, instead of reproducing the dreamlike atmosphere of the book by filmic manners such as multiple exposure, meltings, and daring transitions, has (while relying on the spoken word as guide) sought out the most concrete action behind the words as being the most susceptible of transposition into regular physical terms. We see naturalistically filmed actors, naturalistically filmed sets—a dream world transposed back to the very sense of place and physical reality which it was the aim of Joyce's language to displace and dematerialize into placelessness and pure mirage. In the most accurate sense Miss Bute has created a simplifying film scenario from a given literary text of great complexity. Her film becomes a Surrealist version of the work's transcendental action because it photographs people and things in their true physical aspect, regardless of their strange relationships and the necessarily illogical sequence of the continuous dream action.

Exactly this, of course, is what happened to both *Finnegans Wake* and *Ulysses* in the stage versions made from them. That of the former became a dance pantomime with words and music, *The Coach with the Six Insides*, performed by Jean Erdman and her company. As theater, it was a remarkably successful and a very perspicacious (necessarily edited) adaptation of the original. Miss Bute's film, as courageous and enterprising as it is, turns out to be not so successfully edited an adaptation. Her chief error, I think, was to neglect rather than exploit the more resourceful filmic devices for making the physical world illusory and changefully fluid, compact with the sort of visual hallucination conveyed by Joyce's prose.

Ed Emshwiller's *Relativity* deals with much the same sort of material as *Finnegans Wake*, in that it shows us the night-mind experiences of an ordinary Little Man and telescopes both life and death into the dream state. Much more restricted, and starting with much simpler premises, *Relativity* still creates a fluid, shifting kind of vision that is more relevant to Joyce's visually kaleidoscopic prose. Such a film as Miss Bute's *Passages* is to be classed among filmic "translations," the fact being that, in trying as it were to make the densely elliptic more coherent, more lucid, she has brought Joyce's work as close as possible to conventional film narrative.

In a parallel way, the film version of *Ulysses*, made by Joseph Strick, also conventionalized the original work by inflecting it toward the traditional novel as usually transposed to the screen. Some of it, well acted, turns out very creditably in this respect, but such scenes are exactly the ones which in the original use the most nearly conventional novelistic techniques. When it comes to Joyce's elaborate stylistic parodies, and especially to the sustained fantasy of the Nighttown, or Walpurgisnacht, episode, which is full of Stephen's drunken hallucinations, the film falls down badly. It should have been evident that the only method by which to interpret the violence and visual grandeur of these scenes would be a broader, more pungent style of acting bolstered by the rich optical manipulations of which film is capable. As it is, the Nighttown scenes are little more than animated slides and the fantasy element turns out to be very weak. As respectful, and in many ways as intelligent, an adaptation as the film made from *Ulysses* is, it must be added to the large historic group of commercial failures to equate filmic versions of novels with the original works.

The ethics of film history, I maintain, must obey a rule

that criticizes all efforts, Underground, avant-garde, and independent no less than routine commercial work, from the viewpoint of a *basic filmic enlightenment,* of which the true avant-
garde film is, be it added, the abiding torch. This torch
illuminates the basic film forms as sustained in works (however
long or short) that have a true and deep visionary scheme.
This is why *The Cabinet of Dr. Caligari* and *Potemkin* are as
much "underground" films, historically considered, as anything by Maya Deren, Andy Warhol, or Gregory Markopoulos.
If today's avant-garde position, as I believe, is vulnerable because of the bad habits and bad standards of the Underground,
this state of things can be historically explained by the fact
that the more imaginative of Europe's leading commercial filmmakers have lately adapted the avant-garde spirit by making
works that are neither routine commercial scenarios nor con-
ventionalizing adaptations from radically different literary
works like *Finnegans Wake.* Take Resnais' *Last Year at Marienbad,* Antonioni's *Blowup,* Fellini's *8½,* Bergman's *Persona,*
and almost any film by Jean-Luc Godard. All are works, like
true avant-garde works, written *for the screen* (the brief story
on which *Blowup* was based provided merely the germ of
Antonioni's film, which resulted in a totally different work).

It is not only that these films are filmically more adept
than most so-called Underground films, but that (as futile and
trivial as most Godard films are) they are more filmically
ingenious and more generally imaginative. It seems to me that
the contrary position—namely, that all these works are obliquely
tainted by commercial formulas—can be founded only on an
arbitrary desire to support the ideal of the small-cult film, the
film (whatever its proportions) that is "little" because it is
economically underprivileged and "big" because it insists on the
absolute primacy of the "personal statement" apart from all
aesthetic credentials.

There is no reason why firmness of outline, a shapely plot
sense, and a feeling for "musical" form (that is, poetry in the

largest and best sense) should be considered defects or taints just because such things are sometimes the approximate achievements of films mechanically to be classified as commercial. For such are also the achievements of the best avant-garde films still being circulated in our Underground era. If commercially produced films can approach an independent art and mature the art of the film, it would seem that, rather than commercial films' having profited as a result, the film art has suffered where it hurts the most—in the avant-garde! For apparently the avant-garde's militant Underground prefers anything (even self-destruction) to resembling the commercial category with its classic taint—a taint which, in fact, is sometimes a baseless superstition.

No matter what charges may be laid against Underground films of recent years, the small independent avant-garde as a whole can always come up with a fresh approach, a new technical method, an isolated "idea," even though such virtues may be wasted in imaginatively poor and inept ventures in filmmaking. One of the most loyal of customers for independent film products, as rented from their distributing organizations, has been the big television studios, which screen them privately for the sake of borrowing tricks from them. The sad irony is that some technical feat, some piece of Underground ingenuity, is exactly what, since it is free-floating, is the easiest to steal. Not in the "imaginative" works shown on TV are the best montage and technical effects to be seen, but in the commercials that intersperse these works. For one thing, the commercials must be very short—sometimes less than a minute—so that the trickier they look, the better. A technical device can be easily abstracted from its context and duplicated in whatever terms are desired. What cannot be stolen, on the other hand, is the precise imaginative context in which the device appears, for that context is an original art—that is, the very opposite of a technical device.

history and manifesto

This book has a conception of history itself that is specific and positive. As I indicated earlier, recorded history should be more than a complicated set of statistics taking up a lot of space; such an apparatus is worth nothing if the historian fails to establish the existence of cause and effect in action or fails, above all, to imbue such an account of true relationships with a system of values.

Take the useful example of Abel Gance, whose formal devices in *Napoléon* I have just been describing.* When we see a still from this film composed of the triplicate screen, showing one panoramic vista as Napoleon surveys his troops from a cliff to one side, we observe the plastic form of a large military camp; in another such scene of the same army, now arrayed in marching order, another plastic form is presented: soldiers on each side march toward a third scene in the center. Both scenes

* Though an authentic version of Gance's film was shown at the Fifth New York Film Festival, in 1967, it entirely omitted the triplicate screen.

reveal a collective organism capable of extension into battle action. In other words, an army is an activist form governed by certain basic laws of both passive discipline and active battle-strategy.

In film, an army is a changing unit worked along with the plastic design of each separate shot of it. The "chaos" of many battles is well known. Yet the chaotic aspect of war exists for individuals and small units that are surrounded by what may look like (and to some extent be) confusion mainly because of the narrowness of immediate perspectives. History can look the same way as a battle does if immediate, limited perspectives are not transcended by an overall conception of form, a visionary logic of action. The most confused battle in a work of film art can be photographed as something with a visible plastic logic—something with beauty. Just so could a military analyst figure out afterward the inherent logic of some great battle in which both armies, at various times, lost their bearings.

When I compared Gance's deliberate organization of his triptych screen with Warhol's generally makeshift duplex screen in *The Chelsea Girls*, the point was a very important one. So far as the effect goes, Warhol could have meant the device of the double screen from the beginning, since his film tells of various supposed residents of the Chelsea Hotel and their friends; the film's actions, to all intents and purposes, are simultaneous in time if separate in actual space. This spatial separateness and contiguity is expressed by the side-by-side reels being simultaneously run off. Although they are related in mood (all the actors are hippie-bohemian types enjoying trips of different sorts) there is no conscious "musical" relation between the two units, any chiming between them being, presumably, accidental. But of course there do occur certain amusing coincidences that, while the two scenes are technically in competition with one another, give off mutual rhyme and reason; for example, one actress (Mary Might, now Mary Woronow), while acting a domineering, exhibitionistic lesbian in one scene, takes the part of a young man's shy, mute fiancée in the contiguous scene; here, since the two actions could not be physically simultaneous, the dualistic dimension is purely psychological: two personalities of the same individual.

Like all Warhol films, *The Chelsea Girls* has drag-time sections as well as sections that hold the interest. The duplex device is helpful because of the tension of trying to take in two scenes at once; it provides an artificial sort of mental stimulation to make up for the lack of development in both scenes. All the same, a certain force builds up attention because most of the actors are plainly indulging in their own sorts of hallucination, usually conveyed in monologue and dialogue as well as limited action; there is very little moving into or out of the camera range, although now and then the optical set-up is altered within the same scene. This holding on as if for dear life to single-scene action, usually mild as such, is both fixated and to some extent fixating. It creates a spectator suspense that does not go entirely unrewarded, as when the quarrel between the fake psychiatrist and his fake patient bursts into sadism when (on the eventual return of the scene) he beats her up.

This male character (played by Ondine) is a homosexual megalomaniac whose obsession is to imagine himself the Pope. His victim also appears in other scenes as a passive lesbian type over whom dominant lesbian types can run roughshod. A residential community (the hotel) is also a community of sexual and nervous sensibility—and here is the visionary plan of Warhol's film that makes it, despite all its faults of clumsiness and ineptitude, important. The time stretch (temporal anamorphosis) acquires for the spectator a kind of reluctantly accepted weight. One senses that these people are acting within a different duration from one's own—that is, in drug time rather than clock time—and their more or less hysterical monologues and desultory wrangles convey this psychically contagious state (at least to some degree) to many spectators.

What I have called the terrifyingly childlike quality of

Underground films emerges proudly and with some effect in *The Chelsea Girls*. As many films I have discussed prove, neither the child nor the madman can be overlooked as valid dimensions of Underground aesthetics. It is just that only in a very few films does childlike or lunatic imagination achieve real poetic articulation, and then perhaps but fragmentarily. Both Jack Smith and Taylor Mead, actors with mad and infantile qualities, have only "moments": they cannot quite dominate the form of the films in which they appear any more than Warhol's actors can dominate his films; Gerard Malanga, for instance, seems to dominate *Vinyl*, and Paul America *My Hustler*, only because the films themselves disintegrate around them. A character, establishing his personality, can create a whole mood, even a limited ambience, but not a whole action— and the art of the film must base itself on whole actions.

Flaming Creatures (as well as its successor, *No President*) is another example of an offbeat erotic sensibility (male transvestite) which is powerful enough, despite all technical filmic handicaps, to create a cohesive atmosphere in which appears the dim vision of a communal muse and the gestures of an authentic rite. If the gestures are gelatinous, rather fragmented even when brilliant, this is owing entirely to lack of imaginative discipline—lack of that shunned thing, artistic conscience. The film's climax—the cunnilingual rape—is expressed with calculated crudity and very primitive photography. This climax to a great deal of transvestite posing around literally begins to shake the room in which it takes place: there are jostlings, slanted angles, and a chandelier sways perilously, as if in an earthquake. The final shots are of the orgy, photographed from above, in a shapeless mass on the floor and experiencing its exhausted farewell tremors. Beyond doubt the filmmaker, Jack Smith, has set down a fantasy eloquent because of its very grotesqueness, the uneven result of madly obsessive emotion.

Warhol's main strength in filmmaking is still as a kind of

personality promoter who can pick real performers and knows enough not to let the camera interfere with them. This strength is in the *visionary plan* which distinguishes his more ambitious films: he has exposed certain type sensibilities whose efforts to achieve their identity molds, à la psychodrama, are recorded by a passive film camera. The "house plan" of *The Chelsea Girls* has the virtue of concentrating a set of performing personalities into a collective mold. Are the personalities inept, unfledged? That is their Underground charm. In a sense the same is true of *Flaming Creatures*: the implication of visionary plan is there because of the cumulative force of a communal mood, at once inspired and rather preposterous (i.e., campy). Such achieved unity (though it may be too lax) is outside the workings of the conventional plot because its "script" is finally the result of collaboration between story idea, director, and actors.

To approximate the regular plot logic and at the same time create a special spontaneity by letting the actors ad lib and improvise their own gestures is a difficult feat, but it was attained by John Cassavetes in his extraordinary film, *Shadows* (1957), done with relatively inexperienced actors and nonprofessionals. Aiming at an effect of cinéma vérité, it belongs to the avant-garde because of its success in avoiding commercial cliché and the positive ease it displays in catching people so realistically in dialogue scenes that one might suspect a hidden camera. The story concerns a couple who are younger half-brother and -sister to a Negro jazz player. They are so light in skin color as to pass, if they wish, for white. We witness the ordeal of their temptation to deny their Negro identity and join a different social world. Their decision is difficult especially because of the kindness of their black half-brother, who is willing to support them as they live in suspense, drifting, hesitating, and completely dependent on him. A young white man suddenly falls in love with the girl and the mutual crisis of brother and sister is set into dramatic motion. At the end, after shock and trouble and bitterness, they seem unable to break with their Negro social identity. The same plot could have been sham and a miserable anticlimax of "good" intentions. But Cassavetes achieved the very rare feat of making it real with an uncompromising use of vérité technique. Unfortunately, after that Cassavetes seemed lost in the arms of Hollywood, where he was first a director and then an actor. Nevertheless, *Shadows* survives as a unique specimen of independent filmmaking, a courageously poetic use of cinéma vérité.

More than ten years later, I was surprised to see Cassavetes come forward at the 1968 New York Film Festival with *Faces*, a film made not for a commercial studio, but on his own, with a dedicated cast who for three years had worked (whenever they could get together) without pay. All were rewarded with a very successful first run in New York City. The title itself came as a pleasant surprise too, for in an article I did for *Film Culture* in 1963 I had written of *Too Late Blues*, a film Cassavetes made for Paramount: "In all his characters . . . we see head-on (in pitiless, breath-taking close-ups of faces and speeches) the automatic reflexes of daily, hourly emotions." It was the vivid authenticity of the *faces* that stood out in my recollection of *Too Late Blues*. By no means a perfect film, *Faces* explores with rich results the same terrain of human nature as the previous film, but more patiently and intensively, as the director always wished to explore it.

Along with the virtues of Cassavetes' method (really a revival of "human interest") come certain defects which it is a critic's duty to notice. None of the actors is a star; some had little or no professional experience. All are interesting and some are very good indeed. I don't think the mature male lead, John Marley, is varied or lucid enough for the great expressive burden which he and his face, like the rest, must carry. Yet Seymour Cassel and the chief female players are up to the mark in proving just how vivid, appealing, and meaningful an actor, properly directed and photographed, can be. Cassavetes has the depth method in dealing with his players and is tireless in getting the most out of them; unhampered by "studio schedules," he brought out their best. The discarded portions of *Faces*, for example, are much, much longer than the long feature film we see: whole shooting sessions were stopped or thrown away because one actor or another couldn't strike the right note in a scene.

So relentlessly explorative a method, concentrating at length on human behavior in given situations, is hard to manage, especially in the final editing stage. Thus *Faces* has a little "underground" informality and monotony to contend with. I feel that Cassavetes should work less experimentally and more consciously, more with a dominant idea in view. Once more the problem is that of form and plot. How "easy" is it to do without a positive conception of story climax, without clear character motivation? In this realistic study of middle-class sexuality, both on- and offbeat, Cassavetes assumes that human motives today tend to be mercurial and rather bafflingly opaque to the interior individual, that people are still "repressed" as well as frustrated, that love and its behavioral laws are still puzzlingly elusive. This is a rather safe, rather traditional modern proposition. The final issue must be that of aesthetic and dramatic values. How much "humanity" can be revealed, how beautifully and how excitingly, by this deep-digging, leveling-out inspection of the commonplace?

Personally, I would complain of the general inconclusiveness of *Faces* as well as a certain meagerness in its imaginative outlook. I think Cassavetes has a lingering documentarist fault, a desire to accept human nature in a dimension where it is too commonplace, too passive. He needs more boldness, more intellectual incisiveness, and above all he should cultivate more *filmic* sensibility.

underground film

A filmmaker working in Europe, Chris Marker, with two films shown at the First New York Film Festival, in 1963, provides a startling confirmation of arguments in behalf of formal vision, meaningful plan, as against loose, naïve documentary technique. One film is *The Jetty*, the other *The Koumiko Mystery*. The latter is another personality portrait, not done head-on, in complete confidence with the subject (a Japanese girl met while Marker was filming the Olympic Games in Tokyo), but rather by way of an interview in cinéma vérité style. The film makes no attempt to penetrate consciously proffered, merely polite surfaces; it is a sort of sensitively photographed album of animated studies of the girl Koumiko. Nothing comes from inside her or the filmmaker, except what one may casually make of her answers to rather conventional questions. The whole thing seems a sentimentally indulged caprice.

Quite the contrary, *The Jetty* is an intense, imaginative piece of filmmaking which depends for its form on the psychological flashback, here told very effectively with still frames selected from a regular film. The skip time—also skip space, since the action is filmed originally was continuous—becomes extremely eloquent as, under the influence of a drug, a man relives or imagines a love affair. The method is apt because, either with or without drugs, the memory is made up of visual pieces which the mind strings together to make a coherent action; even if one invents an action, it is likely to be "true." The idyllic affair leads up to an unexpected incident on a pier (the jetty), when a fighting plane sweeps out of the sky and kills the dreamer.

The planetary time of *The Jetty* is the future, when society will have been driven underground by radioactivity on the surface and the remnant of mankind (so scientific experts say) cannot survive beyond the current generation since everyone has become sterile. The ideal escape from reality is thus the use of this dangerous drug, permitting the subject to live a dream life of past or future but causing pain and perhaps death. The question left hanging is whether the man has been dreaming the past or the future. Marker's skip time, literally the other extreme of Warhol's unblinking solid time, is another temporal anamorphosis, one with holes as it were, so that the emergency economy of time by which people live desperately in a post-atomic period is melodramatically staggered by a super-speed-up induced by a drug. There is no time for "psychology" or "motivation" in this human action. It is entirely objective in its physicality, while its emotional and psychic content is perfectly lucid—that is, has a form determined by beginning and end.

We have only to turn to the example of Maya Deren's films to see that even the filmmaker's own most secret self can be objectively plotted (just as much so as in *The Jetty*), provided he is a good enough filmmaker. I have called the Deren trilogy a symbolic autobiography. In any case, the heroine we see in her films is a high-keyed, deeply neurotic and subtle personality whose love life is clearly, if also mysteriously, charted for us in the form of a surreal fable full of dream symbolism, such as automatic shift of identity and a variety of object symbols undergoing metamorphosis. The work has the pervasive pattern of the stages of an elaborate ordeal. Without a concrete grasp of film rhythm (which Miss Deren seemed, as a trained dancer, to know instinctively), without a whole and shapely idea into whose action she could mold her personality, the satisfying self-portrait she achieved could never have been brought off. On grounds of strict taste one could quarrel with details of Miss Deren's execution, but they are no more than details.

The profoundest sense of film form is not merely an instinctive and musically replete rhythm but moreover a sense of human action as importantly centered in certain ritual incidents and episodes which can be ordered by such a rhythm. This kind of action automatically creates about it those harmonious frames or margins which are able to contain it comfortably, in which it can rest (find its stable center) as well as move with freedom.. It is avant-garde film which teaches us the still "underground" fact that aesthetic space is as relativist as the advanced scientific conception of real space. Otherwise how could we feel the cosmic dimension of an ingenious "pad" film such as *Handwritten*—made from the pages of a book of verse, some Paleolithic drawings, a simple pantomime by the poet, broken glass, the illusion of a starry sky, and spoken poetry? All the *Finnegans Wake* films do not have to be based on Joyce's work. The form of the book actually implies principles of fluid transition, sudden spatial shifts, and multiple dimensions of time/space that are found in the more imaginative avant-garde films.

It is right here, however, that a distinction of immense importance is to be made between medium and message—unless we wish to bow to the fatal premise of Marshall McLuhan that a medium, in effect, has nothing to say, all it has to do is to alter and complicate and contradict its own form. There are certain technologists of the avant-garde—VanDerBeek, Landow, Kubelka come to mind—who spend all their time thinking of more or less fruitful ways of modifying the image produced simply by pointing a camera at something and faithfully registering it (Warhol has overparodied that same antediluvian occupation). The ambience of mixed media has suggested to a good portion of the present Underground that the way to achievement lies entirely within the bounds of sensation as produced by extraordinary technical effects (as in *Dom* and *Wave-length*). We ought to remember that "technical effects" is a unit of the commercial agglomeration and always (quite aside from ordinary montage or editing methods) had a role in filling out commercial-establishment films—for example, interpolating dreams into naturalistic action.

If we regard the new historic function of the Underground as complicating our sensations, as producing optical effects for us analogous to, or predicated on, psychedelic states, we have to

esteem the technologists' researches as more important than anything which might be termed a "story," a "poem," a "complete
action," or even an "emotion," for an emotion is not an instantaneous optical reflex but must be tested in the whole con-
tinuum of experience. We have to cope with the challenge of a
new concept of "aesthetics" itself, one that might be called the
new magic-lantern image of film. This concept puts us in the
midst of a type of filmmaking which completely revises naturalistic fiction and documentary ways of looking at life by providing more complex versions of the old magician's tricks that the
movies did so well at the turn of the century.

Nowadays, by using normal or distorting mirrors, by instant
television, by filming film (and using it perhaps upside-down),
by projecting on irregular surfaces, one can get all sorts of eerie
effects that render performers into doubles and even triples and
create a world (an "environment") that parallels the world
perceived in drug states or dream states. Such filmic experiments, when concentrated and limited to action as formulated
by Happenings, have nothing but optical sensations to offer,
sensations that seem to change the individual consciousness by
duplicating it in time and space, modulating normal vision, and
making human beings perform mechanical actions with a minimum of intelligible meaning. Taken far enough as an end in
itself, such avant-garde activity can be chimed with a very old
occupation of the human race: that concerning itself with human existence on transcendental planes. But such activity also
turns film history into something like science fiction without the
romance, without the old-fashioned adventure narrative—
whether of the comic-strip type or not.

The most stylish avant-garde technology of film, as a department of the Underground, simply proposes that human experience as a whole be discarded in favor of enlarging and complicating human perceptions (optical and perhaps aural). *What*
is perceived, and *who* perceives it, or in what kind of life situa-

tion, all have nothing to do with the case. *Finnegans Wake,* on the contrary, is a revision of the mode of human consciousness *because it is a total revision of the novel,* not merely in the technical sense (as a mode of perception) but as the totality we know humanly, and perhaps superhumanly, as life-and-death. Some Underground films, like Brakhage's later work, have a scope of vision which indeed implies the life experience *in the abstract* by certain isolated tokens, but which *in practice* results in little more than miles and miles of modes of perception, merely an elaborate, if sometimes pleasantly exciting, irritation of the retina. Each shot is a subliminal "environment."

All the latest Underground Film toggery for "seeing new" may be legitimately exciting as research pointing toward great possibilities. Assuredly! All might be used in the service of some *future* realization of a "script" such as Joyce provided in *Finnegans Wake.* Yet meanwhile all this technological research must be classified as strictly experimental. "As is," as historic attainment, on the other hand, it is a new variety of parlor trick for the sophisticated.

But if all film, and especially avant-garde film, is to be conceived as the history of an ever maturing art, then we move automatically to a quite different perspective—to, I think, the correct perspective, in which the anatomy of the avant-garde movement can actually be described and systematized. If, as I contend, the ritual forms, the epic sensibility, the mythic premise, the identifiable human situation are mutually indispensable to the true history of Underground Film (Underground Film being an evolution of avant-garde film), then we have to evaluate that history as I have been trying to evaluate it.

There are difficulties, yes, and of course those difficulties must be admitted and dealt with. For example, if the sense of life naturally sustains a continuity of ritual forms (not necessarily related to a particular religion or transcendental system), we must note that this is contrary to the historic inspirations of

Dadaism and Surrealism, to which we have already given attention as authentic developments of the avant-garde. A ritual ordeal such as that in *Le Sang d'un Poète* is schematic and archetypal, however special and elite, so that it precludes the pure automatism of the Surrealist canon as well as the detached free-form absurdism of Dada. Assessing the Underground Film as a whole, at this historic moment, tells us that its decisions about procedure, logically derived though they are from Dada and Surrealist modes, have resulted in practical Underground errors: numerous films that do no more than display self-indulgent obsessions where one might have expected personal adventurousness and plastic imagination. As we have noted, performing personalities often account for the Underground showcase film, whose roots in certain formal premises *might* have led to much more significant ends. He whom we may call the avant-garde technologist, drunk on a technical innovation, becomes the "performing personality" behind the screen. What we have *on* the screen, however much a sensation, is only the showcase itself, tagged with the filmmaker's name. He is giving us anti-Establishment "entertainment."

Yet it would be quite wrong to think all such work amounts to posturing. On the contrary, some young filmmakers who have been working in relative obscurity (perhaps only because they are *too* serious) are technically ingenious and also have a gift for true film. Paul Sharits is one of the newcomers who are not content with simply mirroring the life style of a recently awakened, beat-into-hippie generation, but have developed almost a mania for the filmic, for intensive manipulation of images and sounds and time. This may be reflected even in the most casual Underground filmmaking, such as Jonas Mekas' *Diaries*, a work in perpetual progress; sometimes an episode is all fast motion with incidental frozen frames and glimpses of natural motion. Sharits, however, plays assiduously with distortion of regular projection, treating film somewhat as John

209

Cage has treated the piano: he "prepares" it and issues such comments as: "Projector as pistol/audience as screen/time-colored pills/yes = no." More sensibly, he writes of his *Ray Gun Virus* (1966), "This film must be shown in a completely darkened room. Sprockets are to be played at sound speed [twenty-four frames per second]; volume set louder than usual; tone set at bass."

His 1969 effort, *Touching*, is probably his most novel and impressive work, relatively brief in that into its running time is packed a speeded-up action of two repeated shots modulated by changing color and negatives as well as skip-editing; that is, selected moments from the original, naturally filmed action following each other at subliminal speed. Chiefly, we are shown only the nude bust of an attractive young male in hippie-style hairdo who performs one act and promptly submits to another. The first is to raise a beglittered pair of scissors to his mouth as if to cut off his protruding tongue; the second is to allow a woman's hand to draw its beglittered nails across his cheeks as if clawing them. The effect of the monotonous jerky changes, created by omitting fractional moments of action, together with the incessant change of color, natural and artificial, is that of a Freudian horror dream of castration under strobe-lighting (perpetual quick flash on-and-off). Meanwhile, on the sound-track, the young man's voice doggedly repeats the refrain of one word, "Destroy," each syllable heavily emphasized.

Gradually, however, owing to ensuing variations in this sound, we begin hearing what seems like whole sentences—according to my ear, "His girl—destroyed—his jaw." Seemingly this was pure psychological suggestion, owed to the fact that, besides pronouncing the word in different ways, the man's voice was fractionally "looped back" on the sound track so as to give the word, eventually, distinct variations. Eventually I heard: "His girl—destroyed—his straw." Other auditors heard different phrases, though not a complete sentence. The last

variation, with the word "straw," was doubtless purely suggestive because, interspersing the action just described, came
periodic if very fleeting glimpses of what seemed to me (1)
opened female thighs and (2) a straw swirling water. Later I
was told by Sharits that the first fleeting image was actually a
view of sexual intercourse and the second a surgical instrument
caught while removing an eye cataract. This is a tricky, highly
compressed film which exploits, compulsively, a very limited
fantasy. Yet as a surrealist tour de force it is richer and more
amusing than most extremist "pad" films.

Michael Snow, who made the international-prize-winning
Wave-length, is going further, more ambitiously into intensive
technique. A very recent film, *Back and Forth*, is almost all in
color and is based on a single camera "pan" from one side of a
college classroom to another. The sound track has two knocks,
like the separated ticktock of a clock or a metronome wired for
sound, heard automatically when the right and left limits of the
swinging "pan" are reached. This optic/aural device goes on
continuously, with minor variations, for about fifty minutes, as
if the camera and the sounds had the hang-up of some very
bored student having a mild nightmare. At different points,
dreamlike, various figures appear outside the windows and
inside the classroom, first at the right or the left while the
metronomic camera eye is at its opposite limit. Also perpetually
heard is a rhythmic, rather wheel-like clangor that periodically
accelerates and then decelerates. Once it is so fast as to seem
the sound of a racing railroad train; at this point the panning
too has reached a crescendo of speed, so that the empty classroom and its windows have the blur of an actual train dashing
past.

All this is very suggestive and intriguing if your interest is
geared to it. The casual human incidents interspersing it are
collective and commonplace: students in their chairs listening
to an instructor, a pair of lovers enjoying a sneaked rendezvous,

a social gathering in which two men have a friendly sparring match. An air of dedicated experimentalism imbues such film-making as Snow's: inventive rather than imaginative, compulsive rather than inspired. Here the academic subject matter is not irrelevant; the technical liveliness itself becomes "academic" because it is so repetitious and because of its accent on the abstract plastics of film photography.

Just as dedicated, and more deeply situated, is the plastic exercise created by Ken Jacobs in a film which, though it has had a "première," can be said to be still "in progress." This in-progress note is, of course, typical of the experimental film laboratory. Jacobs shows us a film (explicitly copyrighted in 1905) about the nursery-rhyme fable of "Tom, Tom the Piper's Son." Jacobs names it *Tom, Tom*, doubtless a pun on its aspects of repetition. It is a silent film throughout. We see (in the usual single set-up of old films via static camera) the tightrope act of a traveling circus, spectators milling in the foreground, a fight among them, a somersaulting clown, and then, when Tom has stolen the fabled pig, the wild, funny chase he is given by the villagers and his eventual capture.

First Jacobs shows us the slapstick, childish comedy, brief but entire, just as it survives in its jumpy original movement. Then (in line with the manipulations of *Dom*) he proceeds to reconstruct the entire action in a most interesting fashion by certain ways of refilming it. He concentrates on details of the original as if in close-ups, tending to be more abstractly plastic the less he shows of the original frame, and varies the pace with frozen frames, slow motion, and reverse motion. Time as well as space is expanded, involuted, intensified. It is all a filmically creative inquiry into the possibilities of the dynamics of action, and its variations give us, as it were, an intensive kinaesthetic sensation of the actual violence of the absurd chase—climbing up inside chimneys, sliding down roofs, breaking down doors, escaping through windows, ending with Tom hauled up from a well, still clutching his pig.

Jacobs' pyrotechnics are far from shallow. Not only are we passed into the interior of the wild comic movement of the original film; that movement is strangely solemnized and even dramatized. Through holding on to certain images, overlapping and reversing them in time, and showing framed-off details closer, the filmmaker reveals a vital beauty of plastic pattern that was not noticeable before. At times one is reminded of Seurat's statuesque drawing, the quality of his Post-Impressionist technique corresponding to the crude black-and-white quality of the refilmed details. In other instances one seems to behold a strenuous figure by Delacroix or a placid "cubistic" detail from a picture by Chardin. One catches even the serene compactness of a Cubist still-life. Jacobs has provided so wonderful a demonstration of the virtues of basic montage that it is a pity I must add that his work here seems as much an expert lecture on filmmaking as a creative film. To end, he shows us the archaic original once more in its entirety. But his point is brilliantly illustrated. At this second viewing one recalls the details and variations he has shown us meanwhile, so that the very same action seems fraught now with a fresh plastic meaning: the total space/time sensation has been heightened by his deliberate filmic manipulations of the original material. Yet with less repetition, a shorter and more "musical" editing of his lengthy variations (the film adds up to 110 minutes), Jacobs would have a more creative film to his credit. I think his work would seem more magical, too, if he did not let us see the original film at all. As it is, his method reveals that obsessive temper of Underground experimentalism that continues to shun the ultimate creative commitment. Is this because the "message" in our day tends literally to disappear in the "massage"?

However that may be, let us turn again to Kenneth Anger

and Ed Emshwiller, filmmakers who have something on their minds besides tricks of technique (however creative those tricks may be in tendency). Both sensitive to the language of film, usually bold and temperamentally inventive, these men are still rather vulnerable when it comes to matters of taste and the ultimate finish known as style. Why, then, do their films belong to the central Underground canon? Because they have begun with a tangible idea of an imaginative sort. In *Scorpio Rising* (Anger) it is the fantasy of the Leather Boy cult; in *Thanatopsis* (Emshwiller) it is the traditional and apparently deathless symbolism of the aging male's vision of a young girl (here a dancer) as symbol of the renewal of virile powers; as, in short, death conceived as resurrection. The conception of filmic space as a dimension of ultimate freedom is of the greatest human importance in these two films: the position of man *in the cosmos* has been their concern.

In filmic space *the void itself is a ground.* We do not actually have to see the solidity of the plane on which a performer walks or dances or merely stands; it is necessarily taken for granted. Since filmic space so often omits showing the full-length figure, filmic stability depends on the convention of a continuous space of which we are shown discontinuous, necessarily fragmented pieces, but which are knit together by the action of those who move within that space or by the harmonious transition from one still background pattern to another: the kinetic principle of a shifted kaleidoscope. When we consider the skip time of *The Jetty* the modulative dominance of the action becomes very plain. Abstract animation, which properly speaking has only *back*ground, also makes this point: the movement itself—not the visibility of a surface supporting the movement—creates the space. Thus, aesthetically, the filmmaker is one who molds space the way a sculptor does his clay or the painter his paint. The achieved movement depends upon dynamic thrusts and the way they interlock, not upon the vertical equilibrium of a person, for example, standing stockstill or a building on its foundation. If modern skyscrapers are dull, it is because they look too much like mathematical shafts planted in the earth. Observe that Francis Thompson's *New York New York* makes urban buildings momentarily interesting by anamorphizing and levitating them. Or take the very different, Warhol-produced *Empire*—the Empire State Building viewed uninterruptedly from dusk to dawn; the interest is not in looking all that time at the same building from one viewpoint but at what the changing light, both in the sky and in the building, meanwhile does to the imagery. *Empire*, utterly futile and pretentious as a film to be sat through, remains a good blackboard illustration of this aesthetic point.

No matter how small a film may be, it must have a visionary plan to rate true interest as a film. In Menken's *Moonplay*, for example, the moon might be a single poker chip except for occasional atmospheric elements. The film's dynamism issues from the rhythm of its animation (the moon jumps from spot to spot) and the way it has been so well set off by Teiji Ito's remarkable music score. The presence of traditional mythic themes in avant-garde film, such as *Narcissus* and works by Gregory Markopoulos, is an interesting and suggestive one. Mythology is not only various sets of stories about the creation of the world and the lives of the gods, it is also a *sensibility*— and a sensibility with special relevance to filmic technique.

No individual filmmaker embodies the mythological sensibility and its poetic aura more than Markopoulos—and for this very reason, despite the international attention he has won, he is perhaps the most underrated member of the new avant-garde. His virtues of magical editing to create transcendent effects and his uncompromising eye for the beauty of the nude and its filmic possibilities (evident in one of his newest works, *The Illiac Passion*) do not emerge as pure and unblemished. As notably independent as he is, Markopoulos suffers from a care-

215

fully nourished quirk of the new avant-garde: an armored narcissism. Like many a filmmaker of lesser talents, he is blind to his own faults; more, he is oblivious to the theoretical virtue of self-criticism. Anything that comes to his mind is good because, and only because, it comes to *his* mind. This leads not only to the many lovely and thrilling effects of *The Illiac Passion* (1967) but also to misjudgment of the true value of image as metaphor and, perhaps more important, to misjudgment of the actor's true value in the metaphoric pattern.

Not all performers in *The Illiac Passion* are capable of projecting interesting personalities or of supplying plastically valuable images. Much of the mythological action which Markopoulos has designed for his film "in modern dress" goes flat because of the performers themselves or because of the director's notion that if his performers mechanically do as he tells them, something beautiful and magical necessarily will result. Some shots in *The Illiac Passion* mistake the ridiculous for the sublime without the ridiculous being in any sense an intended quantity in the aesthetic effect.

It would be unfair to say that Markopoulos lacks a sense of humor, but all the same it does not operate *critically*. At times there is a satiric edge, quite conscious, a notion of the beautifully absurd, as in scenes of a monumentally fat Venus and a svelte, painfully reticent Adonis; here the implications are usually sophisticated. But in other myths (notably the Orpheus and Eurydice) nothing works well. Neither scene nor actors are up to the inspiration of the earlier parts, such as those concerning Hyacinth and Narcissus. The film is consciously subjective, seriously playful, as a film poet's declared fantasy about the gods as centered in the events of Aeschylus' *Prometheus Bound.* Markopoulos' own voice supplies the mannered sound track; sometimes it is dramatically evocative, at other times merely confusing.

For all its poetic stature, *The Illiac Passion* steadily disintegrates and eventually looks merely pretentious. Such a gallant failure deserves both notice and study. If Markopoulos could be weaned from the very milieu that has nourished and rewarded him, he might some day live up to his great promise. But this milieu has insidiously, greedily utilized its basic illusions about the film medium in order to aggrandize itself. The "medium," no matter how futilely or faultily used, has veritably become the "message." There is a glaring cause of this false reasoning. It operates unconsciously in a broad field and is due partly to a trend in theoretical speculation.

Some theorists have argued that film is a medium adapted to express primarily the instability of dreams; the way filmic scenes and actions may change, without necessary logical connectives, geographical or otherwise, is exactly that of dreams. But this is to imply that all artistic form imposed on such a medium, all conceptual intentions, are therefore arbitrary. In the "natural" state, supposedly, film has the peculiar ellipsis and fragmentariness, the irksome inconclusiveness, of dreams, whether or not the dreams are strange or wonderful. So far as deliberate filmmaking goes, this only means that tacitly one is advised to follow the single Surrealist canon of automatism or else "copy" a dream on film as faithfully as possible. However, if one were strictly to obey such a precept, visual gibberish, with perhaps neither end nor beginning, would follow. That is, it might well follow; the result would in fact depend on how well the filmmaker could "cheat" by having a poetic and mythological sensibility, so that the dice of dream-mode vision, as it were, could be loaded with aesthetic insights and a sense of form.

Now what is a "mythological sensibility"? It is the assumption that the human being himself has the godlike faculties of going everywhere in space with convenience, and instantaneously, of appearing and disappearing at will, of sustaining a measureless inward power of consummating his desires. The two recent films from abroad, *The Mirage* and *No More Flee-ing*, offer ironic testimony to this mythological faculty because they illustrate precisely its failure: one has a young pariah for its hero, the other pictures the self-destructive end of man's dreams of all spatial conquest. What we should note about the style of both films is the sense of amplitude in the space de-picted by the camera; though it contains tragic failure, this space is universal in its plastic character. Indisputably, it is the *great* scene of action.

In the works of Homer we find the gods capable of these mythological offices and powers just mentioned; if these were limited it was only because of the gods' competition with one another. The important thing about a filmmaker's having this sort of sensibility should be obvious enough: he posits that absolute freedom of movement in space which is necessary to the successful achievement of film; it is a kind of *confidence* of which the human performer, for his part, should be aware as his immediate faculty. No doubt, in the physical world and to some extent in the moral world too, this is an illusion, yet in the ele-mentary aesthetic sense (in the dream and in film) it is not an illusion. The very events of *No More Fleeing* and *The Mirage* are determined by this assumption. It is like mankind's dream of flying, at one time considered only a scientific fantasy. The air-plane was one sort of solution; motion pictures were another.

Gregory Markopoulos' films are based vaguely on certain mythic patterns and their performers have vague mythological identities. How successfully such realizations turn out depends on contingencies of the casting and just what effects Markopou-los has had in mind. His resultant style, even at its best, is only moderately successful. He still tends to dwell too long on an action and an individual, and to have imprecise ideas about the action's nature and thus the individual's role in it. But the importance of his filmmaking attitude still lies in visionary plan, which in him issues from a conscious mythological sensibility. There is a natural feeling of spaciousness in his films and an ease of action in his actors, whom he tries, directorially, to endow with solemn poise. Thus while his exterior backgrounds are natural and he uses for interiors no extravagant sets, only some extraordinary house or suggestive room, he creates for his more mature films a rarefied atmosphere whose meaning is that the most ordinary circumstances of life can sustain heroic action predicated on a mythological plan. His single-frame technique of modulating action enriches with a special excitement the hieratic sort of rhythm in his films.

Narcissus (1956), the Cocteau-influenced film by Willard Maas and Ben Moore, is accomplished with much intuitive acumen considering the simplicity of its means. Its passing tension at times goes limp but it relies on a solid structure. The myth of Narcissus and Echo is set forthrightly in a sort of city slum, a socially deserted warehouse district, where the hero is an infantile young homosexual living a hermit's penurious life of wandering the streets, collecting toylike fetishes, and daydreaming. He makes a prophetic image: a hermit-hippie although one unacquainted with the use of drugs. Echo is the good-looking queen of a neighborhood gang of young toughs. Her sexual overtures to Narcissus rejected, she induces her gang to beat him up and wreck his little shack; crushed in every way, he drowns himself in the nearby river. As in Cocteau's films, a mirror has become the token of passage into the world of fantasy—there are three dream episodes all involving the hero's apotheosis. The first is idyllic and pathetic, the second (set in a gay bar) orgiastic with anamorphic photographic effects, the third tragic and manic: Narcissus' otherworldly union with the company of great heroes represented as statues. *Narcissus* is a serious and sensitive commentary on a deluded type of homosexual whose infantile withdrawal flows from mental and nervous instability. Without its mythological sensibility, however, the film would not have achieved its poetic level.

underground film

In Stan Brakhage, a filmmaker whose qualities are important but very ambivalent, one can trace the evolution of a sensibility ever in search of a visionary form reaching toward the cosmic dimension. That part of his later work, *Dog Star Man*, about the corpse of a dog which, undisturbed in its place outdoors, passes through numerous seasonal changes, itself of course going through the necessary transformation of dead organic matter, has a deep beauty of idea; the reference is to the evolution of the constellation Sirius. The error Brakhage makes is compulsive overworking of his visual range. Technically the camera changes are frequent but also very repetitious, so that quantitatively (again a sort of of anamorphosis) the film is stretched far out of shape. Brakhage is gifted with a film sense whose freedom of action becomes redundant through lack of dramatic and lyric proportion: the absence of a shapely container.

The inverse of Warhol's fixed-gaze camera, Brakhage's stampeding camera has run away with time and space in the avant-garde film, but not without a sense of opening up endless avenues of adventure. Along these and across them, every inch of the way, Underground Film is making history. The point is to understand what this history is.

the shape of things to come?

The great point, nowadays, about trying to write any history is to be sure that the constitution of mankind is itself basic, steadfast. Can one be sure of that? Isn't the truth, rather, that the anatomy of Underground Film, in history's light, is a permanent revolution so fluid that one can never be certain it is in correct focus? Besides, what of the stock on which the image is freshly printed? Happenings, for instance, are antihistorical in that they incarnate a kind of perpetual motion no matter what the rate of speed or the material; they represent something like the quickly replaced light patterns flashed on the "perpetual motion" of go-go girls. In Underground films and certain varieties of the off-off-Broadway stage we find an action-beyond-action that, like the frozen-frame technique telling a film story in still-shot glimpses, travels along with the pulse and image of time-reality and outstrips it in tempo of change . . . in order to be, apparently, *groovy*.

Now the instant—that crazy, glorious, groovy instant (al-

though, by the time this is in print, the word "groovy" itself
may have passed into dead history)—is *here;* now, or tomorrow,
it's *gone!* Moral pathologists might get busy analyzing the
phenomena of quick-change fashion and also the urgency of its
causes. But soberly to go back to causes is itself a way of
standing still to focus on past time, and thus losing time, or at
least "marking" it, in the present. The point is not that every
change must introduce the "new"—that was a dream of the old
avant-garde. The point now is what is usually signified by the
term "change-off." Maybe there *is* nothing new under the sun—
not even colonizing the moon with human beings—for eventually time will probably bring existing science fiction around
to actual fact, and that's that. Today, not novelty but change-off
is the avant-garde filmmaker's own thing.

The paradox put forth by Andy Warhol is that he expects
even his shortest and least monotonous filmic things to provide
backgrounds exactly like old-fashioned wallpaper which wove
"pictures" into its abstract decorative patterns. No longer is
one supposed to sit and watch a film, giving it one's attention
the way one does in the classic movie house; one can fall
asleep, go out for a drink or a sandwich, make a phone call,
come back—or else forget about the whole thing . . . the film
meanwhile is unrolling *as if* it were a picture hanging in its
regular place on the wall. Supposedly it doesn't mind not being
watched. Warhol himself is self-coached not to mind not being
watched. Socially he is usually an alienated, diffident cynosure.
It's part of the great human conspiracy of the twentieth century
to escape civilized anxiety by imitating, pretending to be,
things.

If you take a trip abroad, you close your apartment unless
you lend it to a friend or sublet it. Your *things* don't mind
unless they're living things, pets or plants; then you have to
provide for their care. Not so Underground Film audiences.
Left to themselves, they're on their own. Thus things or people

seen via Warhol's catatonic camera are not supposed to "mind" not being watched (up-ended narcissism) any more than the unwinding reel minds not being watched unwinding. Let us not be pretentious enough to call all this a philosophy of alienation, or even of indifference. It's an etiquette rather than a philosophy —a tacit, relaxed, complex etiquette of informality. In a way, the vanguard of the hip generation substitutes *cool* for *indifference* and tends to exhibit *engagement* (of whatever kind) instead of *alienation*. As for Warhol per se, he is a sort of anatomy of hip sensibility rather than a filmmaker. And other filmmakers, despite their less retiring egos, are getting to be like him by sheer force of his atmosphere. This is why Warhol and the pop milieu he typifies can be called anti-art, or better, just non-art. The single painting is no more than the single film frame, which slips by, supersubliminally, in the service of reflecting the way one instant of action in the world of material things continuously replaces another.

While I've been calling on historical data to help me compose this anatomy of avant-garde and Underground film, filmmakers have not waited for me to finish, but are plunging ahead with their activities at increased speed, calling into play all the new and old ingenuities they know, or care to know. Indefatigable "pad" workers (like Ken Jacobs and Michael Snow) seem to see no horizon to laboratory experiment, and with technical bravura they stretch audience patience to the breaking point and beyond. Such filmmakers represent the fanaticism of the Underground in holding onto the screen with optic/aural gymnastics. Brakhage has gone into childhood with a spirit of investigating what it meant for him to be a child once and now to be a father, a creator of human beings. After copulation and birth scenes come gliding, ingenuous sights of small organisms nakedly becoming aware of themselves and each other.

Not long ago Brakhage premiered in New York a four-part

sex film called *Love Making* (1969). To me it seems that the
rhythm and quality of the shots of a naked young man and
woman having ordinary sex are neither filmically nor humanly
as interesting as Brakhage's earlier film called *Loving*, which,
while not as nude or explicit as the later film, is just as convincing and more imaginative. Yet a comparison of this sort
matters not in the least to the prevailing temper and tempo of
Underground Film fashions. Assuredly, the second part of the
new film, showing two hippie-type males making standardized
love (one active, the other passive) and featuring unmistakable
fellatio, does supply some human interest. It marks, I believe,
the first time such a thing has been exposed to a public audience.
For the strictly built-in audience at this première, the routine
homosexual acts passed with no more than a few semisilent
gloats, some scattered, suppressed gasps. So far as stirring up
articulate moral or emotional reflexes could be observed, they
passed like the eight hours Warhol devoted to looking at the
Empire State Building.

Then Brakhage displayed a sequence of naked children
jumping about and casually, playfully caressing one another.
They are so young that all the play seems pre-erotic as well as
precoital; at least the camera shows nothing else. In the case
of children so young—about four to seven years of age—a
giantism of the film screen comes through. The loving attentiveness of Brakhage's camera, whose eye is full of them, turns the
screen into a Michelangelesque vision, as if we had so many
close-ups of the Sistine wall. Jumping and rolling about on a
springy mattress, the children often get beyond camera range,
so that the effect of giantism—as if the screen were too small
to contain them—is filmically emphasized. Some such glimpses,
if repetitious, are undoubtedly beautiful foot by foot of film.
Yet because the playing children offer no filmic shape or
sequence, we must conclude that they are not necessarily meant
to be more than the sort of environmental image nonchalantly

projected by Warhol. Once, I know, Brakhage was provoked
into despising Warhol's lack of craft, his flouting of the importance of movement as well as rhythm and editing. Perhaps
the stylist of *Flesh of Morning* and *Reflections on Black* has
grown more lenient, just as he has patched up his quarrel with
the Film-Makers' Cooperative in order to form an Underground
front, if not merely a working relationship.

Regarding Warhol's latest activities, it is no secret that, in
the domain of film, they are headed as fast and as far as possible toward more commercial success and a revised popular
formula based (humorously) on the new supertolerance for
nudity and sex display. It was amusing to witness the press conference held after a screening of *Lonesome Cowboys* at the
Fifty-fifth Street Playhouse, New York City, just before its
simultaneous premières at that theater and Warhol's Garrick
Theatre in the Village (the scene of *Flesh*'s marathon triumph).
Paul Morrissey is now the production manager of Warhol's
films and his presence is obviously what has given the conven-
tionalizing turn of "entertainment" to Warhol's absorption with
the groovy scene in terms of camp, sex, and young-male beauty.
Although at the press conference Andy and Paul lined up with
a female player from the Underground-influenced film *Midnight
Cowboy* (1969) and a male superstar from *Lonesome Cowboys*,
Morrissey was the authoritative spokesman and even "trans-
lated" some of Warhol's laconic, undertoned answers to questions from the press, which incidentally was largely collegiate.

Warhol continues to be eloquently wide-eyed, open-mouthed,
and deadpan in public; the last can be considered a pun. Warholism is surely pagan and owes a lot to Pan, god of earthiness
and naïve sexuality. Yet the revival is strangely constrictive.
The orgiastic element is still pretty playroomish. At the press
conference Morrissey underlined Warhol's admission that his
own painting was "junk," a form of "decoration" at best, and
that in any case his films bear no conscious relationship to his

225

painting. His films seek now to be "entertaining," Morrissey declared, and entertaining only. "No art, please," is the tacit gimmick. However, one must note that in *Lonesome Cowboys* a big concession has been made in the direction of coherent story and coherent dialogue, both (however much "tripped-up") based on recognizable human relations. *Lonesome Cowboys,* publicized as an erotic spoof of old-fashioned Westerns (something even commercial Westerns have become in late years), actually is a charade using long-time conventions of Hollywood Westerns to show off the various hang-ups and the various sexes of the underground set from which Warhol's films are cast.

Seen here are three very photogenic, long-haired, picturesque youngsters combining good looks and sex appeal: Eric Emerson, Joe Dallesandro (of *Flesh*) and Tom Hompertz. If, in fact, they weren't so far on the hippie side, they'd be very possible Hollywood material. The point is that they, their personalities in their roles, live in that special, ambiguous realm which may, I think, properly be called ambisexual. Patent if youngish virile traits are mixed interestingly with homosexual reflexes familiar to those who know borderline or uncrystallized male types. In one dimension a psychoanalyzing of cowboy sexual loneliness and isolation from women, turning in another dimension into bed relations among the characters, the film is not at all a put-on, but a crude sort of poem expressing the temptations (and occasional capitulations) of young men that are brought about by the massive homosexual pressures of the metropolitan scene.

Together with some older cowboys (including the classic "elder brother" of the cowboy clans) the three young men encounter a lady ranch owner and her homosexual male companion; the latter two are what make *Lonesome Cowboys* a stark camp-parody. At the press conference Morrissey dropped the admission that the "plot" of the film is modeled on *Romeo and Juliet;* the admission itself was tongue-in-cheek inasmuch

226

as one could appreciate all the points of *Lonesome Cowboys* without having set eyes on Shakespeare's play. Still, the play is one basis, seemingly, for alluding to the lady ranch owner's male companion as "the Nurse." This part is taken by the Underground veteran Taylor Mead, whose style, with the relentless tread of time, has grown definitively faggot.

As for Viva, the superstar filling the only female role in *Lonesome Cowboys* (Ramona, the ranch owner), she is a true offbeat vamp of the Underground: modestly breasted, thin and angular, with a beaky nose, a hard prettiness, and frizzed-out hippie hair. Her willingness to appear undressed, and to undress, before the camera is less sexy than blasé Living-Theatre boldness. She is also willing to seem to get laid – as she positively is in *Blue Movie* (*Fuck*), a Warhol film of 1968– but this activity in both films looks less sensual than it does human-sexual-response. The same is true of the virility of her partner, Tom Hompertz, whom she enjoins in seductively schoolteacherish tones, "Take off your pants!" Hompertz is a longish, muscularly beautiful youth with an oddly seraphic and detached look, much enhanced by a pre-Raphaelite hairdo. Both partners seem to *like* rather than *love* doing it. The ensuing love-death parody is impossible to miss.

Perhaps we have a new sexuality here: the superstar's. This would be a sort of mutually tolerant, good-natured narcissism in which sex is a public demonstration whose feelings are best relished by the participants later on, in the screening room. This goes for homosexual as well as heterosexual playacting. Which is all deeply part of the ambisexuality. Whenever or however someone fucks, he fucks himself as much as another. Unless I'm much, much mistaken, this is something that modern gay guys and gals—and even straight ones—naturally dig. In other words, human confrontation (peace-and-love type) has replaced human copulation. Sex as passion? That can be left to those square kids in Zeffirelli's *Romeo and Juliet*. One won-

227

ders if heterosexually inclined females have some cause, these days, to worry. Here, of course, Viva is only a parody of such a woman. Yet the parody may be significant in itself.

Ramona, before the cowboys gang-rape her in a scene that reeks of put-on, remarks to "Nurse" that one or two of the cowboys are wearing mascara, and later she screams that they're all queer, anyway. Only one of them, it turns out, has any real desire to disillusion her on this point. One might say that *Lonesome Cowboys* makes ridiculous not just the female sex but sex itself. The Sheriff rather needlessly reveals himself a transvestite, and all overt sex between the males is shown in the form of schoolboy roughhouse, boyish flirtation, or innuendo. At the same time the proportional emphasis of the action, and the few drops of emotional validity, are heavily on the homosexual side. The truth is that the film's whole action is an ad-libbed, masquerade-ball charade of the kind of sexual game that goes on in one segment of the underground set. It's a milieu in which a female is perpetually reminded that she was once only a rib; as a rib, Viva gives a remarkably articulate performance.

In the interests of film, one must add that *Lonesome Cowboys*, which is in color, has much the best photography of any known Warhol film and also is much the least boring. Many of the laughs are well earned, both because and in spite of their being camp laughs. A comic art (as much as the Factory would scorn this term) now shows up in the Morrissey-Warhol formula—an art that is disconcertingly informal and disconcertingly documentary. The whole documentary trend of the filmic avant-garde—emerging in the fusion of leftism with aesthetics and uniting finally in the term "life style"—means an entente between documentation and aestheticism which leaves the latter, embarrassingly, at a loose end.

From the very beginning the twentieth-century avant-garde has had its own way of being anti-art: it has denounced both decadent and academic aestheticism and flirted seriously with radical politics. This movement soon resulted in a schism dividing Stalinist Surrealists from Trotskyist Surrealists. Yet now that Stalinism has officially been laid to rest, even in the Soviet Union, the issue is no longer so burning, if only because the historic quantity, Surrealism, has been dialectically turned into post-Dada pop formulas. In this way the modern avant-garde almost instantaneously entered the museum; that is, the Establishment. A recent development on these lines is the holding of a Film-Makers' Cinémathèque series at the Gallery of Modern Art, New York, built by Huntington Hartford, and in many ways antimodernist.

But what are the relevant facts? The filmic Underground, insofar as it deals with life styles, is fully as anti-abstract as the institution whose founder believes (or at least believed) that God was insulted by certain Abstract and Abstract-Expressionist art. Still, Hartford's museum has been "surreal" enough to hold major one-man exhibitions for the modern painters Pavel Tchelitchew and Salvador Dali. Both Dali and Tchelitchew, if it comes to a question of retaining the human image intact, have special and personal ways of distorting and fragmenting the human image at their pleasure. All the same, the human image remains for these two painters a kind of mutable symbol of organic life, a vignette or a mural as might be, but something based on "photographic" likeness. Well, such has the human image been, basically, in the history of the avant-garde film and the current Underground Film! The Underground assumes that humanity still wants its reassuring truthtelling mirrors: still wants the statistics (however touched up) of its own daily life and daily fantasies to surround it, to form an intimate semipermanent environment. Thus there is nominal aptness in the harmony established, via the Film-Makers' Cinémathèque, between the Gallery of Modern Art and the Underground forces.

229

underground film

To the *anti-aestheticism* of the Underground must be added *anti-intellectualism*. This is clearly affirmed by the curious aversion of in-under commentators to supplying criticism of Underground film works. There is, properly speaking, very little such "criticism." Rather, what there is of it verges on a more or less restrained cult mania, such as that printed in all-out-appreciative program notes. This sort of commentary is instanced in the notes written by P. Adams Sitney for the series of repertory showings recently sponsored in various spots, including the Jewish Museum, by the Film-Makers' Cinémathèque. Sitney's notes are quite literate, at times perceptive, but taken at their word, are more or less flattering bouquets extended to a big round of in-under filmmakers. As pointed out by Stanley Kauffmann,* Underground Film criticism may sound persuasive and to the point till one actually witnesses the creative work it pretends to interpret; an appalling gap then appears between the object in view and the description itself. By and large, Underground Film criticism is an occupation to be termed blurbing; statistically, it is most inaccurate unless both film and commentary are viewed as one homogenized life style. Then the argument (I think this is the wish of the Underground as a whole) becomes entirely empiric, and really is neither argument nor criticism, but an appeal or invitation to join up. It's as much a matter of faith as any religion. Such commentaries are not criticism in the classic sense, but only part of the same life style that produced the films.

Take the question of know-how. Some Undergrounders have it; some don't, and don't want to have it. Professionally, the term know-how used to signify the proper way to tell a story or represent an action on the screen. Logically it implied good photography, good (i.e., formal) editing, and of course good direction. It implied these because filmmaking was assumed to

* In his *A World on Film* (New York: Harper & Row), pages 424-425. Comment on an exposition on Underground films by Ken Kelman, *The Nation*, May 11, 1964.

relate to prose narrative and theatrical drama as known, established historical quantities. But even by midcentury, lucid
story and lucid human situation were art factors which had
already lost some prestige, and now, when the century is almost
three-quarters over, what was once known as a complete action
(either as episode or whole story) is something which even
commercial films are finding less and less essential to filmmaking. The episode has quite surmounted the story-plot in all
those commercial films which take their cues from the pop rage.
This is why such a semicommercial film as *Head,* attempting
dizzily to drown itself in the hippie milieu, is much more like
a prolonged number in an old-fashioned musical revue than like
an old-fashioned movie. The emphasis—even as in the Beatles'
animated-cartoon *Yellow Submarine*—is on spectacle-plus-fable.
The reality of the standard term "plot" has been supplanted by
the reality of the drug-and-dream inspired term "trip," as we
saw in our previous discussion of *The Trip* and *Chappaqua.* If
such films as these are occasionally denounced by the inside
Undergrounders, it is because they resemble commercial films
enough to be suspected of making a play for the biggest possible
pop audience—and that's hardly avant-garde cricket.

I take it that Underground reaction against coherent action
(the basis of the standard plot) stems from drug experiences as
these have been converted into the Drug Attitude. Actually being
turned on by a drug is simply the physical path of achieving
what numerous filmmakers usually put into film via the Drug
Attitude. A very impressive Swedish film, *I Am Curious (Yellow),* one with a *plot,* has lately had a long run in New York
after being banned by jury trial as obscene and then permitted
public showing by a decision of the U. S. Circuit Court of Appeals. Despite its epoch-making sexual candor, *I Am Curious* is
probably resented by a large faction of Underground Film as
well as held in suspicion by a good portion of the New Left.
The reasons are one reason. Vilgot Sjöman, its writer-director,

231

has conceived not only a life style but also a life experience, and he has told it with notable coherence and completeness, even risking a dual-reality dimension by directly inserting scenes of making the film into the fictitious action. This same rational dualism, emerging with ironic implicatons about the New Left life style, is apt to seem too intellectual and a bit offensive to many Undergrounders. In the same way, Cassavetes' *Faces* could be indicted by the more in Undergrounders because it actually tries to present human character through coherent actions, however dramatically inconclusive these are.

The whole action of *I Am Curious (Yellow)*, however, is pretty conclusive. Its conclusion is the disillusion of a young woman with New Left politics in Sweden (a politics notably international) because the nonviolence on which it is dogmatically based proves inconsistent with the manifest violence of a great sexual experience. Sex and politics are here exhibited coherently in terms of an individual's moral problem. And it is the moral problem per se which is taboo to the militant inner reaches of the filmic Underground.

This is why Norman Mailer's films, especially the ambitious *Beyond the Law,* must remain moot, debatable quantities to the doctrinaire Underground. The film form here is the treatment —a loose vérité treatment—of the daily milieu of a police captain, played by Mailer himself. It is the exposure of an occupational predicament and of contingent human reflexes; the best of the latter are the performances of Rip Torn and the poet Michael McClure as hippies calamitously fallen into the clutches of the police. Obviously the film is not intended to be either a "plot" or a complete statement about anything.

Strangely enough, one large dialectic end product of a movement that began *against* the decorative in art, as too aesthetic, has now embraced a decorativeness of the anti-aesthetic or nonaesthetic. For examples: Pop Art, Happenings, Environments, the extemporaneous actor/audience theater. That is, without being beautiful in any formal sense of plot, idea, or conscious visuals except dancing (and thus of any rhythmic sense except swing or rock), a film is still "decorative" because it is a recorded image, a wall-illusion, a temporary environment. It is a new variety of interior decoration—and this includes, of course, all the people who are seen in fetish-footage films projected as environments. This emulsion of the real and the illusive is one reason why the result is ephemeral, can appear and disappear at will, seem to have neither end, beginning, nor middle. The most sensitive Underground nodes are exactly at the point where film as dream-flow and film as reality-flow indistinguishably mix.

The filmic image cast on a wall during a cocktail party or rock-society session might as well be instant television. In fact, the function of such mirror-environment films (whether in discothèque or private studio) is to give the illusion that the people on the wall are the same, or might as well be the same, as the people dancing and/or making love in the room where the film is being projected *but not necessarily watched*. Light patterns projected onto dancers was seen in *Revolution*, the semicommercial paean to the hippie-drug milieu on the West Coast. Once again we are reminded that a prime Underground factor is a kind of narcissism. Via Underground Film, modernism has brought the twentieth-century art movement full circle from anti-illusionism and antirepresentationalism to this downright narcissism—more or less illusionist—of a given elite: the Undergrounders, the hip-swingers and cool-cool babies, the warholites and the mekassianics . . .

As I have hinted before, it is a form of self-advertisement, a real social propaganda. In the truly radical underground sense, film becomes an automatic variety of cosmetics: a magic-mirror extension of the costumes and baubles and long hair of the hippie milieu with its paraphernalia luxury dream, its Leather Boy and Daniel Boone cults, as departments of special effects. "Life is a dream" is a very old myth. It is one which has now utilized Underground Film as a style of modern living; or maybe, vice versa, modern life has utilized "life is a dream" as a tangible, revivified myth. It makes no difference which, for the logic of cause and effect is quite irrelevant to fetish-footage psychology.

Therefore (naughty word if Undergrounders are listening!), the problem of the historian, re Underground Film, is to decide whether our time's most radical phase of filmmaking—I mean that sector to which Jean-Luc Godard, say, seems an opportunistic square—may not be the symptom of a historical movement *to end all history*. History (written or pictorial) has documentary importance only if certain constants exist, certain means by which we can, understanding the past, make the present more lucid and whole to the consciousness, to the mind, and thus afford means of relative judgment: what to *keep*, what to *discard*. In the most significant sense, history is the basis of the agenda of life—how it can be best arranged for human advantage, convenience, and (if one can presume to be so aesthetic) pleasure. But in fetish-footage psychology—the very heart of Underground Film—all conscious arrangements for the future are too logical, too explicit, too "conservative." Why too conservative?

Because of the idea of historic continuity, which means the responsibility of relating end to means, effect to cause, result to intention. To insist on this responsibility, from the widest Underground standpoint, is to betray the very life blood of the avant-garde, whose prevalent aim is to exist without being measured or weighed by anything but its own self-approval. Underground Film and Pop Art represent the only elites in human history which insist on the privileges of an elite without any visible means of earning or sustaining those privileges; that is, without any values that can be measured, or even, properly speaking, named except by its own labels. A distinct

234

irony of the Underground is that here the film, the only complete time art of the theater, exactly duplicating itself simply
by starting the reel over again, declines to take seriously its own
historical integrity. Underground Film desires rather to regard
"the record" as both a dispensable and yet ever renewable
"time"; supposedly a thing that, once homogenized with the
current of life, never knows separation or objectivity, can never
be "viewed" as an isolated object, and therefore cannot be
judged, cannot even be accepted or rejected. It simply *is*—in
a kind of automatic, impermissible, endless continuity. . . .

Well, this would not only be the end of film history, it
would be the end of history. I prefer *history* for the film only
because I prefer *consciousness* for the film. Therefore I am
for Underground Film only as I am for its historic avant-garde
values as these exist and can be verified in a total continuity of
aesthetic values. Fetish footage is a dead end . . . or rather, a
trailing filament of the visual void.

coda

If the history of the Underground Film in all its styles and phases has one essential message, it is that the film medium, to achieve its destiny, must not only be pure, free of all commercial taints, it must also have scope of vision and an implacable aesthetic character. The scope of *Un Chien Andalou* and *L'Age d'Or*, the scope of all surreally influenced later films such as *The Lead Shoes* and *Dom*, is the world of human action freed into subjective will and objective chance: reality standing open to fantasy in a domain where the consummation of wish gets magical co-operation from the most ordinary objects and the dailiest situations. Is the word "aesthetic" a true stumbling block to appreciating this argument? By the term "aesthetic character" I do not mean anything which may glibly be called, these days, arty. That is the error of those who misconceive what it is to be anti-Establishment in really constructive and worthwhile ways.

For quite some time now, art works, duly exhibited at gal-

236

coda

leries and museums, have been produced on the tacit basis of being anti-art. Only a minority of these, I think, really deserve their honored places; nevertheless, all of them have technical postulates which amount to an aesthetics, downgraded though that aesthetics may be. As for the iconoclasm of the Dadaists and the Surrealists, that cannot be understood without assessing the role of irony in their shared creeds. New idols (made of the same objective materials and still to be termed "beautiful") were created to replace those destroyed; to do this effectively, labels as well as works had to be attacked. There was urbane irony in André Breton's strategy when, instead of calling something he liked "beautiful" (*beau*), he called it "pretty" (*joli*). "Aesthetic" was simply a label which, because of certain late-nineteenth-century developments in the arts, had gained the bad name of representing decadence and affectation. The greatest irony, in terms of our current problems, is that Art Nouveau— exactly a late-nineteenth-century upsurge of "aesthetic decadence"—has come back today with such a popular bang, and that such an artist as Beardsley—one of the high priests of that decadence—has had such a recent revival.

So for filmmakers today to shrink at sight of the terms "aesthetic" and "mythological sensibility" would be just plain chicken! Pop cults tend to insist on the exclusiveness of idioms and to favor the convenience of slogans. But this is to be snobbish—provincially snobbish. Doubtless it is part of the calculated absurdism and overfluid cultism of the Youth Attitude, wanting fresher and fresher novelties to assert their continued difference from their elders, none of whose icons they can tolerate. Most striking about the youth furor is the lack of consciousness in its cults that some day those now in their teens or twenties will be *(gasp!)* in their thirties. The logic is that in a given time, and rather too soon, perhaps, they will have to rate themselves as old-hat. What will they be doing in their thirties? And in their forties? What will they think of the institutions of teenie-boppers and hippies (not to say yippies and crazies) to which many once belonged? The answer may not matter to them, now or in the future. It does matter to history, that habitual memorizer. Only by annihilating history—that is, only by declining to measure time in terms of values—can Underground Film get its kinky, headstrong way and assert the nonhistorical values of existence over the historic existence of values.

An odd current phenomenon is the increasing use of the word "adult" in all sorts of ads, especially ads for commercial films. The old sign before theaters and in ads, "For Adults Only," held out a promising lubricity that has been somewhat toned down by the new official ratings signified with initials. In general usage the term "adult" is coming to have more and more serious connotation. One wonders if perhaps the word is addressed not to technical adults, but to young artists and students who like imagining they are as good as or better at sixteen or seventeen than those who are classifiable as adults. The popularity of the word may be just another sign of the pervasive Youth Attitude itself.

Is such a discussion to the point at this book's conclusion? I feel it is, owing to a basic truth by which all underground affairs, those of film or any other art, are governed. "Underground" would have a false meaning unless it inevitably connotated something that has yet to achieve its full *visible* stature, its place *above ground*. Film is the youngest art and just for that reason has the most potential of all. Of course, film has so often been called the youngest art, in optimistic as well as pessimistic inflections, that it is risking bad form to mention something almost certain to register with a tinge of banality. Yet I doubt if any serious manifesto about avant-garde film could avoid the tacit assumption that the film art has yet to reach the peak of its maturity. The avant-garde is, I repeat, a *coda*

torch, and it ideally illuminates all underground activity while leading the way up.

If in the "anatomy" of these pages I relate the medium and style of film to traditional forms such as epic, myth, and lyric, as well as to the novel, it is in order to be culturally and critically intelligible; just so, when *Ulysses* and then *Finnegans Wake* appeared, it was necessary to relate those works to the traditional forms of the novel and the epic poem. The profit there was to define the differences as well as the likenesses, and to do this in terms of Joyce's concrete procedures. It seems to me historically most apt that the avant-garde, as a conscious film movement, was born at exactly the time that Joyce was finishing *Ulysses*. It was not that the novel was "destroyed" by *Ulysses* and that *Finnegans Wake* was to be a sort of requiem over its corpse, but that what Joyce did was exactly what the avant-garde filmmakers proceeded to do—and they did it even while the growth of film technique was preparing the commercial film to emulate the novel and surpass the play in the very act of absorbing those forms. Successful or not, that was the aim. Both Joyce and the avant-gardistes of film, who thus established the existence of Underground Film, set out to show that art could feed at the very sources of the poetic imagination without using conventional narratives or respecting the naturalistic mode of the novel.

The format of classical qualities in representational painting had already been progressively eliminated by modern schools: Impressionism and Post-Impressionism, Cubism, Expressionism, and then Surrealism. This is why it is historically inevitable to include *The Cabinet of Dr. Caligari* as well as the Dali-Buñuel films in the early Underground canon. Without such precursors, and without the precursors of the thirties, forties and fifties, the Underground works of the sixties would not have a history, or anything like a true historic meaning.

239

The existence of *film poetry* is also one of the essential factors in Underground beginnings, because the language of film poetry is what separates all imaginative creativity in the film from the vast body of mere filmic documents and commercial film fiction. It is true that sometimes the lines of development, as in *Potemkin,* or in film poems that have been made purely out of documentary footage—such as the brief but brilliant French films, *Dream of Wild Horses* (1960) and *Forbidden Bullfight* (1959)—may cross each other with mutual benefit.

Yet this is just what proves the point about the central value of the poetic imagination, which in film is historically in the keeping of the international avant-garde. In turn, the *historical duty* of the international avant-garde is to consider the poetic imagination as in its keeping. It is because not all workers in Underground Film seem perfectly or thoroughly convinced of this that I have tried to demonstrate it to them while addressing this book primarily to the general film-going public with serious interests. This book is also, in a sense, an interoffice communiqué—which is why, into the objectivity of a history, I have tried to weave the subjectivity of a manifesto and to "draw in" an anatomy, or precise organization of parts.

History writing, we know, cannot be coherent or concrete without a defined sense of values; without a specific interpretation of the sum of significant events. What else is traditional anatomy but an inventory of the sum of the human body's parts? I interpret the body of Underground Film as a true organism, not a hobbledehoy of fads that may—like a Happening—fall apart and disappear. . . .

filmography

The following list, composed chronologically, includes virtually all key works stressed by the present writer as indicative, and often important, in the passage from avant-garde to Underground film; it contains as well some other films of related interest. If not all films by every outstanding filmmaker are listed, it may be because those omitted add nothing special to the filmmaker's significant sum of work, at least in the eyes of this critic. In certain cases it might be fairly logical to substitute another film by the same filmmaker for one mentioned here. Above all other concerns, the effort has been to render in this list a rounded picture of the avant-garde/Underground Film as it exists historically. Dates given refer usually to year of release: a number of these films took more than a year to make.

1915   *Le Folie de Docteur Tube* (Abel Gance)
Les Vampires (Louis Feuillade)

1919	*The Cabinet of Dr. Caligari* (Robert Wiene)
1921	*Rhythmus 21* (Hans Richter)
	Manahatta (Charles Sheeler/Paul Strand)
1923	*The Crazy Ray* (*Paris qui dort*) (René Clair)
	Rhythmus 23 (Richter)
1924	*Ballet Mécanique* (Léger)
	The Fall of the House of Usher (Harrington)
	Entr'acte (Clair)
	Ménilmontant (Dimitri Kirsanov)
1925	*Potemkin* (Eisenstein)
	Rhythmus 25 (Richter)
	Twenty-four Dollar Island (Flaherty)
	Metropolis (Lang)
1926	*Emak Bakia* (Man Ray)
	Brumes d'Automne (Kirsanov)
1927	*Anemic Cinema* (Marcel Duchamp)
	Berlin (Ruttmann)
1928	*Tusalava* (Len Lye)
	The Life and Death of a Hollywood Extra (Vorkapich/Florey/Toland)
	La Coquille et le Clergyman (Dulac/Artaud)
	The Fall of the House of Usher (James Sibley Watson)
	The Passion of Joan of Arc (Dreyer)
	L'Etoile de Mer (Man Ray)
	The Telltale Heart (Charles Klein)
1929	*Un Chien Andalou* (Buñuel/Dali)
	H₂O (Ralph Steiner)
1930	*L'Age d'Or* (Buñuel)
	Le Sang d'un Poète (Cocteau)
	Autumn Fire (Herman G. Weinberg)
1931	*Oramunde* (Emlyn Etting)
1932	*Que Viva Mexico!* (Eisenstein)
	Poem 8 (Etting)

filmography

1933   *Zéro de Conduite* (Jean Vigo)
    Ecstasy (Machaty)

1934   *Lot in Sodom* (Watson/Weber)
    Synchronization (L. Jacobs/Schillinger/Bute)

1935   *Colour Box* (Lye)

1936   *Synchrony No. 2* (Mary Ellen Bute)

1937   *Even as You and I* (Hy Hirsch)

1939   *Stars and Stripes* (Norman McLaren)
    Dots and Loops (McLaren)
    An American Dream (Oskar Fischinger)
    #1 (Harry Smith)

1941   *Object Lesson* (Christopher Young)
    1941 (Francis Lee)

1943   *Meshes of the Afternoon* (Maya Deren)
    Geography of the Body (Willard Maas)
    Film Exercise I (James and John Whitney)

1944   *At Land* (Deren)
    Film Exercises 2-3-4-5 (Whitney brothers)

1945   *Visual Variations on Noguchi* (Marie Menken)
    Choreography for Camera (Deren)

1946   *The Potted Psalm* (Sidney Peterson)
    Fragment of Seeking (Curtis Harrington)
    Ritual in Transfigured Time (Deren)
    Dreams That Money Can Buy (Richter)

1947   *Le Bijou* (Lee)
    The Cage (Peterson)
    Fireworks (Kenneth Anger)
    Horror Dream (Peterson)
    Fiddle De Dee (McLaren)

1948   *Meditation on Violence* (Deren)
    Lysis, Charmides, Psyche: a Trilogy (Gregory Marko-
      poulos)
    Picnic (Harrington)
    The Petrified Dog (Peterson)

	Mother's Day (James Broughton)
	Painting and Plastic (James Davis)
1949	*The Lead Shoes* (Peterson)
	On the Edge (Harrington)
	Motion Picture No. 1 (Fischinger)
	Mr. Frenhofer and the Minotaur (Peterson)
1950	*Ai-Ye* (Ian Hugo)
	The Adventures of Jimmy (Broughton)
1951	*Swain* (Markopoulos)
	Four in the Afternoon (Broughton)
	Looney Tom (Broughton)
1952	*Divertissement Rococo* (Hy Hirsch)
	Form Phases I (Robert Breer)
	Mambo (Jordan Belson)
	Caravan (Belson)
1953	*Interim* (Stan Brakhage)
	Unglassed Windows Cast a Terrible Reflection (Brakhage)
	The Pleasure Garden (Broughton)
	Hallucinations (Weiss)
	Eaux d'Artifice (Anger)
	Mandala (Belson)
	Little Fugitive (Morris Engel)
1954	*Inauguration of the Pleasure Dome* (Anger)
	Desistfilm (Brakhage)
	What Who How (Stan VanDerBeek)
1955	*Reflections on Black* (Brakhage)
	The Wonder Ring (Brakhage/Cornell)
	Yantra (James Whitney)
1956	*Narcissus* (Maas/Moore)
	Mankinda (VanDerBeek)
	Nightcats (Brakhage)
	Theme and Transition (Carmen d'Avino)
1957	*8X8* (Richter)

New York New York (Francis Thompson)
A Man and His Dog Out for Air (Breer)
Flesh of Morning (Brakhage)
Adebar (Peter Kubelka)

1958   *A Movie* (Bruce Conner)
The Big O (d'Avino)
#12 (Harry Smith)
Pull My Daisy (Robert Frank/Al Leslie)
Anticipation of the Night (Brakhage)
Loving (Brakhage)
The Mirage (Weiss)
Dom (Walerian Borowczyk/Jan Lenica)

1959   *The Room* (d'Avino)
Dance Chromatic (Ed Emshwiller)
Handwritten (Charles Boultenhouse)
Science Friction (VanDerBeek)
The Very Eye of Night (Deren)
Shadows (John Cassavetes)
Window Water Baby Moving (Brakhage)
Sirius Remembered (Brakhage)
Raga (Belson)
Star-Spangled to Death (uncompleted) (Ken Jacobs)
Forbidden Bullfight (de Daunant)

1960   *The Dead* (Brakhage)
Lemon Hearts (Vernon Zimmerman)
The Flower Thief (Ron Rice)
The Connection (Shirley Clarke/Jack Gelber)
Dream of Wild Horses (de Daunant)
Black and White Burlesque (Richard Preston)

1961   *Cosmic Ray* (Conner)
Guns of the Trees (Jonas Mekas)
Mr. Hayashi (Bruce Baillie)
Arabesque for Kenneth Anger (Menken)

1962   *Moonplay* (Menken)

Flaming Creatures (Jack Smith)
Thanatopsis (Emshwiller)
Blonde Cobra (Bob Fleischner/Ken Jacobs)
Twice a Man (Markopoulos)
Blue Moses (Brakhage)
Dog Star Man Part I (Brakhage)
The Queen of Sheba Meets the Atom Man (Rice)
Happenings I, II (Saroff/Oldenburg)
Shoot the Moon (Red Grooms/Rudy Burkhardt)
The Maze (Preston).

1963   *Dionysius* (Boultenhouse)
Scorpio Rising (Anger)
Totem (Enshwiller)
Fleming Falloon (George Landow)
The Jetty (Chris Marker)
Hallelujah the Hills (Adolfas Mekas)
Chumlum (Rice)
Sleep (Andy Warhol)
Christmas on Earth (Barbara Rubin)

1964   *The Devil Is Dead* (Carl Linder)
Sins of the Fleshapoids (Mike Kuchar)
Kiss (Warhol)
Haircut (Warhol)
Couch (Warhol)
Empire (Warhol)
Blow Job (Warhol)
The Brig (Mekas/Brown)
Lurk (Grooms/Burkhardt/Denby)
Paper Dolls (Preston)

1965   *Peyote Queen* (Storm De Hirsch)
The Art of Vision (Brakhage)
Echoes of Silence (Peter Goldman)
Finnegans Wake (Bute/Joyce)

filmography

Harlot (Warhol)

Screen Test (Warhol)

The Life of Juanita Castro (Warhol/Tavel)

Vinyl (Warhol/Tavel)

Horse (Warhol/Tavel)

Son of Dada (Preston)

1966   *Breakaway* (Conner)

Lapis (James Whitney)

Inauguration of the Pleasure Dome: Sacred Mushroom Edition (Anger)

Relativity (Emshwiller)

Fat Feet (Grooms)

Ray Gun Virus (Paul Sharits)

Galaxie (Markopoulos)

Ming Green (Markopoulos)

Film in Which There Appear Sprocket Holes (Landow)

The Chelsea Girls (Warhol)

Chafed Elbows (Robert Downey)

Poem Posters (Charles Henri Ford)

1967   *Orgia* (Maas)

Titicut Follies (Frederick Wiseman)

The Illiac Passion (Markopoulos)

I, a Man (Warhol/Baker)

Bike Boy (Warhol)

Line of Apogee (Lloyd Williams)

Piece Mandala (Sharits)

Portrait of Jason (Clarke/Holliday)

Wave-length (Michael Snow)

1968   *Third Eye Butterfly* (De Hirsch)

Flesh (Paul Morrissey/Andy Warhol)

Beyond the Law (Norman Mailer)

The Queen (Frank Simon/Sidney Meyers)

underground film

> *Remembrance* (Edward Owens)
> **1969** *Love Making I-IV* (Brakhage)
> *Touching* (Sharits)
> *Lonesome Cowboys* (Warhol)
> *Tom, Tom* (Ken Jacobs)
> *Back and Forth* (Snow)
> *I Am Curious (Yellow)* (Vilgot Sjöman)

Note. Readers who are interested in seeing the above-listed films, most of which are available for rental from sources in the United States, are advised to write the following distributors for their catalogs. It is well to remember that museums with film departments more or less regularly program series of films drawn from these sources and from their own archives. Films to be rented from the sources given below are in 16 mm and in a few cases (for theatrical distribution) also in 35 mm.

Audio Film Center, 10 Fiske Place, Mount Vernon, N.Y.; 2138 E. 75th St., Chicago, Ill.; 406 Clement St., San Francisco, Calif.

Brandon Films, 221 W. 57th St., New York, N.Y.; 20 E. Huron St., Chicago, Ill.; 244 Kearny St., San Francisco, Calif.

Canyon Cinema Cooperative, 58 Verona Place, San Francisco, Calif.

Contemporary Films/McGraw-Hill, 330 W. 42nd St., New York, N.Y.; 828 Custer Ave., Evanston, Ill.; 1211 Polk St., San Francisco, Calif.

Film-Makers' Cooperative, 175 Lexington Ave., New York, N.Y.

filmography

Film-Makers' Distribution Center, 175 Lexington Ave., New York, N.Y.

Grove Press Film Division (including Cinema 16 Film Library), 80 University Place, New York, N.Y.

Janus Film Library, 24 W. 58th St., New York, N. Y.

Museum of Modern Art Film Department, 21 W. 53rd St., New York, N.Y.